M000308753

"Yet there isn't a train I wouldn't take"

Railroads Past and Present
Edited by George M. Smerk

"Yet there isn't a train I wouldn't take"

Railway Journeys by William D. Middleton

Text and Photographs
by William D. Middleton

Indiana University Press
Bloomington & Indianapolis

This book is a publication of

Indiana University Press
601 North Morton Street
Bloomington, Indiana 47404-3797 USA

www.indiana.edu/~iupress

Telephone orders   800-842-6796
Fax orders   812-855-7931
e-mail orders   iuporder@indiana.edu

© 2000 by William D. Middleton

All rights reserved

No part of this book may be reproduced or utilized in any
form or by any means, electronic or mechanical, including
photocopying and recording, or by any information storage
and retrieval system, without permission in writing from the
publisher. The Association of American University Presses'
Resolution on Permissions constitutes the only exception
to this prohibition.

The paper used in this publication meets the minimum
requirements of American National Standard for Information
Sciences–Permanence of Paper for Printed Library
Materials, ANSI Z39.48–1984.

Manufactured in the United States of America

Library of Congress Cataloging-in-Publication Data

Middleton, William D., date
    Yet there isn't a train I wouldn't take : railway journeys / by William D. Middleton
        p.   cm. — (Railroads past and present)
    ISBN 0-253-33699-6 (cl : alk. paper)
    1. Railroads. 2. Railroad travel.   I. Title   II. Series.

TF20.M53 2000
385'.09—dc21   99-046002

1 2 3 4 5   05 04 03 02 01 00

$\mathcal{F}$OR DOROTHY whose company has added to the enjoyment of so many of these journeys.

Dorothy Middleton takes a ride in the cab of a Long Island Rail Road locomotive, August 1956.

Contents

I.   Journeys in North and Central America   1

During a quiet moment between station stops on the long journey west across the North Dakota prairie on April 20, 1959, conductor C. L. Manro read a newspaper.

Preface

The railroad track is miles away,
    And the day is loud with voices speaking;
Yet there isn't a train goes by all day
    But I hear its whistle shrieking.

All night there isn't a train goes by,
    Though the night is still for sleep and dreaming,
But I see its cinders red on the sky,
    And hear its engines steaming.

My heart is warm with the friends I make,
    And better friends I'll not be knowing;
Yet there isn't a train I wouldn't take,
    No matter where it's going.

                    —*Edna St. Vincent Millay, "Travel"**

Edna St. Vincent Millay, whose poem "Travel" has made her a sort of poet laureate of railway enthusiasts, had it just right. For the true railway traveler the destination, appealing though it may be, is not the thing; it's the act of getting there that matters.

It has always been that way for me.

My lifetime of railway journeys began with a trip to the 1932 Chicago World's Fair with an older cousin. We traveled in a parlor car, one of those wonderful big heavyweight cars outfitted with oversized, revolving arm chairs, and the trip made a lasting impression. I have never since declined any opportunity to climb aboard a train to travel almost anywhere.

The pieces in this collection represent close to a half century of train riding. The collection is not intended to provide some sort of all-inclusive representation of railroading around the world; my travels have been far too limited for that. Rather, it is a somewhat arbitrary selection of accounts of journeys that I found particularly interesting. I hope that the reader will find some of them of equal interest.

While several of the pieces in this collection are new, most have been edited or adapted from articles that originally appeared elsewhere. Many appeared in

---

*From *Second April* (New York: Harper and Brothers, 1921), © 1921 by Edna St. Vincent Millay.

Trains magazine over the past 45 years, and I am indebted to its editor, Kevin P. Keefe, for his kind permission to use this copyrighted material. Kevin has also permitted use of the article "Second Morning Chicago," which originally appeared in *Railway Progress*, later consolidated with *Trains*.

Similarly, editor Edwin J. Stauss has kindly allowed use of the article "The Noon Milwaukee," which originally appeared in *Rail Classics*. Michael W. Clayton of Pentrex Media Group has consented to the use of articles which originally appeared in *Passenger Train Journal* and *Vintage Rails*. And finally, Myrna Spark has graciously permitted the use of the Taurus Express article which originally ran in *European Railways*, published and edited by her late husband, Robert Spark.

These accounts of railway travel over a period of close to a half century owe much to the unfailing courtesy, interest, and assistance of people in every part of their railway enterprises. Whether at home in North America or traveling abroad, I have found railroad people to be linked by a common pride in the business of running trains and an eagerness to share what they are doing with interested observers.

My attempts to write about my railway journeys have been aided by many helpful editors and publishers. Chief among them have been the following. The late Willard V. Anderson, one of the original editors of *Trains* magazine, encouraged and patiently critiqued some of my earliest efforts. The late Rosemary Entringer, *Trains*' able managing editor of many years, brought much discipline to matters of grammar and style in my work. And throughout the 33 years that he edited *Trains*, the late David P. Morgan offered much advice, support, and encouragement, and I owe more to this exceptionally talented editor and writer than I do to any other.

Both in developing new pieces and in adapting earlier works for this book, I have been particularly grateful for the contributions of Dorothy, my wife and traveling companion on so many of these journeys. Her advice and criticism have contributed much to the final manuscript. As ever, responsibility for any errors or omissions is mine alone.

—William D. Middleton
Charlottesville, Virginia
June 1999

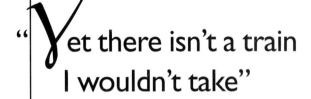

"Yet there isn't a train
I wouldn't take"

A great giant of steam railroading stood in the Fraser (Minnesota) yard of the Duluth, Missabe &
Iron Range Railroad late on a May afternoon in 1959. In a few minutes this 569-ton 2-8-8-4 Yellow-
stone type locomotive would begin the journey to the Missabe Road's Lake Superior ore docks at
Duluth with a 190-car train carrying almost 18,000 tons of iron ore for the steel mills of Pennsylvania.

I.

Journeys in North and Central America

Early on a crisp, bright March morning in 1948 the Milwaukee Road's premiere Madison (Wisconsin)-Chicago train, the *Varsity,* came steaming out across Madison's Lake Monona to begin its three-hour journey to Chicago. An elderly F3 class 4-6-2 Pacific, built by American Locomotive in 1910, headed a train that included a baggage-R.P.O. car, coaches, and a parlor-café car. The eastbound *Varsity* was later shifted to a late afternoon schedule.

The Noon Milwaukee*

Didn't all of us who fancied riding on the cars have some one train that was a special favorite? I'm not thinking about the kind of reverence we bestowed on the *Century*, or the *Panama*, or the other great trains of that sort, which was based on strict standards of excellence, but rather of the kind of attachment that was based entirely on sentiment and long familiarity. For most of us, our special train was one that played a central role in our lives.

For me that train was the Milwaukee Road's *Varsity*.

From April of 1927 until its demise in 1971 the *Varsity* operated over the Milwaukee's 140-mile route between Chicago and Madison, Wisconsin. It was perhaps typical of the better trains that served routes of moderate length and of decidedly secondary importance. Like such contemporaries as—for example—IC's *Delta Express*, SP's *Del Monte*, or GN's *Gopher* and *Badger*, the *Varsity*'s reputation was, at best, regional.

The *Varsity* was never a particularly prepossessing train. In steam days the train normally ran behind one of the Milwaukee's venerable class F3 4-6-2 Pacifics. Although they were still spirited performers, the F3s (Alco 1910) were hardly front rank power on a road that ran the likes of 120-mph class A Atlantics and F7 Hudsons.

When diesels came to the *Varsity* in the late 1940s, they were most often drawn from the ranks of the Milwaukee's earliest (1941) Alco DL-109 or Electro-Motive E6 passenger units, themselves displaced from main line *Hiawathas* by newer power. Later, during the 1950s and beyond, the Milwaukee's postwar Fairbanks-Morse OP's or passenger-equipped Electro-Motive F units often drew the *Varsity* assignment.

Like its motive power, the *Varsity*'s rolling stock was usually handed down from the main line trains. From the 1940s on, the train's consist usually afforded a sampling of the Milwaukee's several earlier generations of *Hiawatha* equipment. Typically, there was a combination car up front to handle the RPO-express-baggage traffic, perhaps a car of storage mail, generally no more than two coaches, and the *Varsity*'s own special café–parlor car bringing up the rear.

At holiday periods there were always extra cars, and on such occasions as a

---

*© 1975 Challenge Publications, Inc., reprinted with permission from the March 1975 issue of *Rail Classics* magazine.

Wisconsin home game, particularly against Northwestern or Illinois, the morning *Varsity* from Chicago would carry as many as 18 or 20 extra cars of football fans that would be switched right out to Camp Randall Stadium, and then returned to Chicago on the southbound *Varsity* in the afternoon.

My long association with the *Varsity* began in 1947, when our family moved into a white frame house overlooking Lake Monona and the Milwaukee tracks at Madison. The northbound *Varsity*—train 117 in the timetable—arrived in Madison right around noon, and listening for the familiar whistle at the edge of town was a lunchtime ritual. Then we'd watch for the string of red and orange (until they became Union Pacific Armour yellow in the mid-1950s) cars to come gliding across Lake Monona toward the West Washington Avenue depot. To us it was never "117" or the *Varsity* but simply the "Noon Milwaukee." All you ever had to do was write, "I'll be in on the Noon Milwaukee," and the family knew just what you meant.

Among the Milwaukee's earliest passenger diesels were a pair of American Locomotive DL-109 units acquired in 1941 for *Hiawatha* service. By the time this photograph was taken in 1948, the two Alco's had been downgraded to lesser trains. This was the westbound *Varsity,* just south of Madison, arriving from Chicago shortly after noon on a wintry February day.

The southbound *Varsity*—No. 118—was no less a fixture. It was always scheduled out of Madison around 5:30 or 6 P.M., and the spirited way the train came booming out across the lake, honking impatiently at the fishermen roosting on the trestle, always helped to enliven the highball hour as the family relaxed on the front porch before dinner on summer afternoons.

During nearly a quarter century the paths of my life and that of the *Varsity* were interwoven. During those years I came and went from Madison many times and in many ways, but as often as any other my journey began or ended on the *Varsity.* Scheduled out of Chicago's Union Station around nine or nine-thirty in the morning, it was almost always the best connection you could make from anything arriving in the morning from the east, south, or west, and I rode it on the last leg of countless journeys home.

Boarding was never the rush that characterized the big main line trains; you always knew there'd be plenty of seats ("Madison?—to your left. Local passengers to the right"). If you'd slept late on the *Capitol* or the *Pacemaker,* and hadn't had time to breakfast at Fred Harvey's in Union Station, a late breakfast in the café-parlor, with the inevitable Milwaukee Road rose on each table, was one of the journey's special pleasures. The cook and waiter that ran the little dining section served up as good an order of hotcakes and sausage as I can remember having, the coffee was hot and plentiful, and business was never so heavy that you couldn't linger over your breakfast.

The run up the main line to Rondout was always made at a good clip, but the further you got from Chicago the slower *Varsity* ran. There was always a stop at

At noon on a summer's day, the westbound *Varsity* came honking across Lake Monona in June 1953. One of the railroad's passenger-equipped Electro-Motive F units headed the train.

Fox Lake—the end of suburban territory—and then the train went rolling across the gentle, rich hills of the southern Wisconsin countryside, pausing at places like Walworth and Avalon, where perhaps a post office truck and a relative or two waited expectantly beside the track.

Janesville was the biggest place along the *Varsity*'s route, and the train always seemed to spend a little more time there while the crew handled the head end

5

Along with the two Alco DL-109s, the Milwaukee also acquired a pair of Electro-Motive's early E6 passenger units for its main line *Hiawathas* in 1941. By 1948 these, too, had been downgraded to secondary trains. One of them brought the westbound *Varsity* across Lake Monona at Madison in September 1948.

business. Beyond Janesville my impatience always seemed to grow as the stops became more frequent—Edgerton, Stoughton, and then McFarland—and finally we were almost in Madison.

There was a quickening sense of anticipation as I watched for Lake Waubesa and the County Fairgrounds on the left. Then the diesel honked for the Lakeside crossing and moments later the train was out on the long Lake Monona fill. To the right the state capitol dome loomed above the lake as the wheels pounded rhythmically across the diamond at the mid-lake crossing with the North Western. Then the coaches slid in between the A. J. Sweet produce house and the Findorff lumber yard on the far side of the lake, past the coal yard and the creamery, and at last into the yellow brick depot on West Washington. I'd look down from the vestibule and see the folks waiting on the platform and I knew I was home once again.

The *Varsity* expired from much the same causes as did its contemporaries elsewhere in North America. After the Illinois Turnpike and Interstate-90 went all the way, you could drive to Chicago in less time than it took the train. And even if you didn't drive, there were express Greyhounds almost every hour, and two airlines could get you from Madison to O'Hare in less than an hour.

By the end of the 1950s trains 117 and 118 had begun their inevitable decline. Parlor car service ended in 1963. For a season café-lounge service was continued with one of the Milwaukee's Super Dome Cars—displaced from the discontinued *Olympian Hiawatha*—and then for a few months more with a regular café-lounge, but after April 1965 the train carried only coaches.

In 1967 the Post Office Department withdrew the *Varsity*'s RPO contract, and the Milwaukee promptly filed for abandonment. There were hearings and then the ICC finally said the train must continue to run on weekends and holidays, and thus the *Varsity* lingered on for a few more years. But finally, with the arrival of the Amtrak era on May 1, 1971, the *Varsity* was allowed to end its now empty journeys.

My train—the Noon Milwaukee—was gone now, and going home would never be quite the same again.

The Journey Today

Rail passenger service to Madison ended with the Amtrak start-up in 1971, and numerous attempts to restore it since then have all, thus far at least, ended in failure. The once-proud Milwaukee Road itself was merged into the Soo Line in 1986. The Chicago–Fox Lake portion of the Chicago-Madison route is now owned by the Chicago region's Metra, while the balance of the route is owned by the Wisconsin & Southern.

A Farewell to the Doodlebug*

Chances are good that most of us who grew up in rural America before World War II remember the gas-electric motor car. Of course we never knew it by that name. It was always called the "doodlebug" or the "galloping goose," or some equally derisive yet affectionate nickname.

During my own somewhat nomadic boyhood my family lived in a good many out-of-the-way places, but no matter where we went there was nearly always a doodlebug local that showed up every day at the local depot. I was only six years old when we lived in Hayti, way down in the southwestern tip of Missouri, but I can still remember the day the whole family went to the depot to meet my mother, who was returning from the East aboard the Frisco's gas-electric local that arrived from St. Louis every day. This was the first time I'd ever seen one, and it seemed a formidable machine, with red and white stripes on the front end. And I recall the long summers on the Montana prairies, when we visited the Wolf Point depot almost every day to watch the Great Northern's "galloping goose" pause to load and unload its cargo of mail, milk cans, baby chicks, assorted merchandise, and perhaps even a passenger or two.

The most impressive gas-electric of all those I remember was the Omaha Road's *Namekagon*, which used to come through Hayward, Wisconsin, on its run between the Twin Cities and Ashland. It was painted in bright green and yellow, and its name, which was taken from the local river, was proudly displayed on the rear of the trailer car, just like a mainline limited.

The first really successful internal-combustion rail car, developed by the Union Pacific's William R. McKeen, Jr. in 1905, wasn't a gas-electric at all, of course, but instead was a machine which used a complicated mechanical drive. The true gas-electric car, employing a gasoline engine–driven generator and traction motors, had been tried as early as 1891; but not until 1908, when General Electric introduced a line of gas-electric cars, did the idea reach the practical stage. By this time reasonably reliable heavy-duty gasoline engines were being manufactured, and rapid development of the electric railway industry had made the necessary motors and electrical equipment available. General Electric sold over 100 of its

*© 1961 Kalmbach Publishing Co., reprinted with permission from the May 1961 issue of *Trains* magazine.

Early on an April morning in 1959, Northern Pacific engineer Ed Williams climbed aboard motor car B-21 at Fargo, North Dakota, to begin his day's work. The car would make a 148-mile, nine-hour journey across the North Dakota prairie to Streeter as train 139, returning to Fargo the following day as train 140.

gas-electric cars to U.S. railroads, but the most successful builder was the Electro-Motive Company, which sold around 500 of them during the 1920s.

Many of the gas-electric's original proponents saw it as a means for the steam railroads to compete with the frequent passenger service offered by their interurban competitors; but as it turned out, the car was rarely used in this manner. Instead, low operating costs found a far wider application for the gas-electric as a means to economically operate lightly patronized local and branch-line services. Most important of all, perhaps, the gas-electric car pioneered the principles that made the diesel-electric locomotive possible a few decades later.

The gas-electric was what you might call attractively homely. Aside from the earliest McKeen and General Electric cars, which had knife- and bullet-nosed front ends respectively and were exceedingly dashing in appearance, most gas-electrics were built without the remotest concession to streamlining. They usually had a front end that was chopped off square, with such locomotive appurtenances as bells, headlights, markers, and air horns more or less haphazardly mounted on them. On the roof in disorderly array were located complicated-looking pipe radiators, mufflers, and exhaust stacks. For winter operation a sturdy snowplow frequently replaced the locomotive-type pilot.

The gas-electric was not a quiet machine. From a distance the snorting exhaust sounded something like that of a large tractor, but from within the engine room, where the unfortunate engineer rode, the clatter of the engine was something frightful. An engineer who valued his hearing always plugged his ears with cotton before setting out. The gas-electric's air horn was, in pre-diesel days, a distinctive feature that earned the car the widespread "galloping goose" title.

What with the generally low estate of branch-line and local passenger service, less and less was seen of the doodlebug during the years after World War II. But in the late 1950s a notable exception to the widespread disappearance of such schedules was the Northern Pacific's network of branch lines in North Dakota. It wasn't that NP was doing any better with this kind of operation than anyone else, it was simply that the obstinate North Dakota Public Service Commission refused to have any part of NP's proposal to substitute less costly highway services. By early 1959, however, NP—with the assistance of the 1958 Transportation Act—was finally getting somewhere with its efforts to discontinue almost all of its branch-line motor-car and mixed-train schedules in North Dakota. This seemed to be a good time for a last fond look at the once-familiar doodlebug, and I promptly invested $15.62 in a round-trip ticket between Minneapolis and La Moure, North Dakota, that was good for a 24-hour circle tour comprising 278 miles of travel aboard two doodlebug locals and a mixed train, not to mention another 371 miles aboard the *North Coast Limited* and the *Mainstreeter*.

At 7:45 one April evening I departed from Minneapolis, and a few minutes before midnight the *North Coast* had me into Fargo in royal style. I was back at the depot shortly after dawn next morning, for motor-car train 139 was scheduled for a bright and early 5:50 A.M. departure on its 147-mile run to Streeter, North Dakota, over the Fargo & Southwestern branch. Motor car B-21 was already in the depot, and the assorted contents of a string of baggage trucks were rapidly disappearing into the mail and express compartments at the front end.

Except for the corporate title displayed on the letterboard, the B-21 had little

11

Stopping at every town along the way, Northern Pacific motor car train 139 worked its way across the North Dakota prairie on a bright spring day in 1959. At Lisbon, a place of some importance as the seat of Ransom County, the station was a bit grander and the stop a little longer than most.

The gas-electric motor car was a versatile "train in one car" that combined several functions in a single piece of equipment. In addition to space for passengers, the NP's motor car B-21 had separate Railway Post Office and Railway Express Agency compartments. The train crew and station agent handled a modest business in both mail and express during a station stop at Verona, North Dakota.

During a station stop at Glover, North Dakota, the baggage man on the Northern Pacific's Jamestown-Oakes mixed train 154 manhandled cans of milk from local dairy farms into the train's combine for the trip to the creamery.

Freight was the principal business of Jamestown-Oakes mixed train 154, and conductor Frank White wore the traditional overalls and cap of freight train crews as he took care of paperwork in the train's elderly combine.

in common with the glossy Loewy-styled *North Coast* I'd stepped off a few hours before. The B-21 was a plain-looking, utilitarian vehicle, finished in serviceable Pullman green, with a bright red and white front end for visibility. There were comfortable leather-upholstered seats for 22 in the mahogany-paneled rear passenger compartment, and roomy express and RPO compartments up ahead. A builder's plate identified her as a 1929 Electro-Motive product with a car-body built by St. Louis Car Company. Like all NP gas-electrics, the B-21 had long since been dieselized—in this case with a Sterling diesel.

Engineer Ed Williams poked around the journal boxes, then climbed up beside the noisy diesel to start the B-21 on its way across the prairies. It was early spring, after the snow had gone and before the fields had turned green again, and I had forgotten how lonely the empty, treeless plains could be. The towns along the way—Woods, Coburn, Sheldon, and Buttzville—seemed little more than a few houses and grain elevators, and perhaps a long row or two of shiny corrugated bins for the surplus grain, huddled close to the track. At almost every one a station agent, elderly and dignified in a trainman-style cap with a metal AGENT badge on the front, waited for us in front of a weathered yellow frame depot. Usually the local mailman was there too, with his battered sedan pulled close to the platform and the trunk lid raised in anticipation of a few sacks of mail. The plain little train order signal above the station's bay window was invariably set at "clear," for ours was the sole train on the line.

Lisbon was the only town of consequence all the way from Fargo to La Moure and its superior status as a county seat was clearly established by a neat stuccoed depot, larger and more substantial than the frame structures elsewhere along the line. The few passengers who remained from the half dozen or so who had boarded the B-21 at Fargo left the car here. Engineer Williams inspected a newly overhauled power truck for signs of overheating, while the agent and baggageman handled a heavy head-end business. Then we headed westward across the Sheyenne River and out onto the prairie again, through more of the lonely little towns—halting momentarily at each to take care of the modest mail and express business, and at Independence just long enough for train 139's Conductor C. L. Manro to register at the junction with the Oakes branch.

La Moure was the end of my ride on the B-21, which paused briefly at the brick depot and then trundled off across the James River toward Streeter. Mixed train 154, scheduled daily except Sunday over the 69 branch-line miles between Jamestown, up on the NP main line, and Oakes, provided the next leg of the circle tour. A black and yellow Geep brought train 154 into town over the James River branch more or less at the 9:55 A.M. scheduled time. If the locomotive seemed modern indeed, the train's consist was very much in the tradition of rural mixed trains of an earlier time. Train 154's long string of box and cattle cars was trailed by a big combine that clumped solidly along on 6-wheel trucks. Arch windows and truss rods marked it as a period piece. The interior décor was equally passé, with dusty leather walkover seats, oil lamps, and a pot-bellied stove. Just ahead of the combine, which accommodated the train's express and passenger trade, was a "peddler" box car for l.c.l. (less-than-carload-lot) freight traffic.

The mixed train stayed in La Moure only long enough to switch a few cars and to handle a little express and l.c.l. business. Then the combine jerked forward as the Geep took in the slack and headed east. We retraced the route of the Fargo-Streeter motor car for some 5 miles, stopped to register with the dispatcher at Independence, then headed south over the 15-mile Oakes branch.

Oakes proved to be the center of a considerable branch-line activity. The town was the terminus for both NP's Oakes branch from the north and the railroad's Fergus Falls branch from the east. Chicago & North Western was represented by a branch which extended northward to Oakes from Huron, South Dakota—the only North Western penetration into North Dakota—and the Soo Line by its Hankinson (North Dakota)-Bismarck branch. The arrival of the NP mixed shortly before noon marked the beginning of a flurry of activity. Soon afterward, NP motor car B-18 rolled in from the east on its daily-except-Sunday round trip from Staples, Minnesota; then the North Western came to life with the arrival of mixed train 1 from Huron behind a green and yellow 12-wheeled Alco road-switcher. Only the Soo remained quiet.

There was time for lunch at the café down the street from the depot before the B-18's 12:20 P.M. departure for Staples on the final leg of my branch line tour. In appearance the motor car was little different from the one I'd ridden over the Fargo & Southwestern branch. Like the B-21 it was an Electro-Motive product—in this case with a carbody built by Standard Steel Car in 1926—and subsequently was re-engined by Caterpillar.

Staples was 170 miles away, and train 112 had a relaxed 5-hour 35-minute schedule in which to make it. For the first few miles east of Oakes, the motor car traveled with a strange bounding motion over nineteenth-century rails laid with opposite joints when the branch was built; then the B-18 settled into a more orthodox gait as newer rail was reached. At Wyndmere, Soo diesels waited impatiently to the north as the agent and crew loaded mail and express at a small depot tucked into one quadrant of the crossing. By mid-afternoon we were passing over the Red River into Minnesota on a curious humpbacked trestle; and finally, beyond Fergus Falls, the monotonous prairie landscape was replaced by Minnesota hills, trees, and lakes. At Wadena the motor car rolled onto heavy rail and crushed stone ballast and followed the semaphores of the NP's main line into Staples.

The sun hung low in the western sky as the B-18 slipped past a long line of dead steam power and then between the platforms at the Staples depot. Baby chicks, crates of eggs, trees from a Minnesota nursery, cream cans, and mail were transferred from the motor car's head-end compartments to baggage trucks to await the eastbound *Mainstreeter*. Across the tracks an already shiny Budd car was being washed down preparatory to beginning its nightly journey to Duluth. With another 12-hour, 340-mile day behind it, the 33-year-old motor car rolled off to the engine house.

Even as I rode them, the trains that transported me on my branch-line circle tour were running their last miles. The Oakes-Staples schedule was gone less than a week later, effective with the summer timecard; and within a short time the Fargo-Streeter run came off as well. For a time the NP continued to operate motor car schedules on its Valley City–McHenry and Jamestown-Wilton branches west of Fargo, but soon these runs were gone, too, and the end had come for the doodle-bug era in North Dakota.

"Yet there isn't a train
I wouldn't take"

Soon after I rode the Northern Pacific's gas-electric locals in 1959, these and similar services elsewhere had disappeared from the North American railroad scene. Mixed train services fared little better. Today, these, too, have vanished from U.S. railroads, and one can find only a few still operating in Canada and Mexico. Much of the branch line network over which these trains operated, too, has vanished. Northern Pacific successor Burlington Northern took up portions of the North Dakota and Minnesota branches that I rode in 1959, and sold what was left to short line operator Red River Valley & Western.

Ore Extra*

In the normal course of events the Duluth, Missabe & Iron Range Railway would have been all-diesel during 1959. But the year wasn't a normal one, and on the afternoon of May 26, 1959, No. 228, some 569 tons of white-tired, articulated, single-expansion steam motive power, waited on the Proctor, Minnesota, ready track with a fire on the grate and 240 pounds of steam on the gauge.

The train of events that built a fire in the Missabe Road's 2-8-8-4 began early in 1959, when United Steelworkers President Dave MacDonald and steel industry bargainers squared off for new contract talks. There were hints of a stubborn strike to come, and big steel users nervously began to stockpile. As the mills stepped up production to build inventories against the July 1 deadline for a new contract, there was a corresponding quickening of activity in the Great Lakes ore industry, which had seen far too little of it during recession year 1958.

The Missabe Road had more diesels than ever before to handle the tonnage that flowed from the Mesabi and Vermillion range mines to the elongated ore boats waiting at the Duluth and Two Harbor docks. (The *Missabe* Road hauls ore from the *Mesabi* Range and passes through the mining town of *Mesaba*. All three names are variations in the spelling of the same word of Indian origin meaning "giant.")

Early in the year Electro-Motive's LaGrange plant delivered 16 maroon and gold units to swell the Missabe SD9 roster to 74, and a half dozen 2400-hp DL-600's rolled west from the Alco works at Schenectady. DM&IR added a dozen leased Great Northern Electro-Motive F-type "covered wagons" to 16 leased Bes-

---

*© 1959 Kalmbach Publishing Co., reprinted with permission from the November 1959 issue of *Trains* magazine.

Tipping the scales at some 569 tons in working order and capable of a maximum tractive effort of 140,000 pounds, a Missabe Road class M4 2-8-8-4 Yellowstone stood among the largest and most powerful steam locomotives ever built. M4 No. 228 was ready to depart from the Proctor (Minnesota) yard with 200 empty ore cars for the Mesabi Range on May 26, 1959.

semer & Lake Erie F units already on the property. But still there weren't enough diesels to go around, and late in April the Missabe began pulling its reserves of Mikes, Santa Fe's, and Yellowstones off the storage tracks at Proctor and Two Harbors.

The 2-8-8-4 Yellowstones that went back to work on DM&IR's Missabe and Iron Range divisions were no ordinary breed of locomotive. Northern Pacific originated the wheel arrangement in 1928, and the Missabe received its first eight, labeled class M3, from Baldwin in 1941. Another ten in class M4, identical to the original in all but minor details, were added in 1943.

By any standard they were big brutes. Stretching 127 feet, 8 inches between couplers, and resting on 18 roller-bearing-equipped axles, the Yellowstones stood 16 feet, $2^7/8$ inches from rail head to top of stack. In working order an M4 and tender weighed in at 569 tons (the M3's were some 3 tons lighter), including the 26 tons of coal and 25,000 gallons of water swallowed up by the 14-wheeled centipede tender. Her vestibule cab, 11 feet long overall and almost as wide, seated four with ample room to spare.

The "Malleys," as they were known to Missabe Road men, were equipped with such miscellaneous efficiency-contributing appurtenances as Type E superheaters, Elesco or Worthington feedwater heaters, Valve Pilot speed recorders, and radio telephones. DM&IR was among the most safety conscious of U.S. railroads, and on the 2-8-8-4's this was expressed in such details as carefully striped footboards, safety chains across the cab doors, and the SAFETY FIRST slogan that was an integral part of the winged Missabe Road herald splashed across the welded tank.

In terms of tractive effort a Missabe Yellowstone could develop 140,000 pounds—more than Union Pacific's Big Boy and exceeded only by some half dozen locomotives in the history of steam. To a Missabe Division yardmaster this meant he could tie 180—or more—ore "jimmies," each grossing better than 90 tons, behind an M3 or M4 and get them over the road in good time. And this was only several cars fewer than what he could hang on a trio of six-motor roadswitchers.

Aside from such adjustments as lengthening of turntables, delivery of what constituted some of the world's largest steam power presented few difficulties to the Missabe Road, which was already accustomed to dealing with massive trains and big power. The contribution of the Yellowstones to the war effort, when DM&IR hauled as much as 45 million tons of ore during a single season (more than any other U.S. railroad), was enormous, and steam was still in the saddle when DM&IR hauled 50 million tons in 1953, its biggest season ever. The Yellowstones' 18 years on Missabe had been a regular cycle of ore-season activity, followed by winter storage and backshop work, and they hadn't missed a season yet (although steam's stint was confined to only a few weeks during the 1958 recession). Among their out-of-the-ordinary activities were several wartime winters of hauling Rio Grande tonnage over Tennessee Pass after the close of the ore season. And on at least one occasion, a 1958 fan trip, a Yellowstone had decorated the head end of a passenger train.

Extra board Engineer Ed App, a blue-eyed, graying man of slight build and a calm, deliberate manner, made a careful circuit of his machine, applying a few drops of oil here and there to the M4's running gear. Fireman John Shovein climbed aboard with the water jug, and head brakeman Ken Montgomery, eyeing low-hanging clouds and a light drizzle, pulled on his oilskin raincoat before setting out to line the switches. Engineer App swapped his gold-rimmed spectacles for a pair of goggles, horsed over the reverse lever and backed 228 down to the lower end of the yard. To the east the W56, the Missabe's dieselized, 1910-vintage Duluth streetcar, came clattering by on its shuttle run between the Proctor shops and roundhouse. The brakeman lined a route to the north end of the yard and the light engine cautiously picked its way through a yardful of dusty red ore hoppers, glossy SD9's, and bright yellow cabooses with the curious overhanging cupolas DM&IR favored for better visibility around its extra wide, extra high ore cars.

It was nearly 2:30 P.M. when 228 backed down what DM&IR still called the "passenger main" (even though the Missabe Division had been freight only since early 1958) onto a waiting string of 200 empty hoppers. The train already had air from the yard system, and as soon as the engine brought the train line up to the required 75 pounds, Engineer App pulled his air test and checked with the yard office by radio. (DM&IR radio-equipped steam engines, which had an inductive type radio, couldn't talk with cabooses or diesels, which had newer type VHF equipment, so messages were relayed via yard offices, which had both types.)

Wearing the traditional cap, goggles, and gauntlet gloves of his occupation, Missabe Road engineer Ed App waited for the brakemen to line the route into the Fraser (Minnesota) yard for Extra 228 North.

It was 2:55 P.M. when the radio speaker rasped, "Released, go when ready." Ed App answered with two short whistle blasts, eased out the throttle, and gingerly began to take the slack out of his 200 cars. The rear brakeman dropped off the engine to look over the train and pick up the caboose. App had his reverse gear set for full cutoff and the big engine began to move slowly through the yard with a soft, offbeat exhaust. Two tracks over, another of the Yellowstones crept by, dragging a southbound ore extra over the scales.

Extra 228's run was strictly a routine operation for the Missabe Road, but it was the sort of performance that could be so labeled on few railroads. Before engine and crew tied up for the night they would deliver their 200 empties to the yard at Fraser, Minnesota, some 68 miles away, and return with a train bearing considerably more iron ore than it takes to fill a good-size lake steamer. Even empty, 200 ore cars represent a train of better than 4000 tons. And pile 70 tons or more into each of nearly an equal number of cars, drag them across the division with a single 2-8-8-4, and you have what can be described quite simply as one of the most remarkable performances ever recorded by the steam locomotive. But

19

on the DM&IR they called it "routine," and went about it with a disarming matter-of-factness.

A darkening sky turned to heavy rain as Extra 228 North picked up speed out of the yard, cinders flying and exhaust sharpening as Ed App shortened the cutoff. His gloved hand reached for the whistle valve and the M4's deep steamboat whistle boomed for a grade crossing just beyond the yard.

The toughest part of the trip comes first for northbound Missabe Division tonnage, which must tackle the division's ruling northbound grade, a mile of 1.4 percent from Proctor to Adolph, before an engineer has a chance to get his train fairly rolling. Ed App worked his sanders as 16 63-inch drivers charged up the hill at full throttle. The 2-8-8-4 had its 200 cars rolling at more than 15 miles an hour as it topped the grade and blasted under the Duluth, Winnipeg & Pacific overhead at Munger. Then the four-cylinder exhaust blurred to a steady roar as Extra 228 rushed the Saginaw hill at a good 30 miles an hour.

For the boatload ore drags moving south on the Missabe Division, a hump in the main line at Saginaw, with 4 miles of 0.3 percent grade from Burnett to Saginaw, constitutes the division's ruling southbound grade. It wasn't an easy pull for the Missabe's super steam power and it still wasn't for the diesels.

The dull thud of a pair of torpedoes above the roar of the stack as we approached the crest at Saginaw served to emphasize the point. A southbound extra, with a trio of leased Great Northern F3's on the head end, had stalled on the grade. The crew had doubled the hill and already reassembled their train as we moved past at reduced speed on the northbound main. Later that night, we reflected, 228 would have to face the same test.

A 2-8-8-4 rides a good deal better when it's working hard, we decided, as the 228 administered a very rough and bouncy ride on the downgrade through Grand Lake to Burnett. Evidently General Roundhouse Foreman O. E. Bjornaas was joking earlier in the afternoon when he told us, "We'll give you 228—she has new springs."

A green distant signal and then a green-over-red home signal for the Coleraine Junction interlocking loomed up ahead. A flashing green order board told us there were no orders as we pounded through the junction where the double track of the Alborn Branch heads off to the northwest. From Alborn to Sax Great Northern's parallel ore line was only a short distance to the west.

The Missabe Road's track and bridges, like its ponderous locomotives and cars, were built for tonnage. The double track of this Missabe Division main line was laid with 112- and 115-pound rail, founded in an ample bed of heavy gravel and crushed rock. The massive bridges that carried us over the Cloquet, Whiteface and St. Louis rivers were designed for Cooper's E-72 loading, as heavy as they come, and were laid with welded 115-pound rail and steel ties, firmly held in place with special patented German tie plates, riveted to steel decks.

For 22 miles north from milepost 38 the Missabe Division was dead tangent track, broken only by a slight 1 degree curve midway, and Engineer App held his train to the 35-mph limit for empty ore cars all the way. Occasional piles of pulpwood at trackside among the desolate, scrubby woods indicated that DM&IR does haul something other than iron ore.

Red over yellow ahead! Our single 19 order read, "Run extra Proctor to Sher-

The massive tender of a Missabe Road Yellowstone could swallow up 25,000 gallons of water. Engineer Ed App topped off the tank of M4 No. 228 at Fraser, in preparation for the return trip to Proctor with 190 loaded ore cars.

wood via Keenan Cutoff," and the Iron Junction CTC operator had the switches lined for the cutoff at Keenan. The Yellowstone negotiated the 8-mile, single-track cutoff in just over 12 minutes, then followed another red-over-yellow signal through the interlocking at Sherwood that took us across the Duluth-Hibbing main line we'd just left, and headed north on the single track Fraser line. An SD9 and caboose waited on the main line to follow us into Fraser.

Extra 228 was on the Mesabi Range now, and huge mounds of waste from the open pit mines dominated the landscape. Fraser was just 6 miles away, and we followed CTC signals all the way in. For the last half mile, as we skirted a vast open pit mine at Buhl, Extra 228 was on Great Northern track.

"Lined for one," called the fireman as we approached Fraser yard, and the slack ran in with a clang as Ed App pinched her down while the head brakeman went ahead to line the switches for Track 3.

"About two car lengths more and you'll be in the clear," relayed the yardmaster by radio as the Yellowstone neared the far end of the yard. The head-end crew doubled five cars over onto Track 1, and at 5:16 P.M. Extra 228 North's run was completed.

While the crew backed the engine through the yard, turned it on the wye, and took coal and water, the SD9 that had followed us in from Sherwood went to work assembling our southbound train from the strings of loaded hoppers in the yard.

The ore we would move out of Fraser came from the Oliver Iron Mining Division's Sherman plant, which washed and separated ore from five nearby mines. To the north of the yard, several Oliver cow-and-calf switchers shoved cuts of side-dump gondolas, bringing the raw ore from the open pits, up a high fill for dumping into the processing plant.

Coaled and watered, 228 backed onto its southbound train at 6:05 P.M. Behind the articulated's drawbar stretched 190 70-ton-capacity ore cars, which added up to a gross train weight approaching 18,000 tons.

"These Malleys were rated at only 180 cars when they were new," grumbled the fireman. And back then, he pointed out, that included some of the smaller hoppers, too. These were all big 70-tonners.

The fireman cracked open the firebox door and blower, while the smokebox-mounted air pumps hammered away at the job of pumping up the train. Three SD9's on a "cross-country" job (an east-west run across the range to Biwabik) came in light for a train, and the two crews chatted about seniority lists and similar matters as they waited for their air.

The rear brakeman walked ahead, looking over his train and setting retainers on the first 55 cars for slow release. These ore cars had an interesting braking feature. Running light a standard 10-inch brake cylinder provided the necessary braking force. When a car was loaded, truck spring deflection limited the travel of a truck-mounted plunger-type piston, which automatically brought an additional 12-inch brake cylinder into action for supplementary braking force.

Getting 190 loaded cars out of Fraser was going to be interesting. Engineer App had an 0.8 percent grade facing him, complicated by wet rail from intermittent rains. The SD9 that had made up our train was coupled on the rear, ready to start shoving as soon as the caboose began moving.

At 7:32 P.M., the air test completed, the CTC signal flashed green. App took slack, cut in his sanders, and eased open the throttle. The M4 moved forward a few car lengths and quit. No go. App heaved back the reverse lever and took slack again. This time the Yellowstone made it. Steam enveloped the cab as he cleared the cylinder cocks, and the engine began to pick up a little speed. The front engine erupted into furious motion as the drivers lost their grip on wet rail heading through the switches. App eased off a little on his throttle but the front engine lost its footing again—and again. Fighting to keep moving, 288 hammered through

Fireman John Shovein checked the fire on the 125-square-foot grate of Yellowstone No. 228 as the locomotive began its southbound journey from Fraser to Proctor with 18,000 tons of iron ore. At full throttle, the locomotive's huge firebox burned more than 500 pounds of Pennsylvania bituminous coal every minute.

Buhl at a slow walk. A small boy stood awestricken on the station platform, committing to memory an unforgettable sight and sound.

Now it looked as if the Yellowstone was losing the battle. Again and again the drivers lost their hold on the slippery rail, and seconds seemed to separate each blast from the stack as the inertia of nearly 18,000 tons pulled the engine to little better than a crawl. One foot propped in front of him to gain leverage, App tried to find just the right throttle setting short of the point where the front engine went out from under him.

Grade crossing ahead! App made frantic motions to the fireman. Shovein reached for the whistle valve, and a low moan from the deep whistle told that the boiler pressure was something less than 240 pounds. A Chevy pulled up short as the Yellowstone inched across the pavement. The driver surveyed the endless string of creeping hoppers in disgust and jerked his car around to look for another way across the track. It was going to be a long wait.

Then suddenly the battle was won. The grade began to level off, and gradually the exhaust cadence quickened. The grade tipped the other way and App shoved in the throttle and started working the air to hold his train back.

Approaching Sherwood a yellow-over-green distant signal indicated that the plant was lined for the Keenan Cutoff again. The red-over-yellow home signal flashed by and Fireman Shovein leaned out in response to a flashing yellow order board to snare the 19 order that told us to run extra to Proctor. App flicked on his cab light, read the order, and passed it around the cab.

Extra 228 South had a slight grade working in its favor on the cutoff, and the cab filled with smoke as App shut her off and drifted. The roar of the stack faded, to be replaced by the sharp hiss of air from the cylinder cocks as pistons flashed back and forth in empty cylinders.

At 8:15 P.M. App sent superheated steam rushing into the cylinders again as the extra approached the junction at Keenan and lurched through the switches to the left-hand main. Behind the dimmed headlight of a 2-8-8-4 nearly a mile of empty ore hoppers waited on the northbound main for us to clear the junction. They were already moving as the three red markers (another DM&IR peculiarity) of the northbound extra's caboose whipped past.

This left-hand running was still another Missabe Road oddity that had almost as many explanations as there were railroaders you cared to ask, ranging all the way from the one that blamed it on English (or Chicago & North Western) operating men in the early days, to the one that says it gave engineers a better view of the track in case logs fell from trains going the other way. Aside from the nonconformity of the practice, there really weren't any disadvantages to it, and a changeover to right-hand operation would have been costly.

The 2-8-8-4 set a steady pace as it rolled off the miles of nearly level and tangent track, with the Valve Pilot speed recorder showing a steady 27 to 28 miles per hour (the limit for loaded ore cars was 30 miles per hour). If the 228 had the devil's own time getting started, she was really rolling now. It was the frequent observation of Missabe Road men that, though the diesels could start and pull more, steam, once rolling, could move tonnage over the railroad in better time. And the M4 was ably demonstrating this characteristic.

Occasionally the cab filled with an orange glare and sudden heat as Shovein

Engineer Ed App tried to find just the right throttle setting as his 2-8-8-4 Yellowstone struggled to accelerate an 18,000-ton ore train out of the Fraser yard on wet rail.

cracked the Butterfly doors to check his fire. Beyond the headlight's beam the red lights of crossing gates began to flash and then dropped into place, a flashing white light indicating all was in working order.

DM&IR mechanical men told me an M3 or M4 would produce 1000 gross ton-miles of transportation from 60 to 64 pounds of coal, which meant that Fireman Shovein's MB stoker was hurling something over 500 pounds a minute of District 8 Pennsylvania bituminous onto the M4's 125-square-foot grate area. And for every pound of coal consumed, the 46-foot-long, 104-inch-diameter boiler was evaporating some 6 pounds of water.

The journey from the iron range complete, engineer Ed App checked around his locomotive following Extra 228 South's arrival at the Proctor yard on a rainy May evening in 1959.

"All black," called the brakeman as the Yellowstone leaned into a curve and he looked over the train. Ahead, a trackside farmhouse stood out momentarily as the headlight beam swept around the curve. Green interlocking signals and a clear order board led the way through Alborn and Coleraine Junction. It was 9:05 P.M. and the Saginaw hill was just 10 minutes away.

Crackling lightning to the south had given way to more rain. Wet rail was going to make the hill just that much tougher. App had the tonnage rolling for all it was worth as the 2-8-8-4 charged through Burnett and stormed the 4-mile grade. At the Cloquet River bridge a diesel came grinding down the hill with yet another string of empties for the range.

Slowly the grade cut into the Yellowstone's speed. The exhaust that had been a continuous rush of sound became a series of separate and distinct reports, as the stack hurled soot and cinders into the sky like a giant shotgun. Steaming beautifully, the big engine never faltered as App laid a fine stream of sand on the wet rail from both sanders and adjusted throttle and reverse lever to get the last ounce of tractive force.

Wham! With a sound like a minor explosion 228 slammed under the Highway 33 overpass. Smoke and steam swirled through the cab, and cinders pelted the cab roof as they rebounded from blast plates under the concrete slab. Just a little over a mile to the crest now.

Minutes later the white frame Saginaw depot loomed up in the headlight beam, and the M4 rolled over the crest with a few miles per hour of momentum to spare. Ed App eased off the throttle and looked distinctly relieved. With a certain smugness I remembered that diesel that hadn't quite made the hill earlier in the day.

From Munger to Proctor Extra 228 rolled downgrade through what was now a fierce downpour. App closed the throttle and worked the air to hold the tonnage in check.

It was 10 P.M. on the nose when Extra 228 ground to a stop short of the Proctor scale house. A half hour later the M4 moved across the scales at a steady 3 mph with half the extra's consist. A yard crew would complete the weighing. By 11:15 P.M. the job was done, the engine in the house, and the crew called it a day.

Later in the night the scale house totaled up the figures. Extra 228 had weighed in with a gross weight of 17,468 tons. The 2-8-8-4 had moved it 68 miles in just two and a half hours. A phenomenal performance for steam? Anywhere else—yes. But on the Missabe Road, strictly a routine matter.

The Journey Today

Steam locomotives like Yellowstone No. 228 disappeared from the Missabe Road soon after my 1959 trip, but big diesel locomotives still move phenomenal tonnages of iron ore down to the ore docks at Duluth and Two Harbors. The rich iron ores of the Mesabi Range have long since played out, but some 40 million long tons of processed low-grade taconite move off the range every year.

Second Morning Chicago*

Muscled stevedores loaded bags of Brazilian coffee into a trailer at New Orleans' Poydras Street Wharf. The coffee was about to begin a fast trip to a Chicago grocery warehouse as a "piggyback" shipment on the Illinois Central's dispatch freight NC-6 on April 23, 1957.

At New Orleans' Poydras Street Wharf two husky stevedores expertly tossed bulky sacks of coffee beans into three orange and brown Illinois Central piggyback trailers. Each of the sacks weighed 133 pounds, but the men's muscled precision made it look easy. The legend on the sacks read Sao Paulo, Brazil; their destination: a Chicago grocery warehouse.

Farther down the wharves lift trucks were shoving half-ton bales of Indian burlap into three trailers destined for a St. Louis bag company, stevedores were loading another trailer with Argentine corned beef for Chicago, and, at the IC's coffee warehouse, more sacks of the Brazilian beans were being hoisted into trailers.

By the time the loading crew arrived at Mays Yard that April 1957 afternoon, ten trailers of high valued freight were ready to roll up the ramp and onto the flats of NC-6, the IC's fastest New Orleans–Chicago dispatch freight. Scheduled for 7 P.M. departure, NC-6 was slated for a 1000-mile dash from the Gulf to the Great Lakes on a forty-hour schedule that would put Brazilian coffee beans and Argentine beef in Chicago in time for second morning delivery.

At Mays Yard I watched as the loading crew secured the last of the trailers. IC used a "circus train" end loading system, backing the trailers up a ramp and down a string of flat cars. All of the road's piggyback flats were modified 53-foot, 6-inch cars with a chain hoist tie-down arrangement which is adjustable to any length trailers. A likely future innovation, the IC told me, would be the use of 75-foot flat cars.

Although the IC was a comparative latecomer in the trailer-on-flat car business, the road was steadily, if cautiously, expanding its operation serving Chicago, Memphis, St. Louis, and New Orleans.

"We're playing it close," is the way Superintendent of Stations M.D. Partelow stated IC's conservative entry into piggyback. As part of this "go slow" approach IC

*© 1957 Federation for Railway Progress, reprinted with permission from the July 1957 issue of *Railway Progress* magazine.

had carefully avoided tying up more equipment than necessary in piggyback operation. Thus far, 46 modified flat cars and 77 trailers had been provided for the service, a "tight" equipment situation that had led to some outstanding mileage records for rolling stock: for example, a 235 miles per day average for piggyback flat cars in the previous February.

"We do a lot of thinking, studying, and surveying before going into new points with piggyback service," said General Merchandise Agent L. A. Schellenberger, who headed up IC piggyback sales and service. With such cautious expansion, piggyback service had been successful in each of the cities where it had been offered. Prospects for additional service included both Jackson, Mississippi, and Birmingham, Alabama.

Thus far IC had handled only railroad-owned trailers at truck competitive rates and regarded all of its traffic as freight "recaptured" from truckers. But the road was now exploring the possibilities of hauling trailers for motor common carriers and shipper-owned trailers. IC was also considering the development of an interchange service with other roads. As Schellenberger put it, "The baby is growing."

NC-6's six trailerloads of Brazilian coffee were typical of an important part of the Illinois Central freight traffic picture—foreign trade. New Orleans was the nation's second largest ocean port, and a large part of its in- and out-bound freight moved over Illinois Central rails. All told, import and export traffic produced some 180,000 carloads a year for the railroad, accounting for better than 10 percent of its total operating revenues.

The import trade had dominated IC piggyback traffic out of New Orleans since the service had started in 1956. Coffee from Central and South America, Ethiopia, and the Ivory Coast of Africa; sisal from Mexico and Africa; canned Hawaiian pineapple; and olives from Spain, Portugal, Italy and Africa were typical piggyback cargoes moving north from New Orleans.

Loader C. P. Windham made the final tie-down connections as a load of coffee was secured on a piggyback flat car for dispatch freight NC-6 at the Illinois Central's Mays Yard at New Orleans.

Soon after six, a switcher came down to pull the ramp in time for NC-6's 7 P.M. departure, and I joined Trainmaster R. L. Warren for a substantial dinner in the yard restaurant before boarding the second of the two GP9 units that would take NC-6 north that night. We would run as Extra 9232 with 62 loads and 41 empties.

Engineer J. H. Clarke eased open his throttle, and 3500 idling horsepower took up the characteristic, even chant of La Grange power. A red board held us a few minutes on the yard lead, as a Missouri Pacific passenger train slid by on its way to the New Orleans terminal. Then signals flashed to green over green and sparks flew from the exhausts, as Clarke got his tonnage rolling in earnest through the warm spring evening.

"Airplane" Clarke wasn't able to live up to his nickname that night. Two units can move 103 cars, but they won't set any speed records doing it. A 35 to 40 mph pace was the best Clarke could do, even on the water level track that carries IC around Lake Pontchartrain.

Clarke braked his train down to the 10-mph limit as we crossed the Manchac drawbridge, the operator at trackside looking us over. We passed Hammond, Louisiana's "strawberry capital," at 8:28 and I recalled reading in the morning paper that IC's "Crimson Flier," a solid strawberry train, had made the season's first trip north the night before, operating with rights over all but first-class trains. Later, at the end of our run, we found a Chicago restaurant chain in the midst of a "fresh Louisiana strawberry shortcake" promotion, made possible by such a redball handling. North of Hammond we counted three local freights busy working the sidings as they gathered the northbound berries.

Dispatch CN-1 slammed by on the southbound main at Fluker, and we spotted a single piggyback load riding ahead of the caboose. North of Chatawa, SN-3 went by with fast freight from St. Louis: two piggyback loads this time.

Ninety-seven miles, and just short of three hours, out of Mays Yard, Engineer Clarke put us into South Yard at McComb, Mississippi, where crews were changed and three GP9 units were substituted for two. A glance at the operating timetable, while the yard crew switched out a bad order tank car, told us that southbound train 1, the streamliner *City of New Orleans*, was due. Typical of Illinois Central's precision operation of passenger trains, the waggling headlight came into sight, on time to the minute; and No. 1 blared through behind two wide open diesels.

"Two units will drag a train like this; three will run it," remarked Trainmaster Warren, and Engineer A. R. Lansing proceeded to illustrate the point. Despite a ruling northbound grade out of McComb, the speedometer soon indicated a 55-mph pace that carried NC-6 into North Jackson in just two hours.

From North Jackson to Memphis, IC freights forsake the main line through Grenada, used by passengers trains, for a single track, nearly gradeless freight route via Gwinn, Mississippi. Dieselization was only a few months old on both the Louisiana and Memphis divisions, and Warren told us of a few of the temporary problems it created for a single track line. Fewer, but faster and longer, freights meant that the line had more sidings than it needed, but with 100-car trains, none were long enough. IC was planning to cut the number of sidings along this important route and to lengthen those remaining to accommodate diesel-length trains.

Diesels had also meant an impressive improvement in IC freight train performance. The 70 new GP9's that IC placed in service in 1957 had helped power new and improved dispatch freights, such as NC-6 and its southbound counterpart CN-5, which had cut schedules by as much as 24 hours. They'd also brought impressive increases in gross ton miles per hour and corresponding decreases in freight train miles and freight train hours.

Actually NC-6 was not a unique train on the Illinois Central: rather it was typical of a fleet of forty-nine dispatch freights that reached every important point on the 6500 mile system, such as the CC-4, which rushed California fruit into

Three brand-new Electro-Motive GP9 units headed northbound New Orleans-Chicago dispatch freight NC-6 over the Illinois Central's Louisiana Division on an April night in 1957. It was past midnight as the train paused at North Jackson, Mississippi, where the railroad's two separate routes to Memphis diverged.

Chicago from connections at Council Bluffs, and CC-6, the "meat train," which usually ran to two or three sections of Chicago-bound livestock and meat products. One of IC's fastest schedules was BC-2, which picked up traffic from Southeastern rail connections at Birmingham and provided third morning delivery at Chicago for Florida fruit. A southbound counterpart, SE-1, provided similar service for Midwestern meat, perishables, and manufactured products.

Nor did Illinois Central fast freight service end with regular dispatch schedules. The IC, for example, moved more bananas than any railroad in the world, most of them through New Orleans. It was a year-around traffic, and the road moved it in solid banana extras, on fast New Orleans–Chicago schedules.

31

At Gwinn, division point between the Louisiana and Memphis Divisions, the yard crew filled NC-6 out to 80 loads and 46 empties, totaling 7515 tons, and there was still more tonnage to come: fourteen loads and five empties to pick up at Greenwood and a carload of brick to set out at Lambert. It wasn't too much train by any means, for NC-6 had water level running all the way to Memphis.

A glance through the waybills told us our new tonnage included box cars of Mississippi cotton, lumber, and fertilizer; tank cars of ammonia, asphalt, and oil; and empty coal cars on their way back to the mines.

Traveling engineer T. C. "Tip" Nelms was at the controls of dispatch freight NC-6 as the New Orleans–Chicago train headed north across western Tennessee after a classification stop at Johnston Yard in Memphis.

As NC-6 eased out of the yard at 3:50 A.M., we were running an hour and forty minutes ahead of schedule; and dawn found the freight making time across the rich farmland of the Mississippi River Delta. The IC originated more cotton than any other railroad, and the Delta was the heart of the cotton country that surrounds Memphis.

By now, it was time for breakfast, and while Conductor Rosson brewed some powerful caboose coffee on the potbellied coal stove, I broke out the box of fresh strawberries that piggyback supervisor Bill James had handed us as we left Mays Yard.

At 9:25 A.M., well fed and better than two hours ahead of schedule, we pulled into Johnston Yard in Memphis, where NC-6 was reclassified. Some of its tonnage was destined for connections, and St. Louis traffic was cut out for other dispatch trains. Four hours later, NC-6 was rolling again, as Extra 9083, with two GP9's on the head end and 43 loads and 43 empties behind.

Traveling Engineer T. C. Nelms took the right hand side for the run across western Tennessee. "Tip" Nelms had a reputation as a good runner, but a clanging low oil alarm noisily ended prospects for a fast trip. Nelms cut out the ailing lead unit while the engine crew worked to correct the trouble, but 9083 continued to act up, and we lost an hour on the run to Fulton, Kentucky, where a replacement unit was waiting.

Engineer R. N. Pennington took over the throttle for the run to Cairo, and the throbbing diesels ticked off the miles at a steady 30-mph clip. Like most Illinois Central men, Pennington remembered the road's outstanding Paducah-built steam power with affection but appreciated what the diesel could do and agreed that it was far easier and cleaner work. "The old steam engine seemed more like railroading though," he observed.

Dusk had fallen when NC-6 slowed to the approaches of the great Cairo Bridge, which carries IC over the broad waters of the Ohio. As the headlight played over the silvery steel work, Pennington recalled how the American Bridge Company had replaced the bridge's main spans a few years before. "They built the new spans on falsework alongside the bridge, pushed the old ones into the river, then slid the new ones into place—with only a few hours interruption to traffic at a time."

Some four miles in length, including approaches, the original bridge was the world's longest river crossing when it was opened to traffic in 1889, completing the Illinois Central's last link in an unbroken route between the Great Lakes and the Gulf of Mexico.

We paused in North Cairo only long enough for car inspectors to look the train over and to get a St. Louis Division crew; and then NC-6 pulled out of the yard still 45 minutes early.

Youthful Trainmaster W. B. Kennedy, who climbed aboard the diesel for the trip to Centralia over his division, called our attention to the curves and grades that typify the line to Carbondale. "Freight trains are allowed 50 mph through here," he told us, "but passenger trains are limited to 45 in order to keep dishes on the tables in the diner."

Centralia was our last division point; we'd be on Illinois Division rails all the way to Chicago now. We waited while the yard crew switched out a "bad order" empty and Engineer "Deb" Barham tested the diesel's Automatic Train Stop equipment. ATS was in use between Centralia and Champaign, and it made this 125-mile stretch of track Illinois Central's fastest. Freight trains were allowed 60 mph and passenger trains a cool 100. ATS cab signals gave the engineer a continuous picture of track conditions ahead with a green "clear" indication or a red signal that limited him to 15 mph. He had six seconds to acknowledge a restrictive indication before brakes were automatically applied.

Barham took us out of the yard at 11:30 P.M., and our pair of 16-cylinder diesels quickly accelerated toward the 60 mph limit. Just north of Centralia, a fast Birmingham-bound train, dispatch freight SE-1, thundered by behind three GP9's. We were in Mattoon before 2 A.M., and it took the crew just ten minutes to set out the 34 cars that left NC-6 there. Alert eyes spotted a hot box south of Champaign, and the offending car was quickly set out on a siding at Pesotum. Twenty-two cars were added to NC-6's consist at Champaign, and from here to Chicago's Markham Yard there was nothing but 100 miles of fast running ahead.

Richton, 29 miles from the Loop, was the beginning of the Chicago Terminal Division and the outer terminal of IC's electrified suburban service, constituting the finest railroad entry into Chicago. North of Richton there wasn't a single grade crossing with streets, highways, or other railroads. Suburban trains had their own exclusive right of way: as many as six tracks as they neared the Loop. Another four tracks handled through passenger and freight trains. It was 6:30 A.M. as our two units roared through Richton, and the suburban fleet was being readied for the morning rush.

At Homewood, the crew dropped the caboose and 21 cars destined for Congress Street on the main line, then took the remaining 50 cars into the big Markham Yard, Illinois Central's largest classification yard. Just a few years before, Markham had undergone a $3 million modernization program to become the nation's first "push-button" yard.

Back on the main line, NC-6 waited while train 4, the northbound *Louisiane*, went by, then crossed over and followed her into the Loop.

On its second morning out of New Orleans, dispatch freight NC-6 was on the last lap into Chicago as the train rolled through the IC's South Side suburban territory on a rainy April morning in 1957. Northbound on its overnight journey from New Orleans, the railroad's *Louisiane* overtook the fast freight on a parallel track.

There was a sharp crack of escaping air from the parted train line as two GP9's pulled away from the train at Congress Street. It was 8:20 A.M. and we were 37 hours and 20 minutes out of New Orleans: a full two hours and forty minutes ahead of NC-6's advertised arrival. A transfer engine and caboose pulled the six piggyback flats from the rear of the train and then shoved them through a heavy downpour to the ramp.

One of the coffee trailers rolled down the ramp, and I swung into the tractor's

Its swift journey on NC-6 complete, a trailer load of coffee was pulled off a piggyback flat car
at the Illinois Central's Congress Street Yard opposite the Loop in downtown Chicago.

cab with the husky teamster who jockeyed it through Loop traffic to its West
Pershing Road destination. As he backed it against the warehouse loading dock, I
glanced at my watch. It was 10:15, and the Brazilian coffee beans I'd seen loaded
into this same trailer less than 48 hours before, and almost 1000 miles away, had
reached the end of their journey.

The Journey Today

The "piggyback" revolution in freight transportation that trains like NC-6
helped to pioneer has since transformed the railroad industry. Intermodal trailer-
on-flat-car and container traffic has long represented the fastest growing segment
of the rail freight business, and U.S. railroads now transport more than 8 million
trailers and containers every year. Today's successor to Illinois Central's New Orleans–Chicago NC-6, intermodal train IO-2, still offers "second morning Chicago" delivery for urgent freight.

Meat Train*

South Omaha's business is meat. Its raw material was livestock, fattened on the plains of the Midwest; and the finished products of its slaughterhouses were carcasses and dressed meat as well as hides and dozens of other packing house by-products. The pens, runways, and loading ramps of its Union Stock Yards Company covered 100 acres of land; and no less than 18 packing plants, including four major producers, were included in its unexcelled facilities. Every year South Omaha received nearly 6 million head of cattle, calves, hogs and sheep from 30 states and Canada; shipped over 1½ million head to Mexico and every part of the United States, both for feeder stock and to packing plants; and sent out nearly 360,000 tons of processed meat from its packing plants. Bawling, steaming, malodorous South Omaha could produce figures to show that it had nudged out Chicago as the world's largest livestock market and meat packing center.

For most of South Omaha's nearly 15,000 packing house and stockyard workers, the day's work was almost finished on that October 1957 afternoon. But for hundreds of transportation workers—truckers and railroadmen alike—the work day was just reaching its peak. Shortly after noon switch crews of the South Omaha Terminal Railway, which switches all but two of South Omaha's packers, had started their early pulls from the packing house sidings and livestock loading tracks; and they would be making late pulls up to 5:30 P.M. Union Pacific and Burlington crews switched the other two plants.

Transfer runs from the North Western, Milwaukee Road, Rock Island and Illinois Central began drifting into the crowded South Omaha Terminal yard. Each crew set out its caboose on a yard track, then dropped down to the lower end of the yard to wait in the clear while the Terminal switchers began putting together their eastbound meat and livestock trains. In its own yard Burlington was assembling its eastbound hotshot, and in the Union Pacific yard a westbound counterpart was being made up.

To call the meat traffic situation competitive is an understatement.

Most of South Omaha's meat production and a good part of its outbound livestock movement was eastbound traffic; and no fewer than five railroads, not to mention a growing, aggressive trucking industry, competed for a share. All five railroads offered comparable fast, overnight Omaha-Chicago dispatch freight schedules designed primarily for meat traffic. To get a better-than-average share of the traffic takes a little something extra in the way of service and dependability. One railroad, Illinois Central, and its premier meat train, CC-6, provided just that.

---

*© 1958 Kalmbach Publishing Co., reprinted with permission from the October 1958 issue of *Trains* magazine.

Early on an October evening in 1957, transfer runs are ready to move out of the South Omaha (Nebraska) Terminal Railway yard with processed meat and livestock from the South Omaha packing plants and stockyards. From left to right were Chicago & North Western, Rock Island, and Illinois Central runs. Out of sight was another for the Milwaukee Road.

To begin with, CC-6 was fast. Illinois Central operating men regarded it as the fastest of the system's considerable fleet of dispatch freights; and in matters of freight train speeds Illinois Central deferred to few railroads. Then there is the matter of dependability. Much of Omaha's eastbound meat traffic was headed for Chicago connections with eastern railroads. For Illinois Central this meant there was a daily connection to be made with the Indiana Harbor Belt at Broadview Yard, west of Chicago. There was a 1:30 P.M. cutoff time at Broadview, and if CC-6 wasn't there with the meat, IHB went without it. A look back through Illinois Central's daily records of connections made showed few days when CC-6 wasn't at Broadview by the appointed hour.

Illinois Central's advertised schedule for CC-6 called for a 4 P.M. departure from South Omaha, but on this particular October evening it wasn't going to even be close to that. It was almost dark before the Terminal switchers were really in the swing of making up the meat trains.

A little after 6, MoPac's domed *Missouri River Eagle*, the "Bird" to the railroaders, came gliding through the yard on its way to Omaha Union Station from St. Louis and Kansas City. Then the Terminal switchers waited in the clear while a Union Pacific switcher delivered a long cut of reefers from the Wilson plant. I joined Illinois Central Trainmaster Bill Johnson for a steak dinner at one of the stockyard eateries while the switchers continued their work.

By the time we returned our train was almost ready.

An eastbound Rock Island dispatch freight soon showed up behind a pair of striped Geeps to deliver five cars of stock for Waterloo for which we'd been waiting. Then a Terminal switcher shoved in the last of our 16-car transfer cut, a glass-lined, refrigerated tank car of animal blood for a Chicago laboratory.

After the four meat runs were made up, the transfer engines came up from the lower end of the yard, coupled on, and began pumping up the train lines while car inspectors looked over the trains.

Burlington's meat train was the first one off that evening. It came booming out of the Q yard to the north behind three Geeps, headed through the Terminal yard, and disappeared to the south. The Milwaukee Road transfer run was ready next, and it headed out on Union Pacific tracks to Omaha and Council Bluffs. Close on its markers followed the North Western run. We were next in the parade, and at 8:12 P.M. Illinois Central GP7 No. 8976 eased 16 cars and caboose into motion. I tossed my camera and bag at the caboose platform and made a stab at the grab iron. Our fast freight run to Chicago was under way. Behind us the Rock Island run, with too many cars tied to its single Geep, was struggling out of the yard.

Our 16-car consist was made up of two parts. In what Illinois Central terms a "city block" were a half dozen cars destined for Hawthorne and Congress Street yards in Chicago. Among them were four carloads of meat due out next evening on IC's crack southeastern dispatch freight, SE-1, for Birmingham and Miami destinations. The rest of our consist was blocked for set-out at other points en route. There was a single carload of vermiculite for Fort Dodge; and there were nine loads for Waterloo—one meat reefer and eight cars of stock for the packing plants.

Strictly speaking, this was not yet dispatch freight CC-6, for CC-6 was a Council Bluffs–Chicago train, eastward second-class train 76 on the timecard, operating daily. More than 15 miles away in Council Bluffs Yard, the main body of CC-6 was being put together.

The back end of the North Western caboose stood out in the Geep's headlight beam as we followed the train upgrade to Summit. Still on Union Pacific rails, we dropped down into Omaha, passed below the Union Station, through an industrial district, then headed north to Illinois Central track and the Missouri River bridge.

At 9:10 P.M. we were in Council Bluffs Yard, and the rest of CC-6 was waiting, ready to roll. The transfer engine shoved the Waterloo and Fort Dodge cars on the head end of the train, then took the "city block" around to the rear end. Three waiting GP9 road units backed on and began pumping up the train line; and a switcher coupled on at the rear end to speed up the job.

At 9:55 P.M. Omaha District Engineer A. A. Kullman eased open the throttle and took out the slack, and CC-6 was under way. Congress Street Yard was 511 miles beyond the Geep's double-beamed headlight. Sparks and a thin blue exhaust shot skyward as the units accelerated out of the yard. Engineer Kullman held his train to 30 mph for a slow order just out of the yard, then he picked up to a steady 50 mph pace. We were almost 4 hours behind the advertised schedule for CC-6, and Mr. Kullman was going to make up a little time. Back in the second unit I adjusted the cab heat control against the chill October night, made myself comfortable in the roomy cab, and prepared for the 135 miles of nonstop running that separated us from Fort Dodge.

Behind Engineer Kullman's three GP9's were 4529 tons of fast freight. In Conductor Ed O'Connor's waybills for our consist of 77 loads and 9 empties were listed not only the predominant cargoes of meat and livestock that gave CC-6 its unofficial title of "meat train," but such items as hides, soap and oil; salt, wine, grapes and canned goods; lumber, plaster, glass, and copper.

Between Council Bluffs and Tara, just 6 miles west of Fort Dodge, CC-6 ran on the Omaha District of Illinois Central Iowa's Division. It was a part of Illinois Central you'd never see from a passenger-train window, for the Omaha District existed only for the movement of freight trains. It was single track, operated by timetable and train order; not a block signal was in sight until the Cherokee District at Tara.

CC-6 was on the Iowa Division all the way until it reached Broadview, less than 15 miles from Congress Street. The largest of Illinois Central's 13 divisions and terminals, the Iowa Division embraced all of what Illinois Central termed its "western lines." Its 964 route miles reach Illinois, Iowa, Nebraska, South Dakota, Minnesota and Wisconsin.

The Iowa Division was a railroad in itself. It was an east-west traffic artery on a system that was otherwise almost entirely a north-south railroad. And it was almost entirely a freight railroad, for the Iowa Division operated but two passenger trains: the Chicago–Sioux City *Hawkeye* and the Chicago-Waterloo *Land O' Corn*.

Iowa Division freight trains hauled many things: coal, manufactured products, gypsum, lumber, agricultural implements, and machine tools. But more than anything, Iowa Division trains moved food.

Although it did in fact reach six states, the Iowa Division was largely an Iowa railroad. On the black loam surface of the state of Iowa is located a quarter of America's finest farmland, and within the state's borders one-tenth of the nation's food is produced.

Nine large packing house centers and three major livestock markets were located on Iowa Division rails, and the division handled nearly 50,000 carloads of meat and packing house products a year. Illinois Central moved more meat and meat products in Iowa than all other railroads in the state combined.

Both Omaha and Sioux City had grain exchanges; and grain storage and shipping were an important industry all along the division. Some 125,000 carloads of wheat, corn, oats, and soybeans moved over the division yearly.

Illinois Central moved not only the food produced along its Iowa Division lines but a lot more delivered from its western connections.

CC-6 was only one of 13 dispatch freights operated over the Iowa Division. Similar to CC-6 were SCF-6 and SFC-6, which moved eastbound meat and livestock tonnage from the packing plants at Sioux City and Sioux Falls. AC-2 was the "apple train," originating at Albert Lea, Minnesota, where it picked up fruit and other freight from the Northwest from an M&StL connection. CC-4 was another Council Bluffs–Chicago schedule, specializing in the movement of California fruits and vegetables delivered by Union Pacific. Waybills of their westbound counterparts listed such items as eastern manufactured goods, Florida citrus fruits, and Central American bananas, which had moved north to Chicago on fast schedules from the Port of New Orleans.

Fast freight was second nature to the Iowa Division.

Green home signal ahead! CC-6 was an hour and a quarter out of Council Bluffs and bearing down on the North Western crossing at Dow City. The steady pounding of 48 diesel cylinders dropped to an idle as Engineer Kullman shut off just before the units hit the diamond, then they resumed their even beat.

The headlight beam picked out the gaunt form of an abandoned concrete coaling tower at Denison. The Iowa Division was Illinois Central's first division to go all-diesel (in 1955), but steam's mark was not yet gone from it.

Red order board! The fireman scooped up a clearance form from the waiting op as we hit Cherokee District trackage at Tara. It was 12:52 A.M., and we'd picked up an even 20 minutes over CC-6's scheduled running time on the Omaha District.

We were in a block signal territory now, and a procession of green lights led us through 6 miles of sweeping curves as 3669 tons of fast freight dropped downgrade into the Des Moines River valley. Engineer Kullman's night's work was all but wrapped up as he took his train across the river bridge, past the big Hormel packing plant, and into Fort Dodge Yard at 1:05 A.M.

Westbound Waterloo–Council Bluffs dispatch freight WC-3, train 71 on the timecard, was holding the main line, and CC-6 went into a yard track. The low-pitched chant of the diesels bounced back at us as we slipped between two strings of cars.

Kullman brought his three units to a halt opposite the depot for the change in crews. The new head-end crew brought out a lead to test the diesel's Automatic Train Stop equipment. Then Waterloo District Engineer Louis Kruse took his

40

train through the yard to clear the main for WC-3's departure and pulled off to let the yard switcher work the train's head end.

Just 50 minutes after it had come to a halt, CC-6 was off and running again. During that time IC had managed to change crews, test its ATS equipment, switch out 7 cars and add 9, inspect 88 cars, and test the air.

Eastbound tonnage from Fort Dodge had to fight its way up a stiff 2 1/2-mile grade out of the Des Moines River valley. Engineer Kruse had 4384 tons of train and 500 feet of 1.40 percent maximum grade working against him—and a night mist to make the rails slippery. With the diesels at full throttle and the sanders working, the three GP9's cut the hill down to size.

Not too many years before, 2-10-2's were taking the tonnage up this hill, and no doubt it was a satisfying sight and sound. But the purposeful roar of three wide-open GP9's piling into the grade with close to 100 cars of fast freight behind them was an event of nearly equal drama.

The 100-mile run from Fort Dodge to Waterloo over the Waterloo District was the Iowa Division's fastest piece of track. The district was equipped with ATS and had a 60 mph limit for freight trains. Elsewhere on the division, with the exception of high-speed track shared with the Burlington, the limit was 50 miles an hour.

Green over red ahead at the Gypsum interlocking! As CC-6 hammered over the Fort Dodge, Des Moines & Southern crossing, I noted the absence of a trolley wire over the one-time electric interurban. All-diesel and freight-only since 1955, the "Fort Dodge–Des Moines Line" was still an important short line.

Gypsum Tower drew its name from one of the Fort Dodge area's leading industries. Local plants manufactured plaster, wallboard, roof decks and dozens of other building products from the versatile white mineral. Clay products were important to Fort Dodge, too; and the city ranked as the world's largest single producing center of gypsum and clay products. Trainmaster S. M. Frank, who joined us in the cab at Fort Dodge, pointed out some of the strip mines and plants along the tracks. "They're good for some 75 to 80 loads a day for Illinois Central," he told me.

Webster City was half an hour out of Fort Dodge. There was a "clear" order board at the North Western crossing, and just north of the tower a green and yellow diesel waited with a southbound freight. Webster City is in another river valley, this one the Boone River's, and the eastbound grade out of the valley dropped our speed to a steady 30 mph as the diesel strained toward the summit.

Meat traffic from Sioux Falls, South Dakota, moved to Cherokee, Iowa, on dispatch freight SFC-6, No. 776 on the division timecard. At Cherokee the Sioux Falls meat train was combined with a similar Sioux City–Fort Dodge schedule, dispatch freight SCF-6, No. 676 on the timecard. From Fort Dodge to Chicago the meat traffic from both of these trains moved on CC-6's schedule, as train No. 76. Because of CC-6's late start from Council Bluffs, the Sioux City–Sioux Falls traffic had arrived at Fort Dodge well ahead of us and was already on its way over the Waterloo District as First 76. Our Council Bluffs section of CC-6 would run the rest of the way to Chicago as Second 76.

The Iowa Division had just two stretches of double track, and when we hit the beginning of one of them—at a place called Susie—it meant we were just 2½ miles from Waterloo, the location of the division's largest yard and a centrally located headquarters for Division Superintendent J. W. Dodge. The double track, which eased congestion outside the yard limits, extended some 4½ miles beyond Waterloo to Hilltop.

Once again, at West Tower, CC-6 crossed the rails of a onetime interurban, the Waterloo, Cedar Falls & Northern. Although the "Cedar Valley Road" was now diesel operated, the trolley wire was still up. It was required for trips to and from the yard by the line's Waterloo–Cedar Falls trolley, Iowa's last passenger electric line. WCF&N had been known as the Waterloo Railroad ever since IC and the Rock Island teamed up to buy it in 1956. WCF&N's strategic industrial belt line at Waterloo was the big attraction for the steam road buyers.

In the pre-dawn hours of October 12, 1957, the IC's eastbound CC-6 had pulled alongside the railroad's big icing dock at Waterloo, Iowa, to add chipped ice to a carload of meat. Before dawn the train would be underway again.

There was a lot of work to be done on CC-6 at Waterloo, but it wouldn't take long—less than an hour. Illinois Central put its fast freights together with speed in mind, both over the road and in the yard.

Waterloo was an icing point for perishables, and its big icing dock could accommodate a string of 60 cars. If necessary another 60 could be doubled over to the other side of the platform. This time we had just a single car of meat that required an application of chipped ice. When the occasion demanded, though, the crew could ice some 60 to 70 cars an hour.

It was 4:25 A.M. as Engineer Kruse braked his train to a stop alongside the icing platform, waited for the head brakeman to cut off the train, then headed for the roundhouse with the diesels.

While the icing crew started to ice down the carload of meat, the yard crew went to work on the switch list. Waterloo was one of Iowa's leading packing house centers, and a good many of the 49 cars blocked for set-out at Waterloo were livestock for the packing plants. Almost all of the 52 cars added to CC-6 were colorful yellow Rath meat refrigerator cars, owned by the city's biggest packer. Depending upon their eventual destination, they were switched to the head or the rear of the train.

Two GP9's and a GP7 locked couplers with 81 cars of fast freight. Fresh power and a new crew were taking CC-6 over the 160-mile Dubuque District to Freeport, Illinois. Couplings banged in a chain reaction as Engineer Jerry Colgin took out the slack. He eased his train to a stop at Rath Tower; then the home signal flashed to green and CC-6 pounded across the east side of the Waterloo Railroad's belt line around the city. It was 5:28 A.M. and the first dim light of the dawn was showing in the eastern sky.

Our meet with westbound train 11, the *Hawkeye*, was overdue. The overnight coach-and-Pullman train had been reported close to an hour late, and we would probably meet her at Wise or Independence. Sure enough, a yellow block was ahead as we approached Wise siding, then a waggling headlight made its appearance. No. 11 had already taken siding, and two brown and orange passenger units were slowly moving their heavyweight train through the long siding as Second 76 moved by on the main line.

For mile after mile of sweeping curves, Engineer Colgin worked the air brake valve as he dropped his 4620-ton consist downgrade through the hills approaching Dubuque and the Mississippi River valley. CC-6 rolled into a final cut and emerged on northbound track above the riverbank, parallel to the Milwaukee Road's north-south line which followed the west bank of the river from Muscatine, Iowa, to Hastings, Minnesota. Colgin brought his train to the brief halt required at the Milwaukee crossing, then headed through Dubuque Yard. It was the only time wheels stopped rolling on CC-6 during the 160-mile run to Freeport. Dubuque was another of the important meat-packing centers on the Iowa Division, but the tonnage moved on other trains.

Westbound CC-3 was waiting in the yard for us to clear the single-track line. Its three GP units already had their train rolling as we passed. CC-3 was a Chicago–Council Bluffs merchandise run and had an early evening departure from Congress Street Yard in Chicago.

Our trio of Geeps plunged through a silvery lattice of structural steel as CC-6 bridged the Mississippi. The Dubuque bridge, owned by Illinois Central, was shared with Chicago Great Western mainline trains as well as with Burlington switch runs. The structure ended abruptly with a right-angle crossing of the Burlington's Twin Cities–Chicago line and a sharply curving tunnel that carried the rails through a vertical riverbank cliff. For 13 miles, between East Cabin and Portage, Illinois Central became a double track, high-speed railroad, shared with Burlington and Chicago Great Western trains. Freight trains were allowed 60 mph over the line, and we were crowding the limit as CC-6 headed southward along the river.

Chicago Great Western was noted for its long freight trains and its prodigious application of diesel motive power. A good example was provided by Chicago-Oelwein manifest freight 91 which came hustling along near Portage behind six units, trailing close to 200 cars. Behind the diesels rode a string of piggybacked common-carrier trucks. I recalled that Great Western was one of the piggyback pioneers.

Form 19 orders at Portage! Engineer Colgin leaned out and snared a clearance form, a wait order on west-bound local freight train 61, engine 9060, and a wad of messages from the operator.

Burlington rails continued south along the river another 13 miles beyond Portage to Savanna before turning away from the river toward Chicago, and the Great Western followed Burlington another mile before leaving the valley on its own track at Galena Junction. But CC-6 took a sharp left turn at Portage and followed Illinois Central's single track up the Galena River valley for the long, hard pull out of the Mississippi Valley. The summit at Warren was some 30 miles away and it would take a good hour's running to make it.

It was still early on the morning of October 12, 1957, when engineer Jerry Colgin braked the 81 cars of eastbound train Second 76—dispatch freight CC-6—to a halt for the required safety stop at the railroad's crossing with the Milwaukee Road at Dubuque. It was the only time the wheels would stop rolling on the train's 160-mile run between Waterloo, Iowa, and Freeport, Illinois.

Over a century ago Galena was a thriving river town and the center of a prosperous lead mining industry. Described as "one of the foremost commercial and industrial centers north of St. Louis," Galena was the goal of Chicago's earliest westward railroad construction. The pioneer railroad, the Galena & Chicago Union, later became a part of the Chicago & North Western, but it never did reach its original goal. Now, Galena was just another station stop on IC and the end of a Burlington branch line. It was hard to imagine Galena's onetime importance as CC-6 roared through the pleasant little city, shattering the early morning tranquility.

The speed recorder needle dropped to 40 mph, then to 20 as the diesels began to feel the 7 miles of 0.80 percent grade from Bowden to Scales Mounds. At Scales Mounds a track gang was at work lengthening a siding, a reminder that dieselization was more than just a new look in motive power. Diesels have meant fewer but faster and longer trains. All along the Iowa Division IC had been pulling out no-longer-needed sidings and was lengthening the remainder to an average of 150 cars to accommodate diesel-length trains.

Waddams Grove was passed at 9:20 A.M. and the subject of our wait order—westbound local freight 61—was safely in the clear for us.

Hot box! Just east of Lena, sharp-eyed Engineer Colgin caught a telltale trail of smoke half way back in the train. Freeport was just a few miles away, so the crew could set out the offending car in the yard.

Ever since CC-6 had left Fort Dodge we'd been picking up time on the Sioux Falls–Sioux City meat train, running ahead of us as First 76. The train was still in the Freeport yard when Colgin brought CC-6 to a halt on the westbound main, but First 76 was soon under way again behind a trio of GP9's.

There was no switching to be done on CC-6 at Freeport, only a change to fresh motive power and a new crew. A Freeport District crew backed on with three more of the ubiquitous black GP9's, then pulled out the box car which Engineer Colgin had spotted on the way in. Its dry journal squealed in protest. Engineer Don Schlegel put his train back together and made ready for the last fast lap on the meat train's run for Chicago.

Eastbound train No. 14, the daytime streamliner *Land O' Corn*, was past due when CC-6 was ready to roll. Almost half an hour late, the *Corn* came in behind a pair of brown and orange Electro-Motive units, made a brief station stop, and raced off for Chicago. The block cleared, Engineer Schlegel wound up his three V-16 diesels, and CC-6 was rolling again. It was 10:20 A.M., and he had a comfortable 3 hours 10 minutes to cover the 102 miles that separated CC-6 from its 1:30 appointment at Broadview.

Once across the Mississippi River into Illinois, the Illinois Central's Iowa Division followed the river southward for several miles on trackage shared with the Burlington and the Chicago Great Western. At Portage, where IC trains turned away from the joint track to their own line, engineer Jerry Colgin leaned out to pick up a Form 19 train order from the tower operator.

CC-6 had no scheduled stops, and the three GP9's were putting the miles behind them at a steady 50 mph pace that would have us into Broadview well ahead of time. Then, east of Rockford, the steady procession of green block signals changed to yellow and finally, at Charter Grove, to red. Traveling Engineer D. D. Fulfer was at our throttle, and he eased his 80-car train past the red block and brought it to a halt several hundred yards behind a stalled First 76.

The train was having engine trouble and the crew was setting the malfunctioning GP9 out on a siding. By the time the train was out of the way and CC-6

was moving again, it was 12:10. With First 76 ahead of us short of power and Broadview still 43 miles away, our extra time margin was gone.

But two units were making a remarkably good showing with First 76, and Traveling Engineer Fulfer was soon following a steady series of green signals. At 12:45 CC-6 bridged the Fox River and began to cross and re-cross the railroad web that surrounds Chicago. Grade crossings and the gaudy colors of new suburban tracts became more and more frequent as the Geeps throbbed along on the last few miles into Broadview.

Thirty cars back, the head brakeman pulled the pin. Engineer Don Schlegel moved ahead, then shoved the block of yellow reefers into the Broadview interchange track. It was just 1:30 P.M. and CC-6 had chalked up another "IHB connection made" for the record. An Indiana Harbor Belt switcher and a transfer caboose were waiting to hustle the meat cars to their eastbound connections.

First 76 had already made its delivery and was waiting in the yard. It was scheduled to tie up at Hawthorne Yard, on Chicago's West Side, so the crew had 8 cars for Congress Street to trade for our 11 Hawthorne cars. We picked up two more Congress Street cars from a local freight, the "Hawthorne Job," and were under way again by 2:10 P.M.

CC-6 threaded its way through Chicago's industrial West Side, and then paused at the 21st Street crossing while three Tuscan red Pennsy diesel units pounded across the diamonds with a 13-car flyer, minutes away from its Union Station destination. Soon on the move again, the CC-6 finally emerged on Illinois Central's lake front trackage opposite Soldier Field.

At Freeport, a Freeport District crew took charge of eastbound train Second 76 to complete the overnight journey into Chicago. Engineer Don Schlegel gave the line ahead his undivided attention as he ran his train through the Illinois countryside.

It was just a quarter after three when Schlegel dropped his train at Congress Street. For some of the meat cars the journey would resume a few hours later when dispatch freights SE-1 and MS-1 headed out on their overnight trips to Birmingham and Memphis. But for CC-6 another run was over. Council Bluffs was 511 miles and 17 hours, 20 minutes behind it. Don Schlegel ran his three GP9's around the train and headed for 27th Street roundhouse.

The Journey Today

Although much has changed in the intervening years, Illinois Central still provides a fast overnight service to Chicago for freight originating or connecting at Council Bluffs. Today's successor to CC-6 is intermodal train I-12, for which IC promises a noon delivery at Chicago.

A Farewell to the Interurbans

Among my earliest and fondest memories are those of visits to the home of an aunt and uncle in Le Claire, Iowa, not far from the Mississippi River. The big attraction there was an electric interurban, the Clinton, Davenport & Muscatine, whose red cars raced up and down the west bank of the river at what seemed to a small boy to be blinding speed. They made a lasting impression, and for me the interurbans acquired an enduring fascination that has remained with me ever since.

An interurban was a very different kind of train. Developed at the beginning of the century out of the new technology of the electric street railway, the electric interurbans were fast intercity railways that often competed with the steam railroads for short-haul traffic, and provided a welcome link between rural America and urban centers before the automobile came along to provide an even better one.

The first interurbans began operating in the 1890s, and for the next two decades the financing and building of interurban railways was a booming industry. By 1917 America's interurban empire had grown to a network of more than 18,000 miles operating in almost every state of the union. By then the automobile was becoming commonplace, and the interurbans declined as fast as they had developed. Well before the end of the great depression much of America's interurban network had been abandoned, and only a few of the strongest lines survived through the World War II period.

In the decade or so after World War II these last interurbans were fast disappearing, and I traveled long and far for the opportunity to experience them before it was too late.

These were a few of them.

" ...YOU'RE ALL OVER DUST!"
A TRIP ON THE CEDAR VALLEY ROAD*

*© 1996 Pentrex Media Group, reprinted with permission from the Summer 1996 issue of *Vintage Rails* magazine.

An electric interurban like few others was Iowa's Waterloo, Cedar Falls & Northern. The line had been started in 1895 by three former steam railroad men, the Cass brothers—Louis, Claude, and Joseph—and when they set out to build a 64-mile southern extension from Waterloo to Cedar Rapids in 1914 they built it to the same high standards that would have been followed by a steam railroad. The line's track, bridges and power supply system were all designed to accommodate fast, heavy trains.

The Cass brothers set out, too, to provide a passenger service and equipment that would equal the luxury and comfort of the finest steam trains. Among the passenger cars ordered from the McGuire-Cummings company for this new service were three deluxe cars intended for extra fare, limited train service. Larger than conventional interurban cars, these big steel cars were equipped as parlor-buffet cars, and for a time they operated with uniformed porters who served passengers à la carte meals from a small kitchenette. Large open observation platforms at the rear of the handsome orange cars were equipped with brass railings and scalloped awnings, and the line's Cedar Valley Road emblem was displayed on the rear platform railing in the grand manner of steam railroad limited trains of the time.

Such amenities as parlor seats and buffet service were long gone when I came to know the Cedar Valley Line, and the three big interurbans were operated as ordinary coaches. Two of them, however, still retained the big observation platforms, while the open platform of the third had been converted to an enclosed solarium.

All three cars were still running in daily service, just as they had since the line opened some 40 years before, when I boarded southbound train No. 18 at the Waterloo station on a May afternoon in 1954. Car 101, one of the two that still had the open observation platform, was assigned to make the two-hour run to Cedar Rapids.

We departed from the downtown station promptly at 4 P.M., and the big car worried its way through the streets of Waterloo, heading north to cross the Illinois Central at West Tower, and then reversing on a wye before following the interurban's belt line around the city to reach the Cedar Rapids line. We passed the electric line's Waterloo roundhouse and yard, dove under the Chicago Great Western several miles later, and then crossed the IC again at Rath Tower to join the Cedar Rapids line at Belt Junction.

Just beyond the junction the interurban sped across the first of the line's two long concrete arch bridges that crossed and re-crossed the Cedar River. At Gilbertville, a steeple cab motor had pulled a long northbound freight into the siding to clear our train.

To better observe the passing Iowa countryside I dragged one of the lounge chairs out on the observation platform, and soon learned that it took a rather hardy traveler, or a dedicated interurban enthusiast, to stay there very long. The big, old car could still top 60 mph with ease as we sailed through open country under the 1200-volt catenary, and the lurching, bounding motion over rough track seemed about to hurl me from my brass-railed perch. Great clouds of dust from the roadbed swirled across the platform, coating me from head to foot.

Still, the experience of open-air trolleying at high speed was an unforgettable one. Nothing ever smelled quite the same as the pungent odor from the grinding brake shoes as we slowed for a stop, or the ozone smell generated by the whirling traction motors—mingled with the heady aroma of Iowa farmyard and river bottom. And nothing ever sounded quite the same as the wail of the interurban's air horn, or the loose-jointed clatter of the racing car over light track.

Stops were frequent as we made our way to Cedar Rapids. An occasional farmer boarded or left the car at rural stops, and once we stopped at a country road

Northbound from Waterloo to Waverly, Iowa, as train 35 on May 14, 1954, the Cedar Valley Road's big observation car No. 102 crossed over the double-track line of the Illinois Central's Iowa Division at West Tower on the outskirts of Waterloo.

crossing to drop a farm wife returning from the nearest town with an armload of groceries. There was even a sudden, unscheduled halt while the conductor chased a stray cow off the track. Most of the passengers seemed to be regular riders, and exchanged small talk with the conductor on a first-name basis. It was a Friday, and payday on the Cedar Valley Road, and the conductor distributed pay checks to the agents at depots along the way, together with a few good-natured insults.

Nearing Cedar Rapids, we lurched to a halt at a country dirt road crossing,

where an old farmer, carrying a cardboard suitcase and a bucket of eggs, climbed aboard. He looked me over with the sort of glance reserved for lunatics, and remarked, "Whyn't you git inside boy, you're all over dust." Upon which, he deposited the cardboard suitcase in a corner of the platform and, still carrying the bucket of eggs, marched on inside.

Like a good many old-timers along the line, the farmer had probably been riding the orange interurbans ever since they'd begun running down the Cedar Valley 40 years before, and by this time probably took the experience and the sights along the way pretty much for granted.

Before long, my interurban journey ended at the converted residence on the outskirts of town that served as the WCF&N's Cedar Rapids station. I didn't know it at the time, of course, but my trip that May would be my last experience with those marvelous open platform cars. Later that same year, their day would come to an abrupt end when a Waterloo car barn fire wiped out the line's two brass-railed cars, 101 and 102. Only solarium-ended No. 100 would remain to operate the WCF&N's last interurban service until it came to an end on February 19, 1956. After a decade in excursion service over the Southern Iowa Railway at Centerville, No. 100, too, would meet its end in a spectacular fire at its new home at Mason City.

Three women boarded Cedar Valley Road passenger car No. 100 at the Cedar Rapids station on April 10, 1955, shortly before its 9:30 A.M. departure for Waterloo. Originally an open platform observation car, No. 100 had been rebuilt in 1928 with an enclosed solarium at the rear.

TROPICAL INTERURBAN

Time has a way of standing still on the railways of the developing countries of the world, where the resources needed to invest in modernization are often hard to come by. Cuba's remarkable tropical interurban was a case in point.

The Hershey Cuban Railway, or Ferrocarril Cubano de Hershey, owed its existence to Pennsylvania confectioner Milton S. Hershey, the "Chocolate King," who built his Hershey chocolate bar into a trademark with worldwide recognition. Toward the end of World War I Hershey set out to secure his own sugar supply with the development of a vast Cuban acreage of sugar plantations and his own sugar mills. The center of this sugar empire was the newly founded town of Hershey, 29 miles east of Havana, where the company's principal mill, or "central," a refinery, and a power plant were located.

A network of rail lines centered on Central Hershey was built to haul cane from the fields to the mill and refinery, and another railroad line was built to transport the refined sugar down to Havana harbor. In order to make this railroad

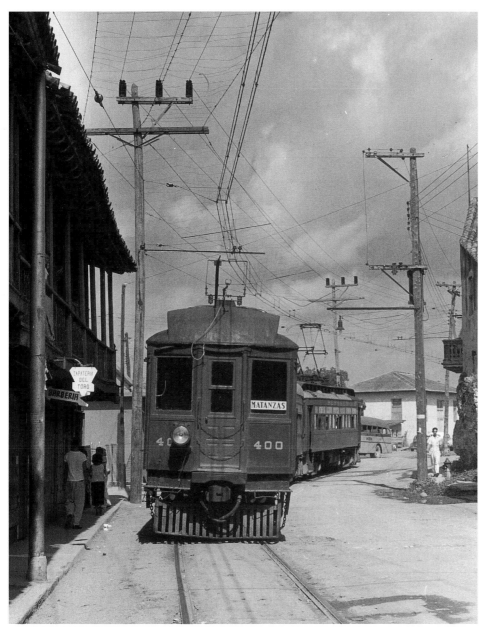

Ready to depart on the 56-mile journey to Matanzas, Cuba, a train of the Hershey Cuban
Railway's big J. G. Brill interurbans waited in the street opposite the Casablanca ferry landing
across the harbor from downtown Havana.

a self-supporting enterprise rather than just a seasonal sugar carrier, the Hershey company extended the line eastward to Matanzas, some 56 miles east of Havana, and established a year-around common carrier freight and passenger service.

The Hershey Company, which already operated an electric railway serving its Hershey, Pennsylvania, chocolate plant, built its new Cuban railway to modern heavy interurban standards. The principal routes of the new railway were electrified with a 1200-volt DC catenary system, and the company turned to U.S. builders for a fleet of standard interurban passenger cars and steeple cab freight locomotives. The first section of the line was completed between Havana and Central Hershey in 1918, and the entire system, comprising some 100 electrified track miles and several times that amount of steam-operated sugar cane trackage, was officially opened on October 5, 1922.

Meticulously maintained in original condition by the railway's commodious and well-equipped shops at Central Hershey, the Hershey Cuban's interurbans rolled on for decade after decade in near-original condition, like museum pieces from the height of the interurban era.

With the electric interurban railways all but vanished from the mainland U.S. and Canada, I had to travel to pre-Castro Cuba to see the Hershey Cuban for myself. Thus it was that Dorothy and I were aboard a Pan Am DC-6 in June 1957 for the hour-long flight across the Straits of Florida from Miami to Havana.

At the sea wall along Cespedes Avenue in the old colonial section of Havana I paid the five-cent fare and boarded one of the little motor launches that shuttled across the harbor channel to the Hershey Cuban's Havana terminal at Casa Blanca. The name—"white house"—came, I was told, from an old garrison once located on the site that had been painted white.

Four daily round trips were scheduled over the main line between Casa Blanca and Matanzas under a timetable that had been in force since 1945, and two additional runs operated to Central Hershey only. I bought tickets for Central Hershey in a noisy waterfront building where the interurban ticket office shared space with the ferry terminal. Waiting for me and a few other passengers in the narrow street outside was a classic interurban train that was straight out of the 1920s.

At the head end of three-car Havana-Matanzas train 4 was a big wood-bodied mail-baggage car built by Philadelphia's J. G. Brill Company in 1920, followed by two Brill-built coaches of wood and steel construction that dated to 1924 and 1920, respectively. The cars were painted inside and out in a dignified deep maroon, and fitted with businesslike pantographs that reached high up to the 1200-volt overhead catenary. Sturdy walkover seats were upholstered in what was very likely the same durable rattan in which they had been delivered almost 40 years before. The upper sash above the windows on each side and the clerestories in the roof were fitted with green "art glass," adding just a touch of elegance to the cars. Signs within the cars advised sternly, *Se Prohibe Hablar con el Motorista*—"don't talk to the motorman."

At the 9:30 A.M. departure time the conductor blew a whistle, and the train's *motorista* nudged the controller around to begin the 2 hour, 20 minute, 56-mile journey to Matanzas. The train crept gingerly along one side of the very narrow street between masonry and tile-roofed buildings that must have dated from

Cuba's colonial era, and then turned to follow a narrow right of way between a row of shacks and an open sewer.

We were soon traveling through a pleasant, lush countryside of fields planted in sugar cane, sisal and corn, all liberally intermingled with palm trees. The right of way, I observed, was anything but private. It functioned instead as a playground for children and dogs, and as a pasture for goats, cows and horses. Sometimes the livestock was tethered to a convenient power pole, but more often the animals wandered free.

"Shiny rails in a trough of vegetation," I wrote in my notebook as the cars rocked along over a track that was overgrown with weeds and grass. The track was rough, and the elderly interurbans bounced, swayed, and nosed from side to side. Weeds that often stood as high as a man waved in the breeze from the passing train. Windows were thrown wide open against the humid warmth of the Cuban summer.

Near Casa Blanca we passed a little open patio where a few people sat at tables. There were thatched huts along the line. Ox carts and men on horseback traveled the dirt roads that ran through the cane fields. High-sided sugar cane cars were lined up on the sidings to await *la zafra*—the winter harvest season. Beyond Guanabo the *motorista* stopped at a path to let off a young Cuban whose natty attire included a pink *guayabera*, the open shirt favored in the tropics, and black and white shoes.

The train's three-minute station stop at Central Hershey brought a flurry of activity. Brown-uniformed trainmen gathered on the platform to exchange small talk, while crowds of passengers boarded and left the train. The *camarero* (baggage-man) loaded and unloaded mail and express. Friends and idlers chatted through open windows, and a boy passed from window to window hawking candies held up on a stick for inspection. There

A Hershey Cuban *motorista* looked back at the station activity during a stop at Central Hershey. The train was eastbound from Havana to Matanzas.

were tracks on both sides of the big tile-roofed station, and the arrival of the westbound train from Matanzas on the opposite side produced much of the same sort of activity. Then the conductors announced departure time with blasts from their whistles and the big red cars went rumbling out of town.

Central Hershey was the railroad's headquarters, and we left the train here to meet with Modesto Suarez Ortega, its chief engineer, who told us something about the railroad's operations and showed us around the shops and other facilities. Central Hershey was a handsome "company town" of elegant residences for company executives, and such attractions as a golf course and lush tropical gardens. There was a company hotel, too, inevitably named the Hotel Hershey, and we joined Mr. Ortega for lunch in its pleasant dining room.

53

A vendor offered candies on a stick to passengers on an eastbound Havana-Matanzas train during its extended station stop at Central Hershey in June 1957.

Later on, we continued the journey to Matanzas through what was surely some of central Cuba's most handsome scenery. The train ran through near-jungle vegetation and deep rock cuts, and climbed grades as steep as 2.5 percent. We caught occasional glimpses of the Atlantic Ocean a few miles to the north. The best part—a circuit of the breath-taking Yumuri Valley—came last. Finally,

Nearing the end of its journey from Havana, the Hershey Cuban's eastbound train 2 followed the lovely valley of the Yumuri River into Matanzas on July 3, 1957.

we rolled between the rock cliffs of the gap which carried a country road, the Yumuri River, and the railroad from the valley to the Bay of Matanzas and came to the end of our journey under the big train shed of the Matanzas station.

From Central Hershey, the railroad operated passenger services over branch lines to Bainoa, Jaruco and Santa Cruz del Norte, principally as an accommodation for employees of the company's refinery and power plant. Most of the schedules were tailored to conform to shift changes, and many runs were operated only during the harvest season when the refinery was operating.

The terminal for almost all of the branch line runs was a siding in the street

55

outside the main gate of the refinery, and I went there one afternoon to begin a circuit over the branches. It was hot and humid and an enterprising ice cream salesman had set up shop with his pushcart in the shade of a nearby tree. I bought a *coco glace*—a delicious coconut ice cream—and boarded the one-car train that was about to depart on the single daily round trip to Bainoa, a few miles south of Central Hershey. The interurban was a handsome, arch roofed steel car. Somewhat smaller than the main line cars, it was one of six lightweight cars built by the Cincinnati Car Company in 1922 for the Hershey's branch line services. It was painted in the same maroon color, with similar seats of durable rattan.

My branch line journey turned out to be a very informal and leisurely affair indeed. The seat across the aisle from me on the Bainoa car was occupied by a mother and her daughter, who held a chicken in her lap. At one point we made an unscheduled stop while the conductor helped a passenger deliver a sewing machine to a trackside thatch-roofed hut.

Later in the afternoon on a trip over the Jaruco branch, the electric car had an unscheduled meet with a buzzard. *Motorista* Alfredo Cerda had the Cincinnati interurban rolling along at a good clip when the big bird came crashing through the front window, chased Alfredo around the platform, and finally flew off, unharmed, through the open door. At the end of the line conductor Antonio Gonzalez borrowed a broom from a nearby housewife and swept up the broken glass.

The author boarded a gasoline motor car for an inspection trip over the Hershey Cuban Railway near Havana in June 1957. *(Photo by Dorothy H. Middleton.)*

The Hershey Cuban's Jaruco local had just lost a windowpane to an unscheduled meeting with
a large buzzard. At the end of the line, conductor Antonio Gonzalez borrowed a broom from
a nearby housewife to sweep up the broken glass.

AMERICA'S FASTEST INTERURBAN

Perhaps the finest interurban property of them all was the Chicago North Shore & Milwaukee Railroad. The North Shore Line was reorganized by redoubtable Chicago public utilities entrepreneur Samuel Insull in 1916 from a typical interurban line that operated between Evanston, Illinois, and Milwaukee.

Insull's men rebuilt the North Shore to some of the highest technical standards in the industry and acquired an entry to the Chicago Loop over the Chicago elevated system that helped make the line a major carrier in the Chicago-Milwaukee market.

Insull's North Shore acquired a fleet of well over a hundred powerful steel interurban cars and established some of the fastest intercity schedules in the industry. In 1926 the Insull management completed a splendid 23-mile high-speed cut-off around the North Shore suburbs through the Skokie Valley. After that, the North Shore was awarded *Electric Traction* magazine's interurban speed trophy in five of the next seven years, and won permanent possession of the award in 1933. In 1935 a British railway trade publication, *The Railway Gazette*, described the North Shore Line as "the fastest electric railway service in the world." And from 1936 until the North Shore ended operation in 1963 the line's schedules loomed large in Donald M. Steffee's annual railroad speed survey for *Railroad*, and later *Trains*, magazines, with almost 2000 miles of operation at average speeds of 60 mph or higher every day.

Powerful steel cars and superb track helped make the North Shore Line the fastest of all American electric interurban railways. A two-car Chicago-Milwaukee limited raced down a long stretch of stone ballasted tangent track north of Racine, Wisconsin, in June 1956.

The North Shore's powerful, fast interurban cars of the Insull era were augmented in 1941 with the introduction of two remarkable *Electroliner* trains built by the St. Louis Car Company. These articulated streamliners were designed to provide passenger amenities that would rival those of competing main line railroad streamliners, and to provide competitive running times. Eight traction motors totaling 1000 hp gave the four-car trains an 85-mph free running speed capability, and they were expected to exceed 100 mph with field taps. In tests, one of the trains reached a maximum speed of more than 111 mph.

With equipment like this, the overwhelming impression created by the North Shore was that of the high-speed, super-electric railroad. The North Shore at its best was represented by the splendid Skokie Valley line, and my most enduring memories of Samuel Insull's interurban will always be those of journeys aboard the electric cars as they raced along this magnificent speedway.

The impressions gained from trips on the *Electroliners* and the standard cars were almost totally different.

The best seats on an *Electroliner* were the pair right at the front of the train,

The finest and fastest electric interurban trains ever built were the two streamlined *Electroliners*
completed for the North Shore by the St. Louis Car Company in 1941. They operated regularly
at speeds in excess of 80 mph, and one hit a record 111 mph in test operation. Southbound
Milwaukee-Chicago *Electroliner* train 802 is seen west of Howard Street on the Skokie Valley
Line in June 1962.

A "panned" photograph captured the breathtaking speed of the North Shore's northbound Chicago-Milwaukee train 415 near Racine in 1962. The car was one of the railroad's steel cars of late 1920s vintage, refurbished in the 1950s in a *Silverliner* color scheme that featured painted *faux* stainless steel siding.

where you had a windshield view of the track ahead and could watch the motorman at work in his cab on the right hand side. The trains were soundproofed and air conditioned, and you felt insulated from the world outside. The *Electroliners* seemed to float along the track, and only a peek at the motorman's speedometer was convincing proof that you were really doing 80 mph or better. But a trip aboard one of the big standard steel cars—that was a different matter indeed.

My very last North Shore journey, southbound on a Milwaukee-Chicago express in June 1962, was aboard one of the heavy 700-class cars of the Insull era, and I'll never forget it. The train accelerated away from its station stop at Lake Bluff, eased through the special work at South Upton, and then the motorman wound the controller all the way around for the exhilarating nonstop sprint down the Skokie Valley to Howard Street. I matched the second hand of my watch against the white mileposts that flitted by and recorded mile after mile at a steady 78–79 mph as we raced south to the Loop under compound catenary stretched straight and taut between the latticework steel bridges that spanned the double track. Windows were wide open to combat the summer heat, and the roar of air rushing past, the screaming of gears and wide open traction motors, and the deep, authoritative blast of the air horn that arrested road traffic at the many crossings combined to make conversation all but impossible. Approaching trains were a widening speck of light from a blazing headlight, and then a sudden blast of air and sound as we met at a combined speed of over 150 mph.

This was electric railroading in the grand manner, and this is the way I want to remember the North Shore, and the interurban.

The Journey Today

Few interurban journeys are possible today. Electric passenger operation ended on the Cedar Valley Road in 1956, and the line became the Waterloo Railroad, a diesel-operated freight subsidiary of the Rock Island and Illinois Central. The line was later merged into the IC, and by 1980 nearly all of the former interurbans had been abandoned.

The one-time Hershey Cuban remains as one of the very last electric interurban railways in the Western hemisphere. Merged into the national railroad system in 1960, the railway continues to operate electric passenger service over its original main line. A few of the original Brill interurbans, two of them refurbished for tourist charter service, still survive, but most service is now operated with a fleet of used cars acquired from Spain's Ferrocarriles de Cataluna in 1997.

The North Shore Line ended operation in 1963, although a 5-mile segment of the celebrated Skokie Valley Line between the Howard Street "L" station and Dempster Street in Skokie survived to become the high-speed "Skokie Swift" route of the Chicago Transit Authority. Both *Electroliner* trains and a number of the North Shore's standard heavy steel cars survive in various U.S. trolley museums.

Although both now operate with modern equipment, the Chicago–South Bend South Shore Line and the Philadelphia-Norristown high-speed line of the Southeastern Pennsylvania Transportation Authority (SEPTA) are former interurban lines that still provide much of the flavor of travel by interurban.

North to Hudson Bay

When making train inspections use extreme caution and be on the lookout for polar bears in the vicinity of Belcher."—Hudson Bay Railway General Bulletin Order 381.

Buried among notices concerning routine track condition slow orders and the like in the railway's daily operating bulletin for August 24, 1998, a warning about unfriendly polar bears suggested that working conditions on Manitoba's sub-arctic railroad to Hudson Bay were anything but routine.

Indeed, this was the case.

When I arrived at The Pas, Manitoba, on VIA Rail's northbound train 693, the *Hudson Bay*, I was met by Hudson Bay Railway president H. Brooke Ruskin, who handed me a copy of the daily bulletin, a timetable, and other material as we began a brief tour of the railroad's facilities at its The Pas headquarters. When the *Hudson Bay* resumed its northward journey, Ruskin joined me to talk about some of these special problems of operating a railroad in the far north.

In addition to polar bears, moose and caribou frequent the railroad's right-of-way. But perhaps the most troublesome wildlife of all are Canada's ubiquitous beavers. The beavers, Ruskin explained, love to build their dams in the streams and drainage ditches along the line, frequently causing flooding problems. The railroad's track maintenance crews remove the dams, the beavers rebuild them, and so on.

As one might expect, however, weather is the most formidable obstacle of all for north country railroaders. Winter begins early and lasts long; snow usually begins to fall before the end of September on the railroad's northernmost Herchmer Subdivision between Gillam and Churchill. Sub-zero temperatures last for weeks, and a -40 degree wind chill is not uncommon. Weather like this makes operating trains difficult enough, but it is particularly hard on track. Some 150 miles of the northern end of the line are built across tundra and muskeg over permafrost—permanently frozen ground with an upper layer that thaws during the summer. Under these severe conditions, track is subject to frequent shifts, frost heaves and sinkholes. For most of the railroad, train speeds are limited to a maximum of 40 mph; north of Gillam the top speed permitted is only 30 mph.

This Hudson Bay line was a relative newcomer to the North American railroad network. The idea of building a railroad was owed to the access to the North Atlantic afforded by Hudson Bay and the Hudson Strait. As far back as the 1870s, farmers of the prairie provinces saw a seaport on Hudson Bay, linked by rail with Winnipeg, as a more direct and cheaper route to the markets of Europe for their grain, as well as a more economical route for imported manufactured goods. Not only would a port on Hudson Bay be closer to much of the great wheat crop of Canada's prairies than any other, but it would also create a route to Europe a thousand miles shorter than that through Montreal or Halifax.

Despite these apparent advantages, however, it was not until 1910 that construction of a Hudson Bay railroad finally began; and it was 1929 before it finally reached Churchill, where the long-sought seaport on Hudson Bay was built.

Our 1054-mile journey to Hudson Bay had begun the night before in Winnipeg's handsome Union Station. A few hours earlier the station's great domed concourse had been alive with the greetings and farewells of scores of travelers detraining from or boarding a swollen westbound summer season *Canadian* of some 20 cars. But as the 10 P.M. departure time approached for train 693, the tri-weekly *Hudson Bay*, the station was quiet and almost empty. At about 9:45 the station agent made the boarding call, announcing stops at places like The Pas, Cormorant, Thicket Portage, and Pikwitonei that recalled a Canadian northland of vast and remote spaces, French fur traders, and the original Indian inhabitants the Canadians now call the "First Nations." A crowd of perhaps 30 departing passengers headed quietly up the escalator to Track 4.

The train 693 that awaited us there was a pleasant surprise. It was entirely made up of former Canadian Pacific Budd stainless steel equipment, gleaming in a recently overhauled newness that belied almost 45 years of service. The six-car train included a baggage-dormitory, two coaches, the diner-lounge *Annapolis*, and sleeping cars *Chateau Vigeur* and *Hunter Manor*. Occasionally, I learned, the train will even include one of the former CP *Park* series dome-observation cars for tour groups or other special parties.

Motive power for the train was a pair of former Canadian National Electro-Motive FP9 units rebuilt with head end power units and gleaming in VIA Rail's dark blue and yellow livery.

Dorothy and I settled our baggage and looked over the accommodations in *Chateau Vigeur*'s roomy drawing room A. The upper walls of the recently refurbished car were papered in a rose-colored, textured material, while the lower walls were covered with gray-green carpeting. The floor was carpeted in a green, figured pattern. The seats were upholstered in a patterned soft gray-green and rose fabric, with a gray-green vinyl trim.

Our route to Hudson Bay was anything but direct. While Churchill lies to the north and a little east of Winnipeg, the train followed a long, curving route to the west over Canadian National tracks, taking us well into eastern Saskatchewan before it returned to Manitoba.

Thus when I awoke the next morning we were in the wheat fields of Saskatchewan, more than 300 miles northwest of Winnipeg. The sun was just coming up in a clear, cloudless sky. I watched the elongated shadow of the train pass along the wheat fields to the west. The fields stretched in every direction. Some were golden with ripened grain ready for cutting, some were newly harvested, and in still others the green shoots of newly planted wheat were beginning to emerge. We passed ponds with ducks, a red barn with white trim, farmhouses, tall wooden grain elevators, and shiny metal grain storage silos.

Shortly after 8 A.M. we slowed for a stop at Hudson Bay, Saskatchewan, where a sedan brought several passengers to the train from the nearby station. There were long rows of covered grain hoppers in sidings, all lettered in Canada's determined bilingualism "Government of Canada / Gouvernement du Canada," alongside an orange-painted Pioneer and two silvery Saskatchewan Pool elevators. A spur curved off to the south, where a plume of smoke and steam marked the location of a large factory.

We resumed a northward journey through a flat countryside that had undergone a rather abrupt transformation from wheat fields to thick forests of pine and birch. In open spaces, occasional patches of yellow and lavender wildflowers grew among tall grasses that glistened with fresh dew. Flocks of birds flew over lakes and marshes, and I noted some of the flooded drainage ditches created by the unwelcome efforts of beavers. I timed our progress past the trackside mileposts at a steady 40 mph.

We headed up to diner-lounge *Annapolis* for a satisfying breakfast of scrambled eggs, hash browns, orange juice, and coffee.

The diner-lounge was actually a full 48-seat dining car, with just four tables in use for meal service and the remainder of the car given over for use as a lounge. Like the remainder of the train, the car was newly and handsomely refurbished. The walls were covered with the same rose-colored, textured paper we'd found in *Chateau Vigeur*, with the same green carpeting on the lower walls, and green, figured carpeting on the floor. Chairs were upholstered in a soft, dark rose–colored material that was reflected in a similar finish on the table tops. Banquettes at each end of the car were upholstered in a gray-green vinyl. Glass dividers toward each end were etched with images of the sandpiper, magpie, kingfisher, and chickadee, while reproductions of paintings by Canadian artists were mounted on the end walls.

At The Pas South we left CN rails for the Hudson Bay Railway. Originally a separate company, the line to Churchill was merged into Canadian National in 1951. Then, in a present-day effort to spin off marginal secondary lines, CN sold the line in 1996 to Denver-based OmniTRAX, Inc., which began operating the line the following year under the original Hudson Bay Railway name. In addition to the Bay Line to Churchill, the new company includes lines extending north from The Pas to Flin Flon and Lynn Lake, Manitoba.

Our stop at The Pas was a long one while we changed crews, the train was serviced, and an extra coach cut into the consist. On an adjacent track, equipment waiting for the late morning departure of the tri-weekly Lynn Lake mixed train included a blue and yellow VIA Rail coach and combine and a 40-foot box car that functioned as a "way car" for delivery of supplies to the remote communities along the line.

The *Hudson Bay* was underway again shortly after 11 A.M. We crossed the Saskatchewan River on a long truss bridge, passed a huge lumber and paper mill, and then headed off into a remote Precambrian shield wilderness of lakes, streams and forests. Around Paterson, some 70 miles north of The Pas, we began to notice great stands of dead trees, the result, Ruskin explained, of widespread forest fires in 1989. The leaves of trees along the line were already beginning to change color, which some say means a long hard winter to come.

The Hudson Bay Railway provides a twice-weekly freight service between The Pas and Thompson, and we had orders to meet southbound train 996, the Thompson–The Pas road switcher, at Ponton. We arrived first and took siding. As the 48-car train came through behind rebuilt Electro-Motive GP7 and GP35 units, the VIA Rail crew climbed down to give the passing train a run-by inspec-

Seen from a rear view mirror on the left hand side of the locomotive, VIA Rail's southbound
Hudson Bay presented an incongruous sight as it cruised leisurely over the forested Hudson
Bay Railway's Thicket Subdivision. Bringing up the rear of the handsome all-Budd stainless steel
train was a string of the piggyback flat cars that carry urgent freight to and from Churchill
through the roadless forests and tundra of northern Manitoba.

tion and gave the crew an "all clear" radio report. Rules require that a cabooseless train must be inspected at least once every 60 miles; train 996 could now run another 60 miles before another inspection would have to be made.

We made scheduled stops at Wabowden and Thicket Portage. Among the crowd boarding the train at Thicket was Bob McCleverty, the town's outspoken mayor, who took advantage of the occasion to lobby Ruskin about the town's passenger service needs.

The dining car crew served up a lasagna dinner and a bottle of wine. Across the table from us the Churchill school superintendent, returning to his post for the new school year, talked of the special precautions that are needed when the potentially dangerous polar bears come to town. Returning to the ice of Hudson Bay from their inland summer haunts, the bears wander through the streets of Churchill from September through November. When that happens, schoolchildren travel by bus and teachers sometimes carry guns, he told us. There's even a special bear alert telephone number ("Dial 675-BEAR") to notify the provincial natural resources authorities when one of the animals shows up.

At Thompson Junction, train 693 left the main line for a side trip over the 30-mile branch to Thompson. CN built the branch in the mid-1950s to serve a huge International Nickel Company mining and smelting operation and the new town that grew up around it; and it's now one of the principal points on the railroad.

In the nineteenth century the railroad served as lifeline for remote communities in the vast, newly settled regions of the North American west, though we seldom think of it that way any more. But to a remarkable degree, the railroad to Hudson Bay still fulfills this historic function. There are few roads in the remote wilderness of northern Manitoba, and none at all that reach as far north as Hudson Bay. For nearly 400 miles north of Wabowden most of the little communities along the railroad have no outside road access, and for the last 159 miles from Limestone to Churchill there are no roads at all. For the hardy people who live here, the railroad is very nearly the only way in and out.

All of this began to come into focus as we approached Thompson. In addition to the tri-weekly *Hudson Bay*, Ruskin explained, a weekly mixed train provides passenger and supply service to the remote communities between Wabowden and Churchill. This runs north from Gillam to Churchill every Monday. The crew switches at Churchill on Tuesday and returns to Gillam on Wednesday. The train then runs south to Wabowden on Saturday and returns to Gillam on Sunday.

The reason for the extra coach added at The Pas became evident when we saw the throng of passengers waiting on the Thompson station platform. Lightly loaded ever since we had left Winnipeg, the train now filled up with travelers who had no other way—except an expensive trip by air—to reach Hudson Bay. The remaining space in the two sleeping cars filled up as members of several tour groups boarded the train to complete their journey to polar bear country. A massive load of baggage, groceries, and supplies—even a pre-finished door for someone's home improvement project—was loaded into the baggage car to accompany their owners to Churchill or one of the back country communities along the way. While the *Hudson Bay* has relatively few scheduled stops, the train makes flag stops at any of the dozens of stations along the line to serve travelers to or from these remote settlements.

The train is the sole link to the world outside for residents of many of the isolated settlements
along the Hudson Bay Railway in northern Manitoba. En route to Thompson and points south,
a sizable throng of passengers boarded the coaches of the southbound *Hudson Bay* at Ilford on
an August morning.

The lifeline nature of the railroad became evident in another way as well. While the train was loading, the new head-end crew cut off one of the FP9 units and ran around the train to a ramp in the nearby yard to pick up six "piggyback" flat cars loaded with highway trailers of refrigerated and other urgent cargo for Churchill. The six "pigs," as the crew called them, were switched to the rear of what had now become one of the most elegant mixed trains operating anywhere.

The train reassembled and, servicing completed, the crew backed into the nearby wye to reverse the train, and then began the run back to Thompson Junction to resume the northward journey. We were on the way again at 8:15 P.M., an hour and 45 minutes behind schedule.

I had joined enginemen Charles Dixon and Francis MacDonald in the FP9 cab for the run to the next scheduled stop at Pikwitonei. In the gathering dusk we looked in vain for a female moose and calf that the crew had observed on their last several trips. The headlight beam picked out only reflectorized flanger signs and an occasional whistle post.

I noted the line of unusual tripod telegraph poles along the right of way. Conventional poles set in the ground had proved unstable in the permafrost; frost heaves pushed the poles out of the ground and toppled them. To provide a more stable support for the lines the railroad developed a novel tripod of cedar poles set on the ground. The railroad has since shifted entirely to radio communications, and the wires are gone, but the unusual tripods are still in place along the tracks as a reminder of yet another problem in sub-arctic railroading.

Several pickup trucks and carts waited at a road crossing as we approached the station stop at Pikwitonei. The engine crew went back to help unload miscellaneous baggage and supplies for the small crowd of passengers that disembarked here.

When I left the cab at Pikwitonei, the crew was expecting further delay behind a northbound unit grain train for Churchill that was running ahead of us. There was no siding long enough to overtake it before Gillam, which was still more than a hundred miles away. I awoke briefly as we passed it there around 3 A.M. These big unit trains represent the railroad's principal traffic, but they run only during the brief "grain rush" season when the port at Churchill is ice-free, from July through October. Most operate with leased or run-through CN power, and I noted that this one was headed by two of CN's big Montreal-built M420 units.

Just north of Gillam the line crosses the turbulent waters of Kettle Rapids in the Nelson River on a remarkable continuous truss bridge, but I would have to wait until the return trip to get a look at the structure. One of the first of its kind on North American railroads when it was completed in 1917, the bridge is made up of two end spans of 300 feet each and a central span of 400 feet.

I was up early the next morning to find the train running at a steady 25 mph over a flat, boggy countryside of muskeg and tundra. The ground was covered with low bushes and carpeted with a light greenish-beige lichen that seemed to grow on everything. The few trees that grew were small and stunted. Shaped by the prevailing northwest winds off Hudson Bay, lobstick pines grew most of their branches toward the southeast. Formations of geese and ducks flew across an overcast, gray sky.

Three times a week the arrival of the *Hudson Bay* from Winnipeg brings high excitement to the handsome old station at Churchill. Tour buses and taxis wait as visitors, come to see Beluga whales, polar bears, and the other attractions of Hudson Bay, retrieve their luggage from the train's baggage car.

Platform lights reflected from the glistening stainless steel flanks of the sleeping car *Chateau Verrechers* as train 693, the southbound *Hudson Bay,* waited for its late evening departure time from Churchill. Visible in the distance is the massive Hudson Bay grain elevator that is the principal reason for the Port of Churchill's existence.

There was little sign of habitation in this desolate landscape; a long stretch of the line south of Churchill runs through what is known simply as "the barren lands." Near milepost 444 we passed a single dwelling and soon after a small shack and a tipped-over outhouse.

At Belcher, one of the few scheduled stops north of Gillam, a metal building beside the track was the only sign of habitation. East of the track, beside a lake, track crew wags had erected a telephone booth and a "Belcher Beach" sign flanked by two pink flamingos.

All through the night and morning we had lost still more time to summer season track work slow orders, and it was almost noon when the *Hudson Bay* finally reached its Churchill destination. Long rows of dusky red covered grain hoppers standing in a long yard to the west carried the names Canadian National, Canada Wheat Board, Government of Canada, Saskatchewan Grain Car Company, and—in dark blue—Saskatchewan. Flocks of geese fed on spilled grain in the yard and along the track.

The Churchill station was an imposing, if down at the heels, two story frame structure surfaced in cement asbestos shingles and stucco, with a high pitched roof. At the platform a long row of taxis, vans, buses, and pickup trucks waited for arriving passengers and their luggage.

The town of Churchill, all of about a thousand strong, had a raw frontier look about it. Wide streets were flanked by dirt and gravel, and the only trees were occasional small evergreens planted in someone's front yard. Most of the buildings were modest, low frame structures or prefabricated metal buildings. Even though it was August, the gray sky had a wintry feel, and I was glad I had packed a jacket and sweater.

By far the largest structure in town, about a half mile beyond the station, was the enormous, 5 million bushel grain elevator that is Churchill's—and the railroad's—principal reason for existence. At the wharf alongside the elevator, a Chinese freighter loaded Canadian wheat for export to Mexico.

Later on I would get a good look at Churchill's sub-arctic deep water port, but now we headed up to the baggage car to retrieve our checked luggage and then hailed a cab to our accommodations at the Polar Inn, lunch at the Gypsy Café, and a search for Churchill's famed beluga whales and polar bears.

The Journey Today

While government budget cuts for VIA Rail and other lines have much reduced Canada's rail passenger network in recent years, trains that provide service to remote areas like Hudson Bay have continued to operate. The *Hudson Bay's* important role in Churchill area tourism is likely to contribute to its survival as well.

The Copper Canyon Train

Few chapters in the story of North American railroad building are more colorful, and none are longer, than that of the construction of a railroad across the rugged mountains of Mexico's Sierra Madre Occidental to create a shorter rail route to the Pacific.

The idea was first advanced in the 1880s by a visionary named Albert K. Owen, who proposed an "International Air Line" that would link Europe and Asia via the U.S. and Mexico though ports at Norfolk, Virginia, and Topolobampo, Sinaloa, on the Gulf of California. Owen's scheme, which included the establishment of a Utopian community at Topolobampo, never materialized, but the idea was taken up again at the turn of the century by Kansas City entrepreneur Arthur K. Stilwell.

Joining forces with Mexican businessman Enrique Creel, who had already built the first section of a railway from Chihuahua across the Sierra Madre, Stilwell organized the Kansas City, Mexico & Orient Railway to complete a route across Texas and Mexico to Topolobampo. A portion of Stilwell's Orient Route across Kansas and Texas, and isolated segments in Mexico, were completed before the project went bankrupt in 1912. It would be another half century before the dream of a new transcontinental route to the Gulf of California was realized.

The project came to life again in 1953, when the Mexican government organized the Ferrocarril Chihuahua al Pacifico (FCCHalP) to complete the line across the Sierra Madre. Track was already in place across the high mountain plateau between Chihuahua and Creel, and 73 miles inland from Topolobampo to Hornillos; but the 158 miles that remained to be built across the Barrancas del Cobre, or Copper Canyon, region of the Sierra Madre would represent some of the most difficult railroad construction ever undertaken.

Over the seven years from 1954 to 1961 Mexico's railroad builders constructed a line that climbed to a maximum elevation of 8071 feet at Los Ojitos before descending to sea level through the rugged peaks and deep canyons of the Sierra Madre. To maintain a grade of no more than 2.5 percent (132 feet per mile), the Mexican engineers built a spectacular line that incorporated great loops and horseshoe curves, 86 tunnels, and 37 major bridges. To do it they moved more than 19 million cubic yards of earth and rock, blasted or built more than 10 miles of tunnel, and erected some 4 miles of bridges.

Although Owen's and Stilwell's vision of a new rail route to the Orient never materialized, completion of the Chihuahua Pacific in 1961 gave Mexico an important new route between the rich agricultural region west of the Sierra Madre and the industrial region to the east; and it created one of the most spectacular railway journeys on the North American continent.

Seeking a fresh look at the wonders of a Copper Canyon railway journey, as well as some insight into the history of the region and its Tarahumara Indians,

Two Electro-Motive GP units propelled the Chihuahua Pacific's eastbound, tri-weekly *Vista Train* up through the rugged canyons of the west slope of the Sierra Madre toward one of the railway's 86 tunnels. Seven coaches, a diner, a dome coach, and a streamlined diner-lounge-observation car made up the long Christmas-week train in 1975.

Dorothy and I joined an Elderhostel group at Los Mochis, Sinaloa, in June 1998 to begin a week-long excursion through the Sierra Madre.

Dawn was still more than an hour away as our party boarded a bus at the Santa Anita Hotel and headed through the streets of Los Mochis to the railroad station. Even in early morning, the heat and humidity of coastal Mexico in June were oppressive.

The former Chihuahua Pacific station on the edge of town was a large, plain masonry structure illuminated by harsh fluorescent lamps. FCCHalP had been merged into the Ferrocarriles Nationales de Mexico (FNM) in 1987, but since its privatization in February 1998 the line had been operated by the new Ferrocarril Mexicano, and a canvas "Ferromex" banner partially covered the big FNM sign on the front of the station.

Waiting for us under a high canopy was eastbound first-class train 73, *Servicio Estrella*—"Star Service," which operates daily between Los Mochis and Chihuahua. A single FNM Electro-Motive GP38-2 unit, former Chihuahua Pacific No. 909, headed a train made up of three Mexican-built "primera especial" air conditioned, first-class coaches; the dome coach *Silver Stirrup* for our Elderhostel group; and an FNM caboose. Except for the dome car, the equipment was finished in FNM's standard medium and light blue colors, with orange-red striping and lettering. A large crowd of passengers waited for the train to open, many of the men wearing broad-brimmed straw hats to help deflect the heat of the sun.

Silver Stirrup promised a comfortable journey. The car was hardly new; it had been built by Budd in 1948 for the *California Zephyr*, but it had been thoroughly rehabilitated and appeared well kept. We would not be disappointed.

Owned by the Denver Railway Car Company and operated under lease by South Orient Express, the car is used for special tour groups such as ours. The exterior was unpainted stainless steel, except for a maroon "Roaring Fork" letterboard reflecting a projected service in Colorado for which the car had originally been reconditioned. The maroon theme carried over to the interior, which had maroon trim, upholstery, and wall carpeting on the main level, with a dark green figured carpet on the floor. Seats in the dome were upholstered in a light gray, with maroon carpeting on the floor.

We took seats at the front of the dome and waited for the 6 A.M. departure time. A long freight train pulled in from the east, and then our train pulled smoothly away from the station platform, right on time. The sky was just beginning to get light.

The lights of Los Mochis glimmered to the north as we passed through the freight yard. Lights were on in a string of camp cars, suggesting that a track gang was getting ready for the day's work.

We traveled northeast from Los Mochis across the fertile plain of the Rio Fuerte Valley. The valley represents some of the richest farm land in Mexico, and we were told that it can produce as many as six a year of some crops. The land is irrigated from reservoirs in the Sierra Madre, and the track occasionally passes over one of the canals that carry the water to the fields. We passed wide fields of hybrid corn and other irrigated crops. Bougainvillea, mango, and palm trees added variety to the landscape. The tallest royal palms, we were told, marked the sites of the original haciendas dating from the 1890s, when developer Benjamin

F. Johnston established the first large scale farms in the valley. Farm workers' dwellings lined the track, many with small cattle pens. Occasional horses and donkeys and a flock of white geese grazed along the track.

The sky began to take on a rosy hue, and shortly after 6:30 the sun rose like a red ball behind the line of sharp hills to the east, climbing in and out of the clouds.

Approaching Sufragio, the line climbed to an overpass that carried us over the north-south line of the former Ferrocarril del Pacifico (FCP)—the Pacific Railroad—that links Nogales on the Arizona border with Guadalajara and Mexico City. Originally the Southern Pacific of Mexico, it became the independent FCP under government ownership in 1951, was incorporated into FNM in 1987, and, together with the former Chihuahua Pacific, was turned over to private operator Ferromex early in 1998.

Our line curved north to parallel the Pacific line into the Sufragio yard and station that serves both lines. Two freight trains were switching in the yard. Food sellers hawked their wares to passengers while we paused next to an elaborate station canopy of folded, thin shell concrete.

Train 73 resumed its journey, paralleling the former FCP for several miles north through San Blas before the Pacific line curved off to the west to cross the Rio Fuerte on a long truss and plate girder bridge. By this time we had climbed to higher ground, leaving the fertile valley behind. There were still occasional palm and papaya trees, small fields of dry-looking corn and grain, and cattle grazing; but more and more the trackside landscape was one of dry scrub growth and cactus.

We were accompanied by Roberto "Beto" Lopez, a native of the area who knew much about its flora and fauna. Beto identified some of the varieties of cactus. There was the familiar *saguaro* prevalent in the Southwest, a variety called *hecho cardon*—"aborigine's comb"—and the impressive *pitaya dulce*, or "organ pipe" cactus.

For the bird-watchers in the dome Beto identified a *caracara* "face to face"— a bird with a white neck and head and an eagle-like beak—perched on a cactus.

The modest houses in the villages we passed along the way were built of brick, concrete block, or the traditional adobe. Occasionally we saw an abandoned adobe house, crumbling away like an ancient ruin. The village cemeteries were made up of brightly painted, above-ground crypts.

Beyond our station stop at El Fuerte, an old Spanish colonial town dating to 1564, we climbed steadily into an increasingly rugged terrain in a landscape of scrub brush and cactus, and a purplish flowering plant. Beto pointed out an occasional kapok tree. We passed several massive crumbling mesas and outcroppings of volcanic rock, and up ahead the jagged peaks of the Sierra Madre began to come into view.

During a brief station stop at Loreto two boys hawked prickly pear fruit to the train's passengers from the station platform. Then we moved on toward the line's longest bridge, an enormous 1637-foot deck-truss span that carries the line over the Rio Fuerte. The view was spectacular as we passed high above the meandering river.

The Chihuahua Pacific's crossing of the Sierra Madre was achieved only by

75

building many tunnels, and a few miles later we were into the first of them and the longest on the entire line, the 5966-foot El Descanso. The line's 86 tunnels are numbered beginning from the Chihuahua end, so this was Tunnel 86. Most of them were drilled and blasted through rock, but more than 20 are "false" tunnels, created by building earth-covered concrete arches above deep cuts at locations where slides or rock falls were common. Actually, as Beto explained, there are now 90 tunnels on the line, since four more of these false tunnels have been added since the railway was completed.

Just above the junction where the Chinipas and Septentrion rivers join to form the Fuerte, we crossed the Chinipas on the line's highest bridge. I leaned out from the vestibule Dutch door to look 350 feet down into the valley below at the battered wreckage of two grain hopper cars that remained from what must have been a spectacular derailment.

For the next 40 miles the climb toward the Continental Divide began in earnest as we followed the rugged gorge of the Septentrion into the heart of the Sierra Madre. One tunnel followed another in dizzying succession; at times the locomotive was into the next tunnel before *Silver Stirrup* had left the last. In one stretch of only 7 1/2 miles just below Temoris there are 20 tunnels, totaling nearly 10,000 feet. Even in this deep, rocky canyon a few hardy families are struggling to subsist; and we saw occasional small farms and corrals tucked into the valley and cattle grazing on steep slopes.

The occasional trackside wreckage of freight cars, victims of runaways or derailments, reminded us that railroading in these rugged mountains could be tough, dangerous work.

At Temoris we encountered the railway's famous loops, two extraordinary horseshoe curves that represent one of the line's most spectacular feats of railroad location engineering. Climbing upstream at river level, the line swoops across the Rio Septentrion on the long, curved Santa Barbara Bridge to reverse direction, climbing up the opposite side of the Santa Barbara Canyon as it heads in the downstream direction. Then it enters the 3074-foot, pear-shaped La Pera Tunnel, where the line curves through 180 degrees to reverse direction again, emerging higher still on the canyon wall as it continues to climb toward the Divide.

High above the Temoris station on this upper level, an enormous sign welded together from pieces of rail commemorates the formal opening of the Chihuahua Pacific on November 24, 1961, by Mexican President Adolfo Lopez Mateos. Just below it stands a bizarre, more recent monument made up of a stack of old hopper cars welded together, surmounted by the orange and black body of one of the railway's original Fairbanks-Morse diesels.

Above Temoris the mountain slopes were more heavily forested in oak and pine; there are said to be more varieties of these species in the Sierra Madre Occidental than at any other place in the world. We passed sawmills, timber yards, and flat cars loaded with sawn lumber. Many of the trackside houses were roofed in wood shingles. Beto pointed out "octopus" cactus, bamboo, and *pinobella*— candle pine—growing in the valley.

At Soledad, at the junction of the Rio Septentrion with its tributary Cerocahui and Plata rivers, the line climbed through another horseshoe curve as it swung

76

away from the Septentrion to cross over the Cerocahui and then curved back to follow the Plata still higher into the mountains.

Not long after noon the train braked to a halt at Bahuichivo, where the crew switched *Silver Stirrup* to a siding and our group clambered aboard a hotel bus for a jolting ride across the mountains for a side trip to the pleasant Hotel Mision at Cerocahui and a look at the spectacular Rio Urique canyon.

In a Bahuichivo siding we noted one of the "market cars" that are an unusual feature of the line. These are box cars hired by fruit and vegetable vendors that are moved from station to station to supply produce to residents of the nearly inaccessible mountain towns along the railway.

Two days later we were back at Bahuichivo to resume the journey east across the Sierra Madre. Train 73 pulled in, once again behind Electro-Motive unit 909, and *Silver Stirrup* was switched to the rear of the three-coach train. We were on our way again shortly after 1 P.M.

The long climb to the top of the Sierra Madre continued. From a canyon wall high above we looked down on the little town of Cuiteco and its mission, established in 1684, and the apple and apricot orchards for which the town is noted. Just beyond Cuiteco, Beto pointed out the ruins of what had been a camp for the railroad construction workers; his father had been among them. In just a few miles we passed through nine tunnels, totaling almost 5000 feet, and crossed nine bridges that added up to another 2100 feet. At Chihuamuicame we pulled into a siding to clear the main line for a trio of Electro-Motive GP38 and GP40 diesels leading a long freight down to Los Mochis, then crossed one of the Septentrion's tributaries on the towering La Laja Bridge.

Food vendors waited on the platform at San Rafael, where we made a long station stop for servicing and a crew change. A candy vendor and colorfully dressed Tarahumara Indian women and girls selling baskets boarded the train to hawk their wares to passengers as we resumed our journey eastward. Our next stop was at Hotel Posada Barrancas, where the basket sellers and candy vendor left the train to wait for westbound train 74, our opposite number, and repeat the process on the way back to San Rafael. On some maps the station name is shown as Ingeniero Francisco M. Togno, honoring the Mexican engineer who located the Chihuahua Pacific across the Sierra Madre.

Ever since the Chihuahua Pacific began running across the Sierra Madre, a brief stop at Divisadero Barranca—"Canyon Lookout"—for the spectacular view from the rim of the Urique Canyon has been part of the journey. Tarahumara basket sellers lined the platform, and train passengers ran a gauntlet of souvenir and food stalls on their way to the overlook. A big hotel perched on the rim offered its guests unparalleled views of a canyon deeper than even the Grand Canyon. We looked down in awe to the silvery Urique some 4135 feet below us, and across the canyon to a south rim some 4 miles away. Altogether, the six principal canyons— Urique, Cobre, Batopilas, Oteros, Tararecua, and Sinforosa—that make up what is usually referred to as the Barrancas del Cobre total over 900 miles and reach depths of as much as 6136 feet.

As we pulled away from the Divisadero stop, a single Electro-Motive unit slipped in on the adjacent siding with the westbound tri-weekly second-class train

Perhaps the most spectacular feature on the Chihuahua Pacific is this engineering tour de force at Temoris, Chihuahua, where trains negotiate a double loop to climb out of the deep canyon of the Rio Septentrion. This view was taken from westbound train 74 above the upper loop. It will negotiate the first loop in the 3074-foot, pear-shaped La Pera Tunnel to gain the track at left below, then reverse direction again on the long loop in the distance that curves back across the river on the Santa Barbara bridge at the right.

76, *El Tarahumara,* made up of five battered second-class coaches and a caboose.

Some 16 miles east of Divisadero, Beto alerted us to another of the railway's spectacular feats of railroad engineering at El Lazo—"the rope"—where the line makes a 360 degree loop as it nears the end of the climb up a 2.5 percent grade to the Sierra Madre summit. As it ascends eastward, the line first passes through Tunnel No. 7 and then crosses over itself on a stone arch bridge directly above the tunnel as it completes the loop.

A few miles later our train finally reached the end of its long climb at Los Ojitos, the highest point on the railway. We had climbed more than 8000 feet from our starting point at Los Mochis. A few miles later a big white "Division Continental" sign indicated that we had reached the Continental Divide.

As the train descended through a long horseshoe curve called El Balcon—"the balcony"—we could see our destination at Creel in the distance. New corn crops were just beginning to grow in fields in the valley around the city. Smoke rose from stacks at a huge sawmill on the edge of town. Beside the track as we entered town was a big green and white tent in a field advertising an appearance of Randu, who was billed as a *hypnotismo colectivo.* What, we wondered, was a "collective hypnotist"?

What is now Creel is as far as Enrique Creel ever got, in 1907, with his project to build a railway across the Sierra Madre. The town has become an important center for forestry and tourism, and it looked like a lively place. Its houses and buildings were an eclectic mixture of typical Mexican masonry, stone, and adobe construction, with a number of what might be called *faux* Alpine structures of logs, with corrugated metal, Spanish tile, and wood-shingled roofs. Just a block from the railroad station, a traditional mission church faced a town square with a bust of Enrique Creel, the town's namesake, at its center.

Befitting the town's importance, the Creel station was a handsome two-story cream-colored stucco structure with a Spanish tile roof, a wainscot and door and window trim in cut basalt, and doors and windows of varnished heavy wood. There was an operator's bay and a train order board, and a radio antenna stood on the roof.

The arrival of train 73 had generated a flurry of activity at the station. Buses and vans from Creel's many hotels waited to pick up their guests. On the station platform the inevitable Tarahumara ladies appeared with their offerings of baskets and crafts, a news butcher advertised his papers at the top of his voice, and a man with a pushcart sold ice cream bars. At a nearby siding, produce vendors sold their fruits and vegetables from another of the traveling "market cars."

Silver Stirrup went into a siding again, and our group climbed aboard one of the buses for the trip to the Cascada Inn, which would be our base over the next two days for outings to some of the area's splendid mountain scenery and a look at the Tarahumara culture.

Two days later we were back at the Creel station for the late morning departure of westbound train 74. *Silver Stirrup* was cut in behind the two diesel units, a GP38-2 and a GP40-2, and we enjoyed a sandwich box lunch served by the car's amiable staff while the train climbed west toward the Continental Divide and the beginning of the descent toward the Pacific.

Aside from the terminals at Chihuahua and Los Mochis, the busiest station on the Chihuahua Pacific is this handsome tile-roofed stucco structure at Creel, named for Enrique Creel, one of the early promoters of a railway across the Sierra Madre. Buses and vans from the tourist hotels, an ice cream vendor, and a few lounging idlers had gathered on the station platform as westbound *Servicio Estrella* train 74 pulled in from the east with Electro-Motive GP38-2 unit No. 909 in the lead.

At Divisadero Barranca we left the train again to spend a night at the Hotel Posada Mirador, perched high on the rim of Urique Canyon. From a hotel balcony we watched nightfall and sunrise on the canyon, and we hiked through pine forest down into the canyon to visit a Tarahumara cave dwelling.

Early the next afternoon, we were back aboard *Silver Stirrup* at Divisadero Barranca, waiting to be coupled into that day's westbound train 74. I hiked around

81

the curve leading into the station to photograph the arriving train, and discovered that No. 74 was probably going to be late that day. Road builders blasting a new highway route across a deep rock cut on the rail line had evidently used an excess of dynamite, and they had a real mess on their hands. The railroad was now several feet deep in rock and debris, and a boulder the size of a small sedan sat squarely in the center of the track.

I watched as the road builders worked frantically to clean up the mess. A maintenance-of-way motor car waited just beyond the blockade, and soon train 74's four GP38 and GP40 diesels had pulled up to wait behind the motor car. A huge Caterpillar front end loader worked to scoop rock and debris off the tracks. Then the machine cleared a path around the boulder, got behind it, and pushed it down the track to a spot wide enough to get it out of the way.

The boulder disposed of, laborers shoveled furiously to clear the flangeways, and then the track crew moved in and measured to make sure the track was still in gauge. It was, and the motor car crept cautiously through the now-cleared blockade. Train 74 came through next and moved slowly into the station, now a good hour or more behind schedule.

We lost more time at San Rafael while three extra diesel units were cut off our train and we waited for eastbound train 73 to arrive, and then lost still more as carmen replaced a defective air hose on *Silver Stirrup*. Underway again, we ran through the siding at Chihuamuicame while the eastbound "segundo"—train 75—waited on the main line. In addition to its usual second-class coaches, the train had a flat car loaded with a power shovel cut in behind the locomotive.

It was late afternoon as the train made its way down the deepening canyons toward Los Mochis, and the deep shadows gave the canyons an entirely different aspect than what we had seen on the way up a few days earlier. As we followed the deep Rio Septentrion canyon we spotted two *aguilas*—white-tailed black eagles—floating lazily in the air currents above the stream.

By the time we reached the massive bridge over the Rio Fuerte it was early evening, and the meandering stream was bathed in the rosy light of a spectacular sunset as we crossed high above the river.

Our Copper Canyon rail journey ended after dark at El Fuerte, where *Silver Stirrup* was switched into a siding with other South Orient Express equipment. Train 73 continued on toward Los Mochis while we boarded a bus that took us to Hotel Posada Hidalgo, a handsome establishment in an 1890 mansion in colonial El Fuerte.

The Journey Today

The outlook is bright for continued passenger operation over the popular Copper Canyon route. The new Ferrocarril Mexicano that took over the privatized Pacific-North segment of FNM early in 1998 has been rehabilitating the equipment used in the daily first-class service between Los Mochis and Chihuahua and is improving the principal stations along the line. Several tour operators offer a variety of tour packages for the popular trip. These include a complete deluxe train operated by Sierra Madre Express, both special trains and deluxe equipment operated in the regular service by South Orient Express, and a variety of tour packages based upon use of the regular Ferromex service.

On a June afternoon in 1998 this mishap just east of Divisadero Barranca disrupted operations
on Mexico's railroad across the Sierra Madre. Constructing a path for a new road across the
rock cut followed by the rail line, highway builders had used a little too much dynamite, leaving
the cut filled with huge boulders and debris. A motor car with a track maintenance crew and
the westbound *Servicio Estrella* first-class train waited impatiently while a big Caterpillar front-
end loader and a gang of laborers worked to clear the tracks. Train 74 was a good hour late by
the time the mess was cleaned up.

Mixed Train to Taviche*

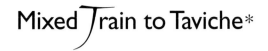

In the soft light of early morning the Oaxaca station was gradually coming to life. In the open breezeway through the center of the building a group of *campesinos* had begun to gather, first depositing their bundles in a neat row on the red tile floor at the entry to the station's single platform and then lining up at the ticket window, chatting quietly while they waited for the 7 A.M. opening time posted on a hand-lettered sign.

In the yard beyond the station a pair of General Electric road switchers throbbed softly, waiting for their train. A compact little Electro-Motive diesel shuttled back and forth on yard switching duties. Two trains were spotted back-to-back at the station platform, waiting for passengers and motive power.

The station was a handsome stone structure, befitting the capital city of the State of Oaxaca and the southern terminal of the one-time Mexican Southern Railway. The stone was a distinctive locally quarried grayish-green volcanic tuff called ignimbrite. Narrow, arch-topped windows and the building corners were set off with raised stone courses, painted a peach color, and there was a large stone arch at the open center entrance to the station. An ornate stone and iron fence surrounded the station grounds, which were elaborately landscaped with banyan and palm trees, croton, and other tropical plants.

My travel plans for this warm July morning in 1994 called for a journey south through the Oaxaca Valley to the little mining town of San Pedro Taviche and back again aboard the Mexican National Railways' (Ferrocarriles Nacionales de Mexico, or FNM) daily mixed train. With me as guide and interpreter was my son Bill, then in his third summer of archaeological field work in the valley.

Promptly at 7 A.M., the ticket agent opened for business. We took our place behind the line of waiting passengers and soon had our turn at the window, where we bought tickets to Taviche. The cost of a one-way ticket was all of N$ 2.50 (then about 78 cents) for the 53.7 kilometer (33.4 miles) journey. The return trip ticket, we were told, would have to be purchased from the conductor.

The pace of activity began to pick up around the station. The two GE road switchers came to life, pulled ahead through a switch, and backed down on a three-car local train for Puebla waiting at one end of the platform. Both were 10000 series "kit built" B23-7 units from a 52-locomotive order built in 1981–82 and assembled in FNM's Aguascalientes shops. One was painted in the current FNM color scheme of medium and light blue, with red trim and white lettering, while the other still wore a faded version of the older colors of dark gray, an orange-red cab and nose, and yellow running board, with a big white road number and NdeM lettering.

---

*© 1996 Pentrex Media Group, reprinted with permission from the January 1996 issue of *Passenger Train Journal.*

Early on an August morning in 1994, the daily mixed train for Taviche was ready for departure from the station at Oaxaca. An Electro-Motive G12 export diesel headed the two-car train made up of a single lightweight aluminum coach and a caboose.

The modest crowd of perhaps two dozen passengers, it turned out, were all waiting for the Puebla train, which went booming off to the north at 7:50 A.M. Our train, Mixtos No. 332, was due out immediately afterward.

The equipment for train 332 waiting at the platform included a single blue coach and a bright yellow caboose. The coach was one of 200 aluminum-bodied lightweights built for FNM in 1978 by then–Hawker Siddeley's Canadian Car Division (now Bombardier) plant at Thunder Bay, Ontario. Interior appointments

85

were austere. The floor was covered with a linoleum-like material, the walkover seats were upholstered in a vinyl imitation leather, and dark brown curtains hung at the windows. There was a single lavatory at each end of the car. The yellow caboose, we were told, was included because No. 332 was a mixed train.

Our motive power for the trip turned out to be the yard switcher, which soon completed its work and coupled up to the two-car train. The diesel, FNM's class DE-18 No. 5876, was an Electro-Motive G12 export unit, which made it something of a novelty in North American railroading. FNM acquired 90 of the 1310-hp V-12 units over the period 1957–64. These, and another two sold to Canada's London & Port Stanley, were the only G12's ever operated in North America. The need for low axle loadings on branch lines, rather than clearance limitations, led FNM to buy the compact export units. No. 5876 still had the older FNM color scheme, with a big yellow shield painted on each end.

Shortly before 8 A.M., with a total of three passengers aboard the 76-seat coach, we were off for Taviche. The *maquinista* (engineer) made liberal use of bell and air horn as we rattled down the center boulevard of the city's busy Periferico Sur (south peripheral road). Near the city center we halted briefly at a platform in the center boulevard, much like a streetcar, to pick up a few more passengers and their bundles. The ratio of passengers to the train's five-man crew was getting a little better.

As we picked up speed again, the line curved to the west to cross over the Rio Atoyac. Another branch curved east to continue in the peripheral road toward Tlacolula, on the north side of the Oaxaca Valley. *Tren mixtos* service to Tlacolula had been discontinued several years earlier, and the track looked as if very little traffic had gone that way since.

Once clear of the Rio Atoyac bridge the rails turned southward toward the central valley. The line took its own route through the valley to Ocotlan and Taviche, well away from the paved highways and the roadside clutter that seems to follow them everywhere, giving us an unspoiled view of agrarian life in the semi-tropical valley.

Up ahead the diesel nosed gently from side to side as it ambled along over the uneven track, while our coach rolled, sometimes alarmingly, from side to side. Vigorous application of the air horn brought a man leading a donkey with a load of straw safely to a stop at a crossing. Dogs raced up to trackside, barking furiously at the passing train and occasionally pursuing us out of their territory.

Voluble head brakeman Florencio Hernandez Perez joined us at our seats and pointed out the passing sights in the *valle central*, while young Bill used the opportunity to practice his Spanish.

All through the fertile valley cultivated fields were intermingled with groves of eucalyptus, oak, and walnut trees. Mixed in with fields of corn were plantings of squash and beans, a pre-Hispanic practice which helps to enrich the soil. The "Meso-American trinity," Bill called it. Off on the horizon, cloud-shrouded mountains ringed the green valley.

An occasional tractor worked the fields, but more often the farmers tilled their crops with horses, mules or oxen, or even by hand. We stopped occasionally for passengers at dirt road crossings or little adobe-walled villages with names like

Ocotlan was clearly the largest and most important point on the line to Taviche, and the mixed train made an extended stop alongside the substantial stuccoed station. The stone base for a water tank at the left stood as a reminder of the days of steam power on the one-time 3-foot-gauge branch line.

Zaachila, La Trinidad, and Zimatlan. At one, the dirt road along the track was labeled Av. Ferrocarrille. "Railroad Avenue" in Central America!

The conductor collected cash fares and carefully punched receipts. We were beginning to carry a respectable load and the coach was soon filled with the pleasant hum of conversation in Spanish and the local Zapotec language.

East of Ocotlan the rails began to climb in earnest toward the mountain mining town at Taviche, and the elderly little diesel that pulled the *mixtos* was working hard as the train followed the twists and turns of the line up through the foothills.

The idea of a railroad to Oaxaca and its valley went back to 1881, when Oaxacan leader Matias Romero organized the American-financed Mexican Southern Railroad to link Vera Cruz with the Pacific Ocean via Oaxaca. Despite none other than General and former U.S. president Ulysses S. Grant as its president, the company went bankrupt scarcely three years later before so much as a mile of track had been built. A new company, the British-financed Mexican Southern Railway (Ferrocarril Mexicano del Sur), finally began construction in 1889 on

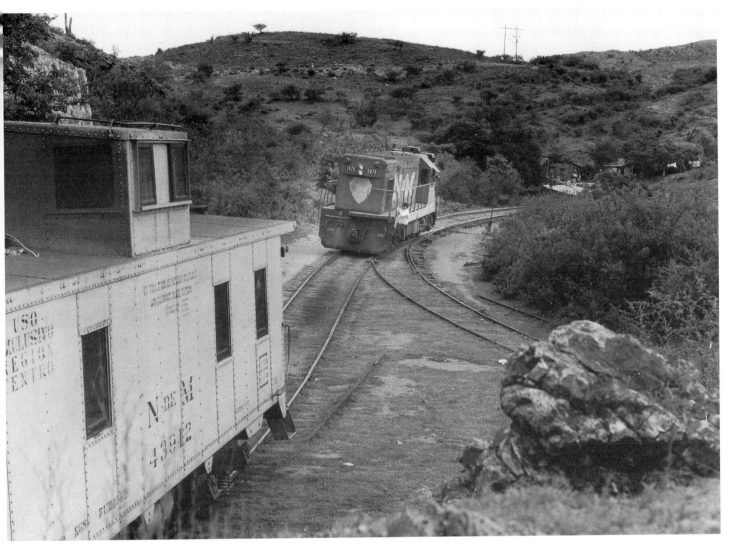

The outbound journey to Taviche completed, the mixed train crew turned the locomotive on the wye and backed on to their train to begin the return trip to Oaxaca.

what was now to be a 3-foot-gauge line from Puebla to Oaxaca. President Porfirio Diaz and other notables welcomed the first train to Oaxaca on November 13, 1892. The line was extended south from Oaxaca into the valley to Ocotlan and Ejutla in 1904, while the branch to Taviche was completed in 1910. Long since incorporated into the Mexican National Railways, everything south of Puebla was converted to standard gauge in 1952.

The train rattled across the Rio Atoyac again on a spindly truss bridge, paused briefly for a few passengers at Santiago Apostol, and before long the little diesel was braking to a halt for an extended stop at Ocotlan, clearly the largest and most important point on the line. The substantial stuccoed masonry station was finished in a sort of salmon red with white trim. Alongside the platform was an empty telegrapher's bay and an idle train order board. Just beyond the station stood a sturdy circular stone structure that had once supported a trackside water tank.

The daily mixed train did brisk passenger business as it headed back to Oaxaca. Loaded down with goods to sell in the city's central market, a group of country women boarded the train's single coach at a rural stop between Ocotlan and Oaxaca.

We had left our hotel too early to get breakfast, so young Bill joined the train crew in a search for something to eat. They soon found a woman food vendor cooking over a wood-fired clay *comal* at a roadside stall, and Bill returned with a welcome stack of hot corn tortillas that were quickly dispatched.

Soon the *mixtos* was on its way again. Just outside of Ocotlan we crossed the paved highway that follows the valley south to Ejutla and the Pacific coast. The rail line to Ejutla was pulled up in 1933, which doubtless had something to do with the coming of the highway. But even today there's only a dirt road up into the mountains to Taviche, and the trains still run.

We were running now toward the eastern edge of the valley through a countryside that was gradually changing as we began to approach the mountains. There were still occasional corn fields, but more and more the hillsides were dominated by organ pipe cactus, yucca, and *aguey*, the plant that rural Mexicans distill into the potent *mescal.* Growing everywhere was a sort of thorny brush that brakeman Florencio called "*spinas.*"

Soon we were into the foothills, and up ahead the familiar chant of an EMD 567 diesel grew louder as the locomotive finally began working hard as we climbed toward Taviche, curving left and right on a steadily rising grade.

The future for FNM journeys like this one was not very bright. In a visit to the railroad's headquarters in Mexico City just a few days before I'd learned that FNM was shedding its money-losing mixed trains and unproductive branch lines just as fast as it could on the way to converting the national system into a high performance double-stack freight carrier for the brave new world of NAFTA.

With that knowledge in mind, the scarcity of passengers on the Taviche *mixtos,* and little sign of any freight traffic at all, I wouldn't have given very good odds on the longevity of the Taviche branch. Thus, I was all the more surprised as we came across a track gang on one of the mountain grades, busily inserting treated timber ties and installing heavier relay rail in place of original stock that looked as if it couldn't have been much more than 60-pound rail.

Just a mile or so short of the end of the line we reached the top of the grade and drifted down into the little village of Taviche. Florencio pointed out the played-out gold and silver mines on the mountainside slopes above the village. A few turkeys hunted for spilled grain between the rails. The train crew turned the diesel on a wye and coupled up to the caboose end of the train for the return journey. A small crowd of passengers climbed aboard and the conductor busily collected cash fares as we began the return journey on what was now mixed train No. 333.

Ocotlan was good for another extended stop as the diesel cut off to collect a box car that had been emptied of a load of bagged fertilizer. We finally had something to warrant our mixed train status!

The passenger business got better and better as we continued on our way back to Oaxaca. A small crowd had boarded at Ocotlan, a much larger group clambered aboard at Santiago Apostol, and still more waited for us at San Pablo. Just before noon we rumbled across the Rio Atoyac into Oaxaca and pulled to a stop to unload most of our passengers at the center boulevard platform in the Periferico Sur. Most were probably bound for the Central de Abastos—the central market— just a few blocks away. We rode on into the Oaxaca station. Florencio bid us goodbye, the crew uncoupled the diesel and headed for the engine house, and Bill and I went to find a taxi to the Zocalo and lunch.

The Journey Today

Over recent years, as the Mexican government has broken up and privatized major components of the national system, passenger services have been severely curtailed. While some trains that serve remote rural areas have been retained, the Taviche mixed train was not among them, and the service no longer operates.

Coast to Coast by 𝒩arrow Gauge*

Given their combination of exotic tropical and subtropical scenery, their narrow gauge, and a certain antiquity, the railroads of Central America have long held a special appeal for me. Paul Theroux reinforced it with his tales of adventurous rail travel down the Central American isthmus on the way to South America in his *The Old Patagonian Express* of 1979. But for a long while, my Central American interest had been strictly from afar.

Costa Rica seemed like a good place to finally experience the trains of Central America first hand. In a country scarcely twice the size of Maryland, Costa Rica encompasses an extraordinary scenic diversity that ranges from the cattle ranchlands of western Guanacaste to the active volcanoes of the central mountain range to the tropical jungles of the Caribbean coast. In a region where the political disorder of an El Salvador or a Nicaragua was the norm, the stability and tranquility of democratic Costa Rica was a hospitable contrast. And no other country in Central America offered quite the railway variety of the Ferrocarriles de Costa Rica (FECOSA). After all, FECOSA ran passenger trains through the valley of the Rio Reventazón on what must be ranked as one of the great scenic railway journeys of the Americas, and—aside from the 3-foot gauge Ferrocarriles de Guatemala—it was the only railway in the Western hemisphere that could take you from the Atlantic to the Pacific on narrow-gauge track. And finally—no small matter for me—it operated two separate and distinct electrifications.

With all of this in mind, I found Costa Rica an easy choice for a brief late winter vacation, so early in March 1985 Dorothy and I were on board an Eastern 727 descending into San Jose's Juan Santamaria airport.

FECOSA was a relatively new system, having been formed in 1977 through consolidation of the two separate railways that reached Costa Rica's Atlantic and Pacific coasts from the capital city of San Jose. Each of these lines had distinct characteristics of its own, with little more in common than some rugged geography, and a 3-foot, 6-inch track gauge, and much of this individuality survived despite the sharing of a common Amtrak-like logo and a certain amount of rolling stock that came with consolidation.

The line to the Atlantic coast was much the older of the two. American railway builder and engineer Henry Meiggs, who had pioneered railways in Chile and Peru, projected the line in 1871 as the Atlantic Railway. Meiggs soon turned the project over to Minor C. Keith, a young Brooklyn-born entrepreneur who subsequently developed railway, mining, agricultural, and shipping enterprises throughout Central America. Building a railway through the jungles of Costa

---

*© 1986 Kalmbach Publishing Co., reprinted with permission from the September 1986 issue of *Trains* magazine.

Rica's east coast and up into the rugged valleys of the Cordillera Central—the Central mountain range—to a nearly mile-high crossing of the Continental Divide proved to be an enormously difficult task. Although it was only a hundred miles from the Atlantic coast to San Jose, it took Keith 19 years to get there with the railway. More than 4000 Chinese, Italian, and Honduran laborers died from malaria, dysentery, and heat exhaustion during construction of the first 25 miles through the jungle lowlands. Later, Jamaican laborers who proved more resistant

to the tropical diseases were brought in to complete the line. Their descendants still populate much of eastern Costa Rica.

Partially to help raise money for construction of the railway, Keith imported banana plants from Colombian plantations and started a banana industry that was to grow into the redoubtable United Fruit Company. Eventually, as the Northern Railway Company of Costa Rica, the Atlantic railway itself came under United Fruit ownership.

Unlike the Atlantic line, Costa Rica's Pacific railway was a government enterprise from the very beginning. A contract to build the first 56 miles out of San Jose was awarded to Ohio contractor John S. Casement in 1897, and construction was completed as far as the valley of Santo Domingo by 1902. Trains began running over the full 72-mile main line between San Jose and the Pacific port of Puntarenas on July 23, 1910.

For its first two decades, the Pacific railway was operated by wood- or coal-burning steam power, but in 1929 the entire route was electrified with a German-built system that remains the only 15,000-volt, 20-cycle, single-phase AC electrification in the Western Hemisphere. Power for the electrification came from a hydroelectric plant at Tacares

Early on a March morning in 1985 the daily train was ready to depart from San Jose for Puerto Limón on the Atlantic coast. A small boy had claimed a window seat for the scenic journey over the mountains and through the jungles of Costa Rica.

on the Rio Poás. Following electrification, the railway became known as the Ferrocarril Electrico al Pacifico, or Pacific Electric Railway.

The Atlantic railway came under the ownership of a government-run Atlantic zone and port development board in the early 1970s, and merged with the Pacific railway under the FECOSA banner in 1977. An immediate objective of the new national railway was the modernization and electrification of the Atlantic railway's principal banana route across the coastal jungle. Between the Rio Frio and Puerto Limón, 66 miles of line were relaid with welded rail and concrete ties, bridges were rebuilt for heavier loads, and new yards were built at each end of the rebuilt line. The European 50-cycle Group installed a 25-kilovolt, 60-cycle electrification, and electric operation began in February 1982. A dozen new dual-voltage, 1200 kw locomotives, built by Alsthom of France in 1981 and capable of operation on either the new electrification or the Pacific line's 15-kilovolt, 20-cycle system, were divided between the two lines.

The only link between the Atlantic and Pacific lines was a steeply graded line through the streets of San Jose, but I was told that FECOSA planned a new connection near Alajuela, where branches from the two lines were only 2 miles apart.

For international air travelers, San Jose is the point of entry to Costa Rica, so it made sense to begin a narrow-gauge journey between the coasts in the middle. The Atlantic railway was first on our itinerary, so late one morning we rode a cab across San Jose to the old Ferrocarril de Costa Rica station on Avenida 3 to catch the single daily train to Puerto Limón. The trip cost 90 colons (less than $2), and the train was scheduled to make the 103-mile journey in 6 1/2 hours.

Aside from the Puerto Limón train, the Atlantic line station handled several weekday commuter round trips that ran between San Jose and nearby Cartagao and Heredia, east and west of the city.

The station was an aging structure of modest proportions dating from 1908. Broad stone steps led up from street level to a stuccoed masonry building finished in white, with a dark maroon base and trim. A rusting, silver-painted roof of Central America's ubiquitous corrugated iron was surmounted at each end by raised mansard sections inset with ornate dormers. In a bit of pretension befitting the railway's capital city terminal, the streetside roof line was enclosed within an elaborate masonry rail with posts embossed in a winged wheel design. At the center, a crumbling statuary group flanked a circular opening that had once held a clock. Intricate ironwork supported a wooden canopy above the entrance steps.

To the east of the building in the midst of a flower garden rested preserved Northern Railway of Costa Rica 2-6-0 Mogul No. 59, rigged with cab lights, markers, and a headlight that were turned on every night. Just beyond was a statue of General Tomás Guardia, Costa Rica's late nineteenth century dictatorial ruler who promoted development of the Atlantic railway.

The train to Puerto Limón stood under a corrugated iron train shed outside the station. Eight coaches of clearly varied origins were pulled by a pair of General Electric diesels separated by two box cars, evidently because of bridge loading limits. As the 11 A.M. departure time approached, a warning bell clanged in the station, and then Caterpillar diesels cranked up and the train lurched into motion.

"Jungle Train" tours over the Atlantic line were a popular attraction for Costa Rica tourists, and we had booked extra-fare seats on one of the handsomely refurbished tour cars that brought up the rear of the train. Our car was an open-platform, arched-roof, wooden coach of uncertain age built by Gregg of Belgium. The exterior was finished in a dark blue, with white window sash and a silvered roof. Red and white stripes lined each side of the car, with a centered FECOSA logo. The interior was finished in varnished oak, with the only parquet floors I have ever seen in a railway car. The walkover seats were newly upholstered in white vinyl. A cheerful Jamaican tour guide named Sarah in a lavender pantsuit dispensed commentary, sandwiches, beer, and ice cream as we made our way through the green countryside.

Bamboo, bougainvillea, and palm trees mingled with brightly colored little

Headed by compact General Electric diesel No. 83, the eastbound Puerto Limón train waited amid verdant tropical growth at Florencia for a meet with a long-delayed westbound train.

houses with neat yards that fronted on the tracks. We passed the University of Costa Rica with its bizarre school of architecture building, and then ran through San Jose's elegant suburbs. San Jose is west of the Continental Divide, and the twin GE diesels climbed steadily through a verdant countryside toward the summit. Beyond Tres Rios the rails paralleled the Pan American Highway for a few

95

"Yet there isn't a train
I wouldn't take"

Florencia schoolchildren gathered to visit with the foreign tourists aboard the "Jungle Train" tour car at the rear of the eastbound daily train between San Jose and Puerto Limón. A derailment down the line had disrupted operations, and the train spent much of the afternoon in the mountain village.

miles until we came to the Divide at El Alto, close to a mile high at an elevation of 5050 feet. We paused briefly here to drop one of the diesels—U10B No. 78—and then the remaining unit—U11B No. 83—headed downgrade toward the Caribbean.

With the great 2-mile-high Irazu Volcano visible to the northeast, we descended into Cartagao, the colonial capital of Costa Rica that lost most of its status after being destroyed by an Irazu eruption and twice wrecked by earthquakes. We made a long stop at the city's tin-roofed, wooden station, and then moved off down a narrow street past neat little houses in walled yards. Snaking one way and then the other, the red-white-and-blue train wound through coffee and cacao *fincas*, banana plantations, and tropical forests on a track cut high into the mountainside above the silvery Rio Revantazón. Now and again the rails curved left into the opening of a tributary valley, swung right to cross high above it on a spindly silver truss, and then curved left again to continue their descent to the Atlantic coast beside the Revantazón far below. It was a steady downgrade run; in the first 30 miles east of the Continental Divide, the railway drops 3000 feet.

Long before the railway came to Costa Rica, English novelist Anthony Trollope saw much the same scenery in 1858 on a similar journey from San Jose down to the Atlantic coast, traveling instead by mule on a muddy road.

"And here we came across the grandest scenery that I met with in the western world," wrote Trollope, "scenery which would admit of raving, if it were given to me to rave on such a subject. . . . every now and then the declivity would become so steep as to give us a full view down into the ravine below, with the prospect of the grand steep, wooded hill on the other side, one huge forest stretching up the mountain for miles. At the bottom of the ravine one's eye would just catch a river looking like a moving thread of silver wire."

Soon after lunch we pulled up at a little settlement called Florencia, nestled among hills rich with coffee plants and sugar cane high up on the north slope of the valley. What should have been only a brief halt in the journey turned into a stop that lasted most of the afternoon. There had been a derailment somewhere down the line, we learned vaguely from the train crew, and the 18-car *apartadero*—siding—at Florencia, it turned out, was the place where FECOSA was going to try to sort out its thoroughly disrupted operations.

The unusual presence of a 12-car passenger train was obviously an event of high excitement. Uniformed schoolchildren appeared from the nearby schoolhouse to join a pair of disconsolate lady travelers waiting for the much-delayed westbound train for San Jose. A large crowd of loungers gathered on the covered veranda of the trackside *Comisariato Florencia*, which began doing the proverbial land-office business in cold drinks and snacks. A few small children organized a pick-up soccer game in the inevitable town soccer field, across the tracks. An occasional tractor chugged by on a dirt road with big trailers of sugar cane harvested from the nearby fields.

Finally, there was some action at Apartadero Florencia. Several blasts from an air horn and the chug of a Caterpillar diesel announced the arrival of another of the ubiquitous U11B's, laboring up the 3.5 percent grade with what turned out to be a work train of flat cars. The work train ran around us through the siding, and

97

both trains resumed a waiting game. A GE U10B with an eastbound freight joined the queue behind the work train.

Another few air-horn blasts from the east, and the long-awaited San Jose train came struggling in. Yet another of the U11B's pulled a train made up of a tank car, a postal-baggage car, and five coaches. A few passengers got off, and the two ladies boarded one of the coaches in evident relief. Our queue of three trains moved ahead beyond the station to saw by the westbound passenger, which soon resumed its journey to San Jose.

But instead of proceeding, our entire entourage backed up to Florencia siding again, and resumed waiting.

This time we didn't have long to wait. Another U11B soon pulled into the siding with a short train of flat cars loaded with steel billets, bound for San Jose from the port at Limón. A track inspection motor car followed close behind, and then came the final movement of our afternoon at Florencia, a second trainload of steel for San Jose. At last our engineer whistled for a start and released brakes, and soon we were rolling downgrade through a landscape of tall grasses, palm trees, and lush jungle into Turrialba.

By this point the line was well down the eastern slope of the mountains, and beyond Turrialba the descent was less precipitous as the railway settled into the tropical valley of the Revantazón. The train ran through a forest of big trees under a broad, jungle canopy. Tangled vines grew up into the trees. The Revantazón was a broad stream now, flowing swiftly through a boulder-strewn, shallow bed. The river's name, which means "breaking of the waves," was clearly appropriate. Occasionally, the railway bored through short tunnels where steep rock outcroppings dropped down to the river. Dusk was falling now, and up ahead the diesel's headlight beam played back and forth from rocky canyon wall to the bright green of jungle growth.

Finally, the rails followed the river out onto the broad coastal plain. At La Junta, the junction with the newly rehabilitated and electrified route into the banana plantations to the northwest, we paused briefly to set out several coaches for a connecting train to Guápiles. Then the train moved out across a long truss bridge over the Reventazón and into Siquirres.

Here, the special tour coaches were set out, and Sarah helped Dorothy and me move our luggage forward to find seats in one of the regular coaches. A large crowd of uniformed schoolchildren boarded the train; I wondered what they had been doing in the several hours between the end of the school day and our delayed arrival. Up ahead, a big 50-cycle Group box cab electric replaced the GE diesel, and at 7 P.M.—hours behind schedule now—we moved off into the tropical night.

The Puerto Limón train was running over an entirely different railroad now. Carefully surfaced track of welded rail, concrete ties, and deep rock ballast replaced the bumpy and irregular line that we'd followed down the mountains from the Divide. There were no lights in the car, and I leaned out an open window into the warm night air to watch stars that sparkled in a clear tropical sky. The big electric's headlight reflected off the dense jungle growth that crowded close to the right of way, and emerald-green block signals flashed to red as we passed. Inside

the car, the roar of Spanish conversation was punctuated with the periodic squall-
ing of a baby.

We stopped every now and then at little halts to discharge a few of the schoolchildren or other passengers. At one jungle siding, we made a long stop to exchange our electric with the GE diesel of a westbound freight, and then our journey resumed with the throb of a Caterpillar diesel in the night air. At each little
town brightly painted houses stood on wooden stilts, close to the track. At Batan
we stopped in the midst of a lively carnival in the center of town. The huge crowd
that had gathered for the event was largely black, most of them probably descendants of the Jamaicans who came originally to build the railroad and then stayed
on to work the banana plantations that followed it. A red-and-blue neon sign and
a blast of loud music announced a trackside dance hall at Matina.

Here, the railway separates into two routes into Puerto Limón. We followed
the one that leads directly to the Caribbean coast at a place called—at one time at
least—Swamp Mouth. Then we followed the coast south through groves of palm
trees into Puerto Limón.

Just to the north of Limón, the new FECOSA was evident in the form of a
new yard serving a refinery and container terminal at Moin. In the yard, narrow-
gauge flat cars stood with seagoing Dole banana containers, waiting to be loaded
aboard the next container ship. We stopped briefly at a station near the edge of
Limón, then moved on into the main terminal and a taxi to our seaside hotel.

Back in San Jose a few days later, I was ready to try the Pacific end of the
ocean-to-ocean railway. Two trains a day go all the way to Puntarenas. I decided
on the 6:30 A.M. departure of train 1, which would give me time to see the sights of
Puntarenas before returning to San Jose on the last eastbound train of the day.

The former Ferrocarril Electrico al Pacifico station on Avenida 20 in San Jose
was much the grander of the capital city's two terminals—a big, two-story building
of masonry construction, dating perhaps to the 1940s, judging from such architectural features as glass block windows and curved corners. The off-white and gray
building was surrounded with a walled station yard. Beyond the station to the
south were a large yard and the main FECOSA shops. At the east end of the
station there was a well-tended garden and a gate that opens out into Calle Central for the connecting line across the city to the Atlantic railway. Railway patrons
could take refreshment across the street from the station at the Ferroviario Bar or
the Bar El Pacifico.

The interior of the station was arranged around a large concourse that extended to the full height of the building. Ticket offices, a Post and Telephone
office, and some railroad offices opened off the concourse, and a double stairway
led to a second-floor balcony and FECOSA executive offices. A design centered
in the tile floor of the concourse depicting steam and electric locomotives, and
models of a 2-6-0 and an electric locomotive flanking the stairway gave a suitable
railroad atmosphere to the place.

I purchased a one-way ticket for 60 colons (about $1.25) and boarded the
Puntarenas train spotted on one of the two stub tracks at the west end of the station. I took a seat in the rear coach, an arch-roofed wooden car with corrugated
metal siding. The interior was finished in wood, with a plain board floor, painted

FECOSA's Pacific line, the former Ferrocarril Electrico al Pacifico, or Pacific Electric Railway, operated with an eclectic mixture of European-built electric locomotives of widely varying ages. An elderly example, but far from the oldest, was box-cab electric No. 133, built by Germany's Henschel-Siemens in 1956. The locomotive crossed Calle Central as it departed from the Pacific railway station in San Jose with a short freight train for the Atlantic line.

in dark red and medium green, with a cream-colored ceiling. The seats were upholstered in a vivid shade of red vinyl.

Costa Rica goes to work early! It was scarcely 6 A.M., but already a group of shop workers had gathered around a nearby flat car, propped up at one end, to examine some fault with an arch-bar truck. Nearby, a crew got ready to begin work at a rail-welding setup.

Across the yard I could see one of the railway's original box cab electrics of 1930 in switching service. Built by AEG of Germany, these novel locomotives sported impressive plumbing along each side. What at first glance looked much like corrugated siding was in reality cooling piping for the locomotive's transformer. Originally, the units had unusual A1A-A1A trucks, but these had since been simplified to a B-B arrangement by removal of the idler axles. And at least one of the 1930 units had been further modified by application of homemade streamlined ends similar to those of FEalP's second generation of electric power, four B-B box cab electrics built by Henschel-Siemens of Germany in 1956.

Around 6:15, this second generation of Pacific railway electric power appeared on the scene with the arrival of box cab No. 133 on an early-morning passenger train from Orotina. And soon afterward, the very latest thing in Costa Rican electrics, one of the 1981 50-cycle Group dual-voltage box cabs, backed in to couple up with our seven-car train.

Promptly at 6:30, a siren signaled departure time, the big electric's engineer responded with an air-horn blast, and train 1 lurched into motion.

The departure from San Jose provided a varied look at life in the capital city. The train rattled along beside a dirt street, past modest little houses, through an industrial area, and beside several huge cemeteries. Beyond the urban skyline to the west, a splendid vista of the mountains of the Cordillera Central was illuminated by the early morning sun. Beyond Calle 42 the rails paralleled the southern boundary of San Jose's La Sabana, a splendid metropolitan park that had taken the place of the city's obsolete airfield a few years before.

From an elevation of about 3700 feet, the Pacific line descended the western escarpment of the Central range on a twisting stretch of mountain railroad whose scenery was second only to that of the Atlantic railway's descent of the eastern slope of these same mountains. Clearly most of the rain falls east of the mountains, and while the Atlantic line ran through lush forests, the Pacific line traversed arid slopes of scattered trees and dry-looking grasses. Groves of Costa Rican coffee grew on all sides.

The train curved first one way and then the other as we dropped toward the Pacific, stopping occasionally at little towns along the way. Twice the train soared high above the ground as we crossed from one side of a canyon to another on long steel trestles. Just beyond Jugodelana, the train descended around a long horseshoe curve, then rumbled slowly across the great steel arch bridge that carried the railway high above the deep gorge of the Rio Póas, which flows down from the Póas Volcano on its way to the Rio Grande de Tárcoles and the Pacific. At Atenas, we were scarcely 24 miles from San Jose but had already descended more than 2000 feet.

Briefly the rails climbed upward on the west side of the Rio Póas valley, and then we began to drop again, following the north wall of the canyon of the Rio

Heading down Costa Rica's western slope toward the Pacific port of Puntarenas, westbound train No. I from San Jose approached Jesus Maria station on the former Pacific Electric Railway on March 18, 1985. Heading the seven-car train of veteran coaches was one of FECOSA's newest electric locomotives, a big 1200 kw box-cab unit built by Europe's 50-Cycle Group in 1981.

Grande de Tárcoles toward the ocean. We ran through a long horseshoe curve at Conception, and then slowed for a brief stop at the mid-point of another, at Dantas, where one of the big European box cab electrics waited to resume its climb to San Jose with the mixed freight and passenger consist of train 2, our eastbound opposite number from Puntarenas.

Gradually the countryside became more tropical, with palm trees and citrus groves at trackside. At Orotina the train ran down the center of the street and then made a long station stop, while trackside vendors sold hot food, fruit, and drinks to passengers through the open windows of the coaches.

Beyond Orotina, the countryside took on a more western flavor. Big, umbrella-like Guanacaste trees stood in ranchlands of dry grass, grazed by herds of white, humped Brahman cattle. There was an occasional cattle loading pen beside the track. At Mata de Limón, elevation 7 meters (23 feet), the railway finally met the sea. Brightly painted little inns and restaurants were grouped around the station, and open pavilions overlooked the sea from a small park shaded by palm trees.

North from Mata de Limón the railway curved inland again briefly, descended to a crossing of the Rio Barranca, and then turned west to follow a long peninsula out into the Gulf of Nicoya and Puntarenas. Yellow wisteria grew everywhere. Beach villas lined the shore on both sides of the peninsula. At Chacarita the train rattled down a street with brightly painted wooden houses on each side. Then we swung over close to the shore and followed the long volcanic sand beach, where buzzards picked over the carcass of a big sea turtle. We took to the streets for a few blocks, and then the train slipped into a modest terminal yard and halted in front of the Puntarenas station on time at 10:30 A.M.

I photographed the arrival activity, inspected the modernistic beachfront station, and then headed up the seaside Paseo de los Turistas for a visit to downtown Puntarenas and lunch and a few cool bottles of *Cerveza Imperial* at an open-air restaurant along the beach while I waited for the afternoon train back to San Jose.

The Journey Today

Alas, one can no longer travel ocean-to-ocean on Costa Rica's narrow gauge railway. Faced with mounting losses, Costa Rica shut down the entire national system in 1995. At last report, however, efforts were underway to reopen both Atlantic and Pacific lines under private operation.

Handsomely decorated with British and French flags, a *Golden Arrow* shield on the smokebox door, and big golden arrows on each flank, well-kept Battle of Britain class 4-6-2 Pacific No. 34071, *601 Squadron,* accelerated out of London's Victoria Station with the Paris-bound *Golden Arrow* on a June morning in 1952. A second Pacific pushing from the rear helped to get the long train of gleaming chocolate and cream Pullmans underway.

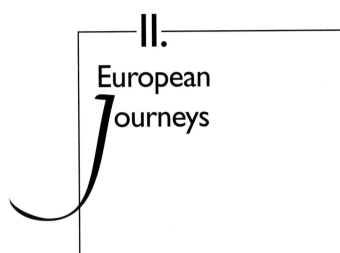

II.
European Journeys

Constructed in an architectural idiom more charateristic of a modern air terminal than a railway station, Oslo's Sentralstasjon is the starting point for railway journeys from the Norwegian capital.

By Rail across the Roof of Norway

It was a curious way to begin a railway journey.

Our taxi deposited us at a dock on the west side of Bergen's inner harbor, where the rakish looking double-hulled express boat *Fjordprins* waited to load passengers for the journey through the Sognefjord. Dorothy and I boarded, stowed our luggage, and found seats that promised a splendid view of the passing scenery.

Our destination on an August 1996 journey across Scandinavia was Oslo, and it would take us two days to get there. We could have made the trip by train in about six and a half hours on any one of several fast trains that operate every day over the Oslo-Bergen line. But Ingerlise, our Norwegian-born travel agent, had suggested the longer way around. The boat trip, she had pointed out, would take us up the wonderfully scenic Sogne and Aurland fjords to Flam. There, our railway journey would begin with a trip over Norway's celebrated Flamsbana. From sea level at Flam, the electric trains of this extraordinary mountain railway climb almost 3000 feet up through the gorge of the Flam valley to Myrdal. Here, the railway connects with the Bergen line for the spectacular railway journey across the roof of Norway to Oslo. It was, Ingerlise assured us, a trip well worth the extra time.

She was right.

Promptly at 8 A.M. the express boat's big diesel engines roared to life, and we slipped out past the elegant old timber buildings of the medieval Bryggen quarter, the Rosenkrantz Tower and King Hakon's Hall, which fronted the harbor on the opposite shore. For the next several hours we sat back and enjoyed the scenery as the *Fjordprins* sped through countless coastal islands and then turned to follow the magnificent Sognefjord to the east. We could have completed the journey to Oslo in one long day, but had opted instead for an overnight stop in the elegant old Kviknes Hotel, overlooking the fjord from the wharf at Balestrand. Shortly before noon the *Fjordprins* set us down on the Balestrand wharf and then roared off to continue the journey up the fjord. We went off on foot to explore the little town and the nearby Esefjord and then watched twilight settle over the fjord as we enjoyed dinner in the hotel dining room.

We resumed our journey the next day with an hour-and-a-half express boat run through the fjords to Flam. A curious note in my *Thomas Cook European Timetable* advised that passengers en route from Leikanger to Flam would "change boats in mid-fjord." Sure enough, they did. In a wide reach of the

107

Sognefjord the express boat swooped around to pull up alongside the smaller ferry *Fanaraken* as she steamed down the fjord. Crewmen deftly handed luggage across, a gangplank was rigged, and a half dozen passengers nervously crossed between the two vessels. Then the express boat pulled away and headed for the Aurland-fjord.

Looming mountains on either side seemed to close in on us as the boat skimmed across the still waters of the ever-narrowing fjord. We stopped briefly at Aurland, and then continued on to Flam, at the very end of the fjord.

Several electric trains were lined up at the platforms of the Flamsbana station, just beyond the wharf. Train 1862, the next departure for Myrdal, was already boarding passengers at Platform 1. We found seats and waited for the 1:45 P.M. departure time.

The Flam railway is barely 20 km. — just over 12 1/2 miles — long, but it took 20 years to build it. It was easy to see why.

The Flam valley is a deep gorge carved out of the rock of ancient mountains by glaciers and rivers. The railway climbs some 2832 feet to Myrdal, running on shelves cut from the mountainsides or in tunnels drilled through solid rock. In its climb up through the valley the railway passes through 20 tunnels, totaling almost 4 miles in length. Each of them was drilled through hard rock at a rate of about 3 feet a month. In one 3-mile section near the upper end of the line, between Vatnahalsen and Blomheller, there are almost 2 1/2 miles of tunnel.

The line crosses from one side of the valley to the other and then back again. Close to 80 percent of the line is laid at a maximum grade of 5.6 percent, with curves as sharp as 13 degrees, 30 minutes, a radius of about 426 feet. Approaching the top, the rails turn around on themselves through an extraordinary series of spirals and reverse curves, passing through a half dozen tunnels in the process. Before the railway was completed, the only way up or down the valley was a torturous mountain road of 21 hairpin turns, negotiable only by Norwegian mountain ponies pulling two-wheeled carts.

Like much of Scandinavia's railway system, the Flamsbana is electrified. Power for the 15-kilovolt catenary, I learned, came from a hydroelectric power station at Kjosfossen, just a few miles below the summit at Myrdal.

The electric train that we boarded at Flam was something of a surprise. Instead of the deep maroon colors of the Norwegian State Railways (NSB) I had expected to see, the equipment wore the blue-gray livery and white stripe of the Swedish State Railways. During the busy summer travel months when the Flam line's schedules expand from four to a dozen daily round trips, a trainman explained, NSB leases the Swedish cars to operate the line. Suggestive of Scandinavian rivalries, however, the Swedish Railways SJ logo on each car had been carefully covered over with NSB's winged wheel emblem.

The six-car train was made up of the class X10 cars that the Swedish system employs in Stockholm suburban service. Built by Sweden's ASEA, a big electrical manufacturer that's the Scandinavian equivalent of GE, these modern cars are equipped with innovative trucks that permit radial steering of the axles in curves. This helps to reduce wheel and rail wear in curved track, just the thing for the tight curves of the Flamsbana. Four 380 horsepower traction motors for each two-car X10 unit promised ample power for climbing the railway's 5.6 percent grades,

A railway journey across the roof of Norway on the Bergensbanen begins under this graceful train shed at the Bergen station. Passengers boarded train 602, an Oslo express, on an August morning in 1996.

while no less than five separate braking systems offered a reassuring redundancy for downgrade journeys.

With a comfortable load of summer travelers on board, our train accelerated away from the platforms right on schedule to begin the climb toward Myrdal. We climbed between sheer rocky mountains on either side and through a lovely valley of green fields and neat farm buildings. A swift flowing river meandered through the valley on its way to the fjord. We stopped occasionally at one of the little villages that dot the valley while sightseers and hikers boarded or left the

109

train. At Berkevam, about halfway up the line, there was a longer halt while we waited in the passing track for a train on its way down the mountain.

Above Blomheller the tunnels came in rapid succession. In the gaps between tunnels and sometimes through "windows" cut into the rock walls of the tunnels, we looked out across the Flam valley toward the great Storaberget and Trollanuten peaks to the west. At some points, as many as three different levels of the Flamsbana could be seen. At Kjosfossen the train made an extended stop, while

The brief stop at Balestrand complete, the express boat *Fjordprins* accelerates away from the wharf to continue her journey up the Sognefjord to a link with Norway's spectacular mountain railway at Flam.

everyone climbed off to enjoy the view of the waterfall just below the power station that supplies the railway. We were soon underway again, twisting and turning through the bewildering series of tunnels and curves the railway's engineers had carved out of the mountains to reach the summit at Myrdal. In scarcely 2½ miles the train snaked through a long double spiral tunnel and three lesser tunnels, reversing direction three times as it climbed steadily up the 5.6 percent grade into the station at Myrdal.

We had more than two hours to wait for the Oslo train. Inside the big red station building we had lunch, and each of us acquired a handsome Flamsbana certificate, numbered and stamped by the station agent.

Myrdal occupied a barren, windswept mountain valley, well above the tree line. It was late August, but snow was still heavy on the peaks around us. The station was tucked between two long tunnels on the Oslo-Bergen line—the Bergensbanen. Just east of the station the line emerged from the mile-long Reinunga Tunnel and then plunged into the even longer Gravehals Tunnel just beyond the west end of the station platform. Drilled through 3.3 miles of the hard granite of the Urhovde Mountains, Gravehals had once ranked as Norway's longest railway tunnel.

Built right across the bare mountains that stretch north to south the length of Norway, the 304-mile Bergensbanen ranks as one of the wonders of world railway engineering. Covering a distance of 304 miles, the line climbs from near sea level at Oslo high above the tree line to an elevation of more than 4000 feet at the high point and then descends to sea level again at Bergen. Within its length it encompasses some 200 tunnels, the longest of them almost 6½ miles long, runs through 17 miles of snowshed, and crosses 300 bridges.

Building the Bergen line took decades. An initial segment completed in 1874 extended 67 miles inland from Bergen to Voss, at the western edge of the mountains; but it was another 35 years before the line was finally driven across the top of the mountains to complete the route between the two cities. Construction eastward from Voss began in 1894 but it was 1907 before the work was complete.

Because of the severe climate of the mountains, construction could proceed in the open for only about three months each year. At the height of work at the

Mountain-climbing trains met at Berkevam, near the midpoint of the Flam line, in August 1996.
Above loomed the rocky heights of Trollanuten peak.

At Kjosfossen, about 3 miles from the summit of the Flamsbana at Myrdal, the trains pause for a view of the waterfall just below the hydroelectric power station that supplies the railway.

turn of the century, as many as two thousand men were on the job, sometimes on 15 hour shifts to take advantage of the long daylight hours of the Norwegian summer. The hard work of tunneling through the granite, gneiss and crystalline schist of the mountains continued throughout the year, but the tunnel workers had to live in isolation for seven to eight months at a time. During the winter of 1902–03 the workers were cut off from supplies for two and a half months. Once a month the paymaster set out on skis, accompanied by a mountain guide, to pay the workers at the remote construction camps. Early in 1905 the two men were overtaken by a blizzard, and their bodies were not recovered from the crevasse into which they had fallen until the following July.

Work was sufficiently advanced by the summer of 1907 that track laying could commence, and track workers advancing from both ends of the line met at Finse, high in the mountains, on October 7, 1907. Some trains began running that December, but it was not until snowsheds and snow fences could be completed that uninterrupted operation could begin in the summer of 1909.

Old photographs of the line show big, double-headed 4-8-0 locomotives hauling trains over the 2.2 percent grades of the Bergensbanen, but the entire line has been electrified since 1964. Today, NSB's big Swedish-built class EL 16 electric locomotives haul the principal trains over the line. They're rated at 5900 horsepower, and they do it with deceptive ease.

The Myrdal station bustled with summer season activity as we waited for our eastbound train. Every hour another train arrived from Flam, discharged its passengers, and then boarded still others for the return trip. Not long after 4 P.M. one of the Swedish-built EL 16 electrics emerged from the Reinunga Tunnel with a westbound Bergen train, paused for several minutes to load and discharge passengers, and then accelerated quietly toward the portal of the Gravehals Tunnel to the west. Hiking and cycling are popular in the Flam valley, and backpacks and bicycles were common among the throngs of arriving travelers.

Late on an August afternoon in 1996, a Flamsbana train emerged from a snowshed at the Myrdal summit, where the line connects with the Oslo-Bergen main line. At the right is a snowshed that leads to the entrance of the Bergen line's Reinunga Tunnel.

Minutes before 5 P.M., right on schedule, another of the maroon EL 16s emerged from the tunnel with the 11 cars of Bergen-Oslo express 604. We loaded our luggage and found seats in the comfortable first-class coach. Big plate glass windows promised good views of the scenery to come.

The train's eastbound climb into the mountains had begun at Voss, some 30 miles to the west of Myrdal. We continued to climb for another 20 miles to the

Bergensbanen summit at Finse, running through a boulder-strewn, treeless land on what NSB calls the longest high mountain railway line in Europe. Low bushes and a mossy ground cover were interspersed with a purplish mountain flower. Tunnels were frequent, and the many snowsheds and snow fences suggested what the winter operating conditions were like on this high mountain line. This far north the snow line is at only about 3000 feet, and the snowfalls along the line are extraordinary. The big rotary snowplows used to keep the line open, I was told, often must contend with drifts that are 25 or 26 feet deep along this barren plateau.

The winter snows are particularly severe around Finse, the highest railway station in Norway, where the line reaches its peak elevation of 4009 feet. The summit crossing became a little easier in 1993, when NSB completed a new summit cut-off that put 6.4 miles of line below ground and lowered the summit elevation by over 200 feet. There's a long passing siding at the mid-point of the tunnel, which now ranks as the longest on the Bergensbanen.

Once clear of the tunnel, the express began the long descent toward Oslo, still running through the rocky, treeless slopes of the vast mountain plateau called the Hardangervidda. Above us to the north towered the mountain range of Hallingskarvet. Across the valley to the south loomed the icy mass of the Hardangerjokulen glacier.

We reached the eastern edge of the plateau at Ustaoset, still at an elevation of over 3200 feet, and then began a rapid descent to the east, dropping some 643 feet in the next 6 miles to Geilo, one of the largest winter sports centers in Northern Europe. Soon we began to see a few trees along the line as we followed a mountain stream down toward the Hallingdalen—the Halling Valley.

In a siding at Hol, just east of Geilo, we met another of the EL 16 electrics climbing toward the Finse summit with our westbound counterpart, Oslo-Bergen express 603. By the time we reached Gol, the beginning of the Bergensbanen's westbound climb across the mountains, we had descended some 3608 feet over a distance of less than 62 miles.

East of Gol the rails followed the curves of the Hallingdalselva—the Halling Valley River—through a lovely green valley of mountain pastures and forested slopes. Overcast skies had begun to clear, the rays of a low sun in the west mingled with occasional rain showers, and for a time the train ran through the arches of colorful rainbows.

Night fell as we ran down the Hallingdalen toward Oslo. It was dark by the time we paused briefly for a station stop at Honefoss. Most trains from the Bergen line turn south here, to reach the capital via Drammen. Our train took an alternate route to the north via Roa and then southward into Oslo's Sentralstasjon, or Central Station.

Express 604 slowed to a halt at a station platform promptly at 9:55 P.M. We gathered up our luggage and headed off into Oslo's great Sentralstasjon. Linked by a tunnel to the city's former west station, the Central Station is now Oslo's principal terminal, with a splendid new terminal building that looks more like a modern airport terminal than a train station. In a nice link with the past, the elegant former East Station adjacent to the new terminal has been handsomely restored as a connecting food service and shopping annex. Clearly, Sentralstasjon

Pulled by a modern, Swedish-built EL 16 electric locomotive, an eastbound 11-car Bergen-Oslo express 604 arrived at the Myrdal station.

was worth a closer look the next day, but now it was time to set out in search of a taxi to our hotel.

The Journey Today

NSB schedules five daily round trips that operate over the full length of the Bergensbanen, including an overnight train with sleeping car accommodations. Early- or mid-morning departures from Oslo or Bergen make the entire trip in daylight. The Flamsbana operates a dozen daily round trips during the summer travel season from June through late September, with just four daily round trips

A link to the past adjacent to the modernistic Oslo Sentralstasjon is the elegant East Station, now restored as a connecting food service and shopping annex.

during the balance of the year. NSB offers several summer excursion packages that include the Bergen and Flåm lines. A coastal steamer and train itinerary includes the Bergen line, while a "Norway in a Nutshell" tour includes both the Bergen and Flåm lines. Best of all is a Sognefjord Express boat trip that combines train travel over the Bergen and Flåm lines with the Sognefjord express boat trip between Flåm and Bergen.

Golden *Arrow**

London is a city of tradition, the focal
point and nerve center of an empire, a
city rich in the monuments, landmarks
and ceremonies of centuries of history—in
short, a great city. Even the antiquated cab
which carried me to Victoria Station on the
morning of June 7, 1952, seemed a part of the
tradition of London.

The trip from the massive Cumberland
Hotel at Marble Arch to Victoria was but a few
minutes through the swirling traffic along
Hyde Park and past Buckingham Palace Gardens. Then I was delivered before the sprawling, soot-stained, typically British majesty of
Victoria. Along with Waterloo, Victoria was
one of the principal terminals of the British
Railways Southern Region (ex–Southern Railway) and, as the big green sign on the front
canopy advised, the terminal for the most im-
portant Continental routes—those via Dover, Folkestone and Newhaven.

Travel on the *Golden Arrow* was something special. This elaborate illuminated
gateway greeted Paris-bound passengers arriving at Victoria Station's
platform 8 for the train's morning departure.

My destination was Paris, and my train was to be the world-famed *Golden
Arrow*—all-Pullman, extra fare and, along with its overnight companion, the
Night Ferry, one of the standard-bearers of British Railways Continental services,
operating via Dover-Calais, the shortest sea route.

Inaugurated on May 15, 1929, the *Arrow* was a comparative youngster by
Britain's standards, where such name trains as the *Royal Scot* had been in continuous service for over a hundred years; but nonetheless it had a well established
place among the elite of European trains. The *Golden Arrow* had operated daily
for hardly a decade before that grim September of 1939 which destined her not to
run again until April of 1946.

There was more than a half hour to spare before the train's 11 A.M. departure,
but I hurried through the neon-lighted GOLDEN ARROW gateway at the train's
regular Track 8 berth to watch the 10:30 departure of a heavily loaded *Continental Express* behind a struggling Battle of Britain–class Pacific. Then I watched the
spotting of the immaculate *Arrow* equipment from the coach yard.

The *Golden Arrow* consist included nine Pullman parlor cars, in addition to a
freight container car and a luggage van. The 10 Pullmans—8 first-class and 2

---

*© 1954 Kalmbach Publishing Co., reprinted with permission from the March 1954 issue of *Trains*
magazine.

second-class—which made up the train's regular consist represented the latest in British car building. They were completed in 1951 by the Birmingham Railway Carriage & Wagon Company. Although the equipment was ordered in 1938, all work on the new train was stopped by the war and not resumed until 1949. The new train went into service June 11, 1951, in time for the 1951 Festival of Britain traffic. These 10 Pullmans with their traditional lines differed hardly one whit in appearance from their predecessors of 30 or more years ago; only wood siding had given way to welded steel. The distinctive oval-windowed doors, chocolate-and-cream livery, scalloped trim and coat of arms typical of British Pullmans remained to provide an air of ornate dignity which left our own American railroading scene with the departure of massive somber-hued Pullmans and brass-railed observation cars from name-train consists.

Heading the *Golden Arrow* for my June 7, 1952, journey to Paris was a polished member of British Railways' first standard class of steam motive power, 7MT Britannia class Pacific No. 70004, *William Shakespeare*. Small boys and Britain's ubiquitous engine spotters had gathered at the head of the Victoria Station platform to admire her.

On the head end was a polished example of the latest in British Railways locomotives: one of the new 7MT Britannia class, a standard heavy 4-6-2 Pacific which first went into service in 1951. The 25 engines of this class then in service were among the first of six standard steam classes to take the rails in British Railways' goal of eventual motive-power standardization.

Our engine was No. 70004, the *William Shakespeare*, already a celebrity among her class. Fresh from the builders at Crewe, the *Shakespeare* spent her first few months on exhibit to thousands of visitors at the 1951 Festival of Britain South Bank Exhibition at London. Since going into regular service in October of 1951 the *Shakespeare* had been working the *Golden Arrow* intermittently together with Pacifics of the ex–Southern Railway Merchant Navy and Battle of Britain classes.

The *Shakespeare* was surrounded by a small knot of the youthful trainspotters that seem a fixture on almost every British station platform, and I joined the eager enthusiasts briefly to admire her classic lines—high drivers, big boiler, cap stack, smoke deflectors, dark-green jacket and silver nameplates, topped off with a GOLDEN ARROW smokebox shield and miniature Union Jack and Tricolor in honor of her blue-ribbon run. This trim Pacific needed no streamlined shroud to proclaim her a thoroughbred!

I boarded Pullman *Carina* in time to hear a soft-voiced hostess announce our imminent departure in both English and French over the train's public-address system. Precisely at 11 we were off with a mellow blast from *Shakespeare*'s chime whistle, which was answered by a shrill wail from *Manston*, a Battle of Britain–class Pacific which gave us a kick out of the station on our 77-mile, 95-minute nonstop sprint to Dover.

The two Pacifics brought us up to speed rapidly as we swung out of the gloom of Victoria, briefly paralleling one of the innumerable dark-green caterpillar-like electric multiple unit trains that race relentlessly over South London's labyrinth of rail lines. Wheels pounded with a hollow thunder as we burst out across the murky Thames and as quickly dove past the great Battersea Park power plant into the industrial jumble which lines the river.

Queens Park was a haze of soft-coal smoke as we passed the huge engine terminal where Victoria's engines were serviced, and crossed over the great steel artery which leads out of Waterloo. South London was seemingly endless banks of row houses with St. Paul's looming to the north, the clatter of frogs and switch points as rail lines joined, crossed and diverged, and occasionally the glimpse of a green playing field. Near Herne Hill, a cricket match reminded us of the Leeds Test Match between England and India which was then being hotly followed in British sport pages.

The Pacific slowed to Sydenham Hill and then gained speed again as we topped the grade in the long Penge Tunnel. Drab row houses were finally replaced by green hills and suburban cottages. At Shortlands we passed the incongruous sight of a trim smoke-deflectored Schools-class 4-4-0, *Kings Wimbledon,* leading a light suburban train. Strange, I reflected, this country where Pacifics are heavy power and modern American Standards operate in mainline service.

I relaxed with a cup of morning coffee served by the car steward in accordance with pleasant British custom, and enjoyed the ever-changing Kent countryside of green hills, pastures, hop fields and rural villages. *Shakespeare* was released at last, and the big Pacific showed us mile after mile of thrilling speed in the famed British tradition. Near Smeeth a track gang stepped back briefly as we passed. I noted that old bull-head rail and chairs were being replaced by T rail, now standard on British Railways.

At Folkestone, brake shoes ground as we slowed for a high viaduct, curved through a short tunnel under the towering white cliffs and swung north along the English Channel toward Dover. The channel was calm and sunny and the gulls floated lazily on the warm air, but as a passenger remarked, "it can be nasty." Ten minutes more brought us to shipside at the Dover Marine terminal where I passed through a cursory customs examination and paused for the inevitable stamping of passports before boarding the waiting steamer.

British Railways appropriately reserved one of their latest turbine steamers, the S.S. *Invicta,* for the *Golden Arrow* service. The ship was built by Wm. Denny & Brothers Limited at Dumbarton, Scotland, in 1939 and went directly into war service as a troop carrier in the Royal Navy Auxiliary. A special plaque in the first-class lounge commemorates her war service, which included the Normandy landings. Not until October 1946 did the *Invicta* go into the cross-channel passenger service for which she was built. After being released from troop service, the ship went on the *Golden Arrow* run six months after it had been reestablished.

As I sunned myself in a deck chair during the one-hour crossing I recalled from publicity handouts that the *Invicta* was equipped with both radar and roll stabilizers—so much excess baggage on a sunny June day but mighty handy during the Channel's more violent periods.

Approaching Calais the *Invicta* made a singularly graceless entrance, turning just outside the breakwater and backing into the harbor. I learned that this was a

With the *Golden Arrow* passengers safely aboard, the S.S. *Invicta* moved away from the Dover terminal to begin the hour-long English Channel crossing to Calais.

standard maneuver, and that the ship was equipped with a special bow rudder to facilitate these backward entries.

Almost before *Invicta* was safely docked, British reserve and quiet efficiency were replaced by the exuberant, boisterous and thoroughly delightful air of France. Hardly had the gangway touched the quay before we were boarded by a blue-capped horde of porters who quickly fanned out over the ship shouting their war cry of *"Porteur! Porteur!"* in a manner reminiscent of a pirate crew searching for a hidden gold cargo.

The Société Nationale des Chemins de Fer Français (SNCF), or French National Railways, version of the *Golden Arrow* (*Flèche d'Or* in French) waited alongside at the Calais Marine terminal. The consist for the 186-mile nonstop run to Paris included six Wagons-Lits parlor cars in their familiar royal-blue and cream scheme with gold striping and the company crest proudly displayed on the side. Fewer parlor cars were required for the run to Paris, since many of our fellow passengers left us at Calais for the Riviera-bound *Blue Train* which waited on an adjoining track. In addition to parlor cars the train included three SNCF coaches in their standard olive green behind the engine. Like most of SNCF's premiere extra-fare trains, the *Flèche d'Or* has carried coaches as well as the luxurious Wagons-Lits equipment since the war.

On the head end was another Pacific, 231E-class engine No. 32. This SNCF Pacific was to British Railways' Britannia Pacifics as Chesapeake & Ohio and Delaware & Hudson Pacifics are to one another. Whereas *William Shakespeare* discreetly concealed its inner workings, No. 32 immodestly displayed its air compressors and other plumbing along the boiler and running boards. Air reservoirs were prominently perched atop its brass-bound boiler, just behind the elongated flanged stack. Smoke deflectors, an oval-windowed cab and a shrill peep whistle gave No. 32 that Continental flair, and a special FLECHE D'OR shield on the cone-shaped smokebox door identified her distinguished run.

With scarcely 10 minutes between docking time and the train's 2:38 P.M. departure, I hurriedly tipped the blue-capped porter who had captured my luggage and scrambled aboard the ostentatious Wagons-Lits. Not as new as her British cousins which I had just left, the Wagons-Lits lacked the chromium-and-glass modernism of her American counterparts; but with her thickly carpeted floors, flowered arm chairs, oversize lamps and massive domed ceiling lights she was nonetheless a symbol of Continental luxury travel in the grand old manner.

As we commenced our nonstop run to Paris, the Calais waterfront area presented a sobering scene of wartime destruction. Out of Calais the Pacific charged into a long, heavy grade, winding above the city. Wheels pounded ever slower, and cinders rattled off the windows as the train slowed to a walk; then, as the grade leveled, 77-inch drivers started to roll! Our schedule called for a 57-mile-an-hour average on a 186-mile run, and this Northern Region of the SNCF was no prairie-state speedway!

Rich farms dominated by solid-looking red-tile-roofed houses slid by. The engineer blasted for crossings with a shrill screeching whistle calculated to raise the dead, and the car waiter served lunch in the incomparable French manner—*consommé*, sole, filet of beef, cheeses and fruit. It was all cooked to a turn and topped off with a bottle of Bordeaux rouge.

Carrying a *Flèche d'Or* shield on her smokebox door, French National Railways 231E class Pacific No. 46 steamed into the Gare du Nord at Paris on a June afternoon in 1952, completing the *Golden Arrow*'s swift journey between the British and French capitals.

Boulogne was passed with only a brief speed restriction, and then the line left the dunes of the channel coast and swung southeast for Paris. Abbeville's huge engine terminal was crowded with steam power of every description, including many of the Baldwin-, Lima-, Alco-, and Montreal-built 2-8-2 Mikados which SNCF bought to help replace their tremendous war losses in motive power. It was amazing to see the lift a trim pair of smoke deflectors gave to the appearance of these transplanted Mikes.

It was amazing, too, to reflect on the tremendous program of reconstruction the French railways had accomplished since the war. Left at war's end with only a fraction of its prewar roster of equipment, many of its terminals and bridges destroyed, and hardly a mainline uncut, SNCF had not only restored service to prewar levels but had launched an ambitious program of electrification and improvement of its major lines. Reassuring indeed was the vitality of these French people.

Near St. Denis, in a flash of red and gray and the murmur of four V-8 engines, a northbound Bugatti autorail streaked by, bound for Liege, Belgium, at a good 80 mph. Permitted higher speeds than any other SNCF trains, these autorails provide extra-fare limited service between most of the principal French cities.

From St. Denis into Gare du Nord was a six-track scramble of mainline trains and Pacific- and tank-engine-powered commuter trains. I noted the unorthodox operation of the Parisian version of the 5 o'clock commuter, which operates outbound in the normal manner but then runs backward on the inbound run. Most Parisian commuter trains were electric powered, however, and the lines out of Gare du Nord were scheduled to be converted under SNCF's electrification program.

Precisely at 5:52 P.M., as scheduled, the *Flèche d'Or* slid under the great shed at Gare du Nord after a 6-hour 52-minute run covering 263 rail miles and 25 sea miles. Not bad time at all for this crack international train.

After a last brief look at our stylish Pacific I joined my fellow passengers in the rush for one of Paris's incredibly dilapidated cabs. Some of them perhaps were making connections with the *Simplon-Orient Express* or the *Nord Express*, but for me it was a trip to my hotel for a quick change and then a Saturday evening in Paris!

The Journey Today

Declining demand for luxury train service in the airliner era brought an end to the celebrated *Golden Arrow* rail-ship service in September 1972, while London-Paris coach and sleeping car services continued on other trains. Rail service between the two cities was revived with the opening of the Channel Tunnel in 1994. Today, luxurious, high-speed *Eurostar* trains make the journey in three hours or less. Its still possible to make the more traditional rail-ship journey, but the trains no longer operate to waterfront terminals, and passengers must make their own way between ferry terminals and downtown stations at Dover and Calais.

By Autorail to Basel

Easter Sunday in Paris that year had been chill and rainy. But in the early hours of Monday morning the sky was clear and the first rays of the sun glistened on the still-wet trees and cobblestoned streets. It was still too early for the morning rush of Parisians to work and the streets were nearly deserted as my cab driver hurled his ancient vehicle down Boulevard Haussman and Rue La Fayette toward Gare de l'Est—the East Station.

It was April 1953 and my destination was Switzerland. The trip was to be a new experience in rail travel aboard one of the French National Railways' (Société National des Chemins de Fer, or SNCF) deluxe, high-speed autorail services, operated with gasoline- or diesel-powered self-propelled rail cars.

First introduced in the early 1930s, SNCF's autorails provided an extra fare, limited service at extremely high speeds over the system's principal routes. With few exceptions, they were permitted higher speeds than any other SNCF trains. One of them, a gasoline-powered Bugatti autorail, achieved a top speed of 120 mph in test operation during the late 1930s. One of the fastest autorail services operates nonstop over the 318-mile route between Paris and Lyon at an average speed of 62 mph, and held the European record for nonstop rail travel. In 1953, SNCF operated some 500 main line autorail services between principal cities in France as well as a number of international services to major cities in Belgium, Holland, Germany, and Switzerland.

Gare de l'Est was an impressive stone structure that ranked as one of the grandest stations of Paris. The original station on the site, designed by architect François Duquesney and completed during 1847–52, was long revered as one of the finest early examples of monumental, expressive station design, with a splendid arched train shed of iron and glass, pierced at the head house end with a great semicircular window overlooking a grand Cour d'Honneur—"Court of Honor"—fronting on Rue de Strasbourg.

Rebuilt in 1931, Gare de l'Est was now the most modern of the stations of Paris, as well as the largest, with 30 tracks. The great glazed train shed was gone, replaced by mundane butterfly sheds over the platforms, but portions of the original station building remained to remind one of its nineteenth-century elegance. Today's Gare de l'Est had its own Metro (subway) station, and its amenities included waiting rooms, a station hotel, shops, restaurants and a buffet. Separate ticket offices were provided for long distance trains (*grand lignes*) and suburban trains (*banlieue*).

Equaling the elegance of the station was the romance of the great international expresses that originated and terminated here. When the *Orient Express*, the first of the Wagons-Lits company's great fleet of international expresses, set out on its maiden journey to Constantinople in 1883, it departed from Gare de l'Est. The *Arlberg-Orient Express* still departed from Gare de l'Est with through cars for

Typical of French National Railways fast autorail services was this northbound Paris to Liege (Belgium) train, seen passing through the northern Paris suburb of St. Denis at speed in June 1952. The autorail was a Bugatti Series B1-B3, an 83-seat two-car unit powered by an eight-cylinder gasoline engine through a hydraulic coupling, and capable of a top speed of almost 90 miles per hour.

such diverse destinations as Budapest, Athens, and Istanbul, where travelers could continue across Asia Minor to Aleppo, Beirut and Baghdad via the connecting *Taurus Express*. Still other international services from Gare de l'Est conveyed travelers to principal cities in Switzerland, Germany, Austria, Czechoslovakia, Hungary, and Eastern Europe.

As I left my cab in the Rue de Strasbourg, a red-fezzed Arab offered Algerian souvenirs. I declined his offerings and passed through the high-ceilinged ticket room to the concourse. My ticket was already bought and reservations made, leaving ample time for a leisurely coffee-and-roll "continental" breakfast at the concourse buffet.

My train for the trip to Switzerland, *Train Automoteur Rapide No. 41*, was typical of SNCF's international autorail services. Offering an early morning departure from Paris, it was scheduled over the 326 miles to Basel in less than five and a half hours, an average speed of better than 60 mph, and this with five intermediate stops and over terrain that is anything but a flatland speedway!

A second Paris-Basel autorail, leaving Paris in the early evening, operated on an identical schedule. By way of comparison, the fastest conventional train over the same route, the crack *Arlberg-Orient Express*, required fully an hour and 45 minutes more to cover the Paris-Basel segment of its long journey.

As on most autorail services, accommodations on the train were limited to first- and second-class seats and an extra fare, amounting to about 13 percent on my second-class ticket, was charged.

The route followed by autorail train 41, double-tracked over the entire distance to Basel, was one of the principal lines of SNCF's East Region, which until the 1938 nationalization of France's railway system was known as the Chemin de Fer de l'Est. Although it was the second smallest of SNCF's six regions, the East was one of the most important, serving the industrial centers of Alsace-Lorraine and linking Paris with Luxembourg, Switzerland, and the Saar Basin of southern Germany.

The East Region was made up of a series of radial lines originating at Paris, and successive transversal lines intersecting these radial lines. The Paris-Basel route met these transverse lines at Chaumont, Belfort, and Mulhouse, which provided direct routes from the east to northern France, the Low Countries, and the Channel ports for England. The Paris-Basel line was the route for a number of important international services to northern Switzerland, Austria via the Arlberg Tunnel, Italy via the Lötschberg or St. Gothard tunnels, and trains to the east from England via Calais, which joined the line at Chaumont.

As departure time approached I proceeded through the gate, pausing while my ticket and reservation were checked, and then headed down the platform to find my seat on the third car of the waiting autorail.

The train waiting on Track 9 was a futuristic looking diesel-electric streamliner called a *rame automotrice triple*. The train was one of a series built in 1936 for the Northern Railway by the Société Franco-Belge de Matériel de Chemins de Fer. It was a three-car train set just over 218 feet long, with a smoothly contoured welded steel car body with skirts that enclosed the running gear, giving the train an appearance vaguely like a giant green and silver cigar. Identical motor cars at each end each provided second-class seats for 47, while a first-class and restaurant car, *la Beauvasis*, at the center of the train seated 42. Big windows with gracefully arched tops were reminiscent of the design of the first generation of *Hiawatha* cars on the Milwaukee Road back home in Wisconsin, also built in 1936, and I wondered who had the idea first.

The two motor cars were each powered by a 404 hp, 12-cylinder Maybach diesel driving the train through a Jeumont generator and a pair of Jeumont traction motors driving each axle of the end truck. Advanced features of the train included roller bearings and an oil-pneumatic braking system with electro-magnetic reserve braking. Rated top speed of the 150-ton train was 150 km./hr. (93.2 mph).

As the hand of the platform clock swung to our 7:45 A.M. departure time the throb of the Maybach diesels was barely audible as we glided smoothly from under the butterfly shed into the scramble of early morning activity in the approaches to Gare de l'Est.

A tank-engined suburban train kept pace with us on a parallel track for a long while, then slowly dropped back out of sight. Then an inbound "Grand Express" hissed by in a blur of blue and gold Wagons-Lits sleepers, half hidden in a cloud of steam from her smoke-deflectored Pacific express engine.

It was April in Paris in 1953, and passengers had begun to gather for the early morning departure of *Train Automoteur Rapide No. 41* for Switzerland from Gare de l'Est. Waiting for them at the Track 9 platform was this sleek, three-car streamliner, whose diesel-electric power plant was good for a top speed of well over 90 mph.

To the left the huge La Villette engine terminal was a pall of steam and coal smoke as we sped past. I recalled that Gare de l'Est would soon become the last stronghold of steam power in Paris. When current plans for electrification of the suburban lines into Gare du Nord were completed, Gare de l'Est would become the only Parisian terminal exclusively operated with steam power, excepting of course a limited number of diesel autorail schedules.

Another tank-engined suburban train scurried by beneath us as we crossed over another rail line. To the right, in a sprawling coach yard, a long string of SNCF's new stainless steel coaches, built in France by a Budd Company licensee, stood out against the dark green of standard French National equipment.

Then, as terminal activity gave way to a Paris of drab stockyards, factories, and freight yards, I turned my attention to the autorail's interior accommodations.

Unlike most European rail equipment, with its side corridors and compartments, SNCF autorails were arranged in the familiar center corridor, open style of North American equipment. Facing pairs of seats provided a pleasant arrangement for congenial travel.

First-class accommodations in the center car were slightly more luxurious than my second-class place. Three, instead of four, seats the width of the car provided a roomier arrangement, while leather upholstery gave the first-class section a more elegant air. I contented myself with my second-class seat, however, remembering the advice of one travel writer who pointed out that only expense-account businessmen and rich Americans traveled first class. I was neither.

129

Finally, as we sped onward, industrial Paris was replaced by pleasant suburban enclaves of small farms intermingled with residential developments. Pink and white blossoms on the fruit trees and newly budding leaves announced that spring had arrived.

A high bridge carried us over the waters of the Marne, flowing toward its junction with the Seine. Soon residential areas disappeared altogether as our route carried us into open country.

A waiter from the restaurant car placed a small table between the facing seats and I enjoyed a second, typically European breakfast of coffee with milk and a *croissant*. I noted that restaurant service, as on all SNCF trains, was operated by the ubiquitous Wagons-Lits company, a sort of international Pullman Company and Fred Harvey rolled into one.

The countryside east of Paris was one of low, rolling hills, woods, and prosperous-looking farms. Save for the houses, with their red-tiled roofs and neat stone-walled yards, and the black, beetle-like French automobiles we overtook and passed on paralleling highways, we might have been passing through the countryside of southern Wisconsin. Occasionally our speeding autorail honked for a road crossing with a two-toned, auto-like horn.

At a little place called Flamboin-Gaudix, some 60 miles out of Paris, our route joined the Seine and for the next 50 miles the train sped along the banks of the historic stream through a series of small towns, all suffixed with the river's name — Pont-sur-Seine, Nogent-sur-Seine, and Romilly-sur-Seine.

My fellow travelers typified the international character of this particular autorail service. Two passengers in the facing seats conversed in German; I took them for Swiss, or perhaps West German, businessmen. Across the aisle a young French soldier, dressed in a bizarre outfit that included khaki trousers, a mottled camouflage jacket, paratrooper boots, and a bright red beret, dozed as the train raced through the countryside. A few sleepy, blue-clad airmen recounted their weekend adventures in Paris as they returned to the U.S. Air Force base at Chaumont. Many of the passengers had the look of tourists, most of them English or American.

A check of my watch showed us on time to the minute as the train slowed to its first stop under the train shed at Troyes. After a brief pause we were off again with a honk of the horn. As we sped out of the yard I noted the autorail's acceleration; good, but not exceptional.

A review of the autorail's performance characteristics suggests that sustained high speed, rather than rapid acceleration, enables it to maintain its fast schedules. Despite a power-to-weight ratio only half that of the Budd Company's RDC (Rail Diesel Car), the nearest thing to it operating in North America, the autorail's 93 mph top speed is nearly 10 mph better than the RDC's 85 mph maximum.

Speed was indeed the most notable feature of autorail train 41. It was speed that was hard to estimate from within the smooth and quiet running train, except for the frequency with which the kilometer markers sailed by.

Another hour's running through an increasingly hilly and forested countryside of the Champagne region brought us to Chaumont, junction point with the East Region's Lille-Dijon transversal line and the route of passenger services between Calais and Eastern Europe.

As the autorail decelerated for the station stop we rode high above the forested valley of the Suize River on a massive masonry arch viaduct, one of the greatest such works on the East Region. The French call their bridges and other structures *travaux d'art*, "works of art." I thought it a particularly appropriate term for this imposing Chaumont viaduct.

The Chaumont station platform was sprinkled with the familiar Air Force blue, and Gallic conversation was mixed with cheerful GI banter as American airmen left the train for the big Chaumont air base and others boarded for the run to Switzerland.

Beyond Chaumont deep rock cuts and tunnels carried our route into the hilly country along the Valley of the Marne. This would be the fastest segment of the journey, and the autorail would cover the 74 miles to our next stop at Vesoul in just an hour and six minutes, for a start-to-stop average speed of 67.3 mph.

Vesoul was another brief station stop. Then, as we got underway again to the muffled hum of the diesels, the Wagons-Lits waiter returned to take my order for lunch. As a countryside reminiscent of upstate New York sped by the windows, I enjoyed an extended luncheon as only the French can prepare and serve it. There was a *consommé*, a fish course, and then a filet, accented with a bottle of splendid Bordeaux rouge, and a dessert of cheeses and cake.

Now we were nearing the great industrial region of Alsace. To the right as we sped into Belfort we passed a huge plant of the Société Alsthom, one of the brightest names in the world of railroading. Builders of locomotives for something like a century, this was the firm that produced the superb series of electric locomotives that have powered the postwar SNCF speedup and have set impressive new world speed marks. Alsthom locomotives daily powered *Le Mistral*, the world's fastest train, on its run between Paris and Lyon.

Beyond Belfort we paralleled the Rhone-Rhine Canal across the valley between the Vosges and Jura mountains into Mulhouse. Switzerland was only a few minutes away now, and the snow-capped Juras were visible to the east as we turned south from Mulhouse toward the international frontier.

The little town of St. Louis was the last point on our route in France. Here in the huge frontier yards the markings of freight cars from nearly every Western European nation pointed up the international character of SNCF's freight operations. There was the SBB-CFF of Swiss Federal Railways, FS of Italian State Railways, NS of Netherlands Railways, and even the BR of British Railways on cars ferried across the Channel in interchange service.

A series of tunnels and long cuts brought us into serene, orderly Basel. As the autorail curved through the last few miles into the station we passed close by the famed Basel Zoo, where small groups of rapt children wandered from cage to cage under the watchful eyes of nurses and mothers. In a nearby street a little green, four-wheel trolley bobbed along the international electric line to St. Louis.

Precisely on time at 1:06 P.M. we glided under Swiss Federal Railways catenary into the imposing Basel terminal. Here, at a crossroads of Europe, trains from France, Germany, and Switzerland came together, and more than two million passengers a year passed through Basel's busy station. Cursory formalities of border police and customs took only a few minutes, and then I dashed for the ticket office and across the platform to a waiting *Lucerne Express* of green-clad coaches and box cab electric locomotive. For our autorail the day's work was only half done. After a brief 15 minute turnaround the green and silver streamliner would be off on the return trip to Paris on an equally demanding schedule as *Train Automoteur Rapide No. 42.*

The trip had been an impressive sampling of one of SNCF's exemplary international autorail services. Train 41 had delivered a dazzling performance in high-speed operation, punctuality, and service that seemed all the more remarkable when I reflected that this was a railway system that had risen from the rubble of World War II in less than a decade. It was hard to believe that this was the same dismembered SNCF that had greeted the Liberation in 1944, unable to run a train between any of the principal cities of France.

The Journey Today

Fast international services like the Paris-Basel autorail I rode in 1953 were the forerunners of an extensive network of Trans-Europ Express services developed over the next two decades to provide fast, deluxe service between the principal cities of Western Europe. Today, a still-newer generation of high-speed international service is represented by Europe's fast-developing network of high-speed trains such as *Eurostar*, France's TGV, and Germany's ICE.

These fast new services have not yet reached the Paris-Basel route, and today's fastest trains make the trip in only 20 to 30 minutes less than the 5 hour, 21 minute timing of the *Train Automoteur Rapide* of 1953.

Orient Express*

Few trains were ever able to rival the cachet of the celebrated *Orient Express*, and probably none will ever exceed its extraordinary longevity. The *Orient Express* introduced the concept of the deluxe international express, and for much of its more than a century of operation the train represented the finest example of the concept of luxury service established by the Compagnie Internationale des Wagons-Lits et des Grands Express Europeens, the great European sleeping car company. It was much more than just a single train, too. For much of its long history it was actually a complex of interconnecting European expresses that were collectively referred to as the *Orient Express.*

The original *Orient Express*—and indeed, a new concept of Continental travel—was born on June 5, 1883, when the train departed from Paris's Gare de

---

*© 1969 Kalmbach Publishing Co., reprinted with permission from the February 1969 issue of *Trains* magazine.

Late on an October evening in 1961 a big Hellenic State Railways Lambda Beta class 2-10-0 Decapod had just arrived at Thessaloniki with a local train from Istanbul and Pithian. On the platform beyond stood through sleeping cars from the *Tauern* and *Simplon-Orient* expresses, en route from Paris to Athens.

l'Est on its initial trip to Constantinople (now Istanbul). It was the first of the great fleet of international expresses operated exclusively with its own luxury equipment supplied by the Wagons-Lits company. Wagons-Lits had been formed in 1876 by a Belgian engineer, Georges Nagelmackers, who was inspired to establish a Continental equivalent of the Pullman Company during a visit to America in 1870.

An all-rail route to Constantinople had not yet been completed, and the first *Orient Express*, normally made up of two baggage-and-mail cars, a dining-parlor car, and two or more sleeping cars, operated twice weekly via Munich, Vienna, Budapest, and Bucharest as far as Giurgiu, a small Romanian port on the Danube. From there, steamers carried passengers across the river to Ruse, Bulgaria, where they boarded another train for the 7-hour journey to the Black Sea port of Varna. Beyond Varna, steamships of the Austrian Lloyd Company completed the trip to Constantinople in 15 hours. Total running time from Paris to Constantinople was 81 hours 40 minutes.

Although the first leg of the journey was made in surroundings of unusual comfort and luxury for the period, the remainder of the trip was often an adventure. The connecting train service across Bulgaria was over a primitive line, unprotected against wandering livestock. An early traveler over the route described the locomotive's huge latticework pilot, which was constructed of iron bars, as "strong and solid enough to sweep away an ox." The port of Varna lacked suitable facilities for embarking passengers on the connecting steamships, and the transfer was made "by means of rough boats steered by boisterous boatmen who waited for passengers at the foot of a muddy bank, in open country."

New double-truck equipment for the *Orient Express* was completed a few months after the service began and made its first trip on October 4, 1883, with a large party of journalists and officials in attendance. Unfortunately, the splendid new dining car developed a hot box and was replaced at Munich by a rough-riding six-wheeler. According to accounts of the journey, however, the quality of the food was undiminished. At Szeged, on the Romanian frontier, Onady Kahniar and his 11 minstrels boarded the diner. Tables and chairs were removed to the baggage car, and the musicians struck up a waltz. The sensation of the festivities was an impassioned rendering of "La Marseillaise" by the black-bearded dining-car chef. After two and a half hours of continuous playing, the minstrels left the train at Timisoara, and lunch was finally served.

By 1885 construction of a new line from Budapest to Constantinople via Belgrade had been completed as far as Nis, in southern Serbia, and the Wagons-Lits company signed an agreement with the Serbian government providing for weekly operation of the *Orient Express* to Nis. Under the terms of the agreement, the train was limited to 100 tons. This was to be reduced to 80 tons in times of bad weather or temperatures under 6 degrees below zero Centigrade (21 degrees Fahrenheit). The tonnage reduction was accomplished by leaving a sleeping car behind, adding an element of uncertainty to a Balkan journey. Beyond Nis Wagons-Lits organized a horse-carriage service which required two days to transport Constantinople passengers and their baggage to Philippopolis (Plovdiv), Bulgaria, where the rail journey to Constantinople resumed.

By 1889 the all-rail route across Bulgaria to the Ottoman Empire capital was nearing completion, and Wagons-Lits sent a representative to Sofia to negotiate a contract for through operation of the *Orient Express*. To complete the arrangements, an audience with Prince Ferdinand was necessary. Strict court etiquette required that one be in uniform to be received by the Prince. The Wagons-Lits representative, Messr. de Richemont, lacking any kind of uniform, appeared before Ferdinand wearing the borrowed uniform of a captain of the Prince's own police. At this, Ferdinand is said to have remarked, "What a ridiculous country!" The contract was secured, however, and on June 5, 1889, the *Orient Express* began twice-weekly operation without change of cars between Paris and Constantinople on a 67-hour 46-minute schedule.

A weekly service was continued over the original route until 1894. In 1895 Romania completed a new bridge across the Danube at Fetesti, opening a new through route to the Romanian Black Sea port of Constanta which permitted a new rail-steamship *Orient Express* route with only a single change en route. Operation over the two routes continued until 1914, when the outbreak of World War I brought a temporary end to the service. At that time the train was running four times a week over the all-rail route via Belgrade and Sofia, and three times weekly over the "maritime" route via Bucharest and Constanta.

The years before the First World War were great ones for Europe's luxury trains, of which the *Orient Express* was a glamorous leader. Royal personages, aristocrats, millionaires, statesmen, and celebrities traveled on the sumptuous Wagons-Lits expresses as a matter of course. The company's cars were constructed of varnished teak, with interiors paneled in mahogany and inlaid with lemonwood in fanciful patterns. Seats were upholstered in thick plush and were provided with lace-covered headrests. Floors were heavily carpeted.

Dining cars were stocked with bone china and Belgian crystal. Waiters wore knee breeches and white stockings. The food was legendary. Caviar, champagne, and the specialties and wines of the countries traversed en route were served. On June 5, 1903, the twentieth anniversary of the *Orient Express*, a special menu for the occasion offered the train's passengers *foie gras*, *saumon fumé*, *oeufs en gelée*, *sole Metternich*, and *poulet en cocotte*.

Completion of the 12 1/4-mile Simplon Tunnel between Switzerland and Italy in 1904 opened the possibility for a new southerly Paris-Constantinople route which not only was 263 miles shorter than the *Orient Express* route, but would permit a direct service to Constantinople from southern Europe.

Simultaneously with completion of the tunnel, the Wagons-Lits company inaugurated the *Simplon Express*, which operated from Calais, connecting with cross-Channel services from London, via Paris to Milan on a tri-weekly schedule. During the next few years the service was extended to Venice and Trieste, and became a daily train.

A proposal to extend the *Simplon Express* service all the way to Constantinople was first advanced at the June 1906 International Timetable Conference at Bremen, but the idea was shelved following refusal of the Austro-Hungarian government to open the Italian-Croatian frontier post of Cormons to the train.

The proposal was again taken up at the Versailles peace conference in 1919. The Allied governments wanted a new train to link the Balkans with the Western powers. The Austro-Hungarian Empire had been broken up, and the new Yugoslav government, which now controlled Croatia, was eager for the new international service. Details for the operation of the train were worked out in only four weeks, and the first *Simplon-Orient Express* departed Paris's PLM terminal on April 15, 1919, to run as far as Trieste. Service was extended to Bucharest six months later and all the way to Constantinople in July 1920. Running time from Paris to Constantinople was 96 hours 30 minutes, of which over 15 hours was consumed in stops for frontier formalities.

Completion of the Greek railway system between Larissa and Thessaloniki in 1916 had made through running to Athens possible for the first time, and a section of the new *SOE*, as it was commonly known to European travelers, began operation to Athens in 1920, leaving the Constantinople train at Nis.

The original *Orient Express* was restored to service in 1919, operating from Paris to Bucharest. Through cars for Constantinople were still carried, running from Budapest to Belgrade with the *SOE's* Prague and Berlin connection, and beyond Belgrade on the *Simplon-Orient*. Another connecting service, the *Ostende-Vienna-Orient Express*, reached Belgium and Holland.

Still another *Orient Express* came into being in 1932 when the tri-weekly *Switzerland-Arlberg-Vienna Express*, which operated from Paris to Vienna via the Arlberg Tunnel in Switzerland, was extended to Bucharest and renamed the *Arlberg-Orient Express*.

The faster *Simplon-Orient* quickly replaced the original *Orient Express* as the favored train of travelers to the Balkans and to Constantinople (which became Istanbul in 1930), and the service flourished in the era between wars, reaching perhaps its greatest glory in 1938–1939. The train was then composed entirely of Wagons-Lits stock. In addition to the through sleeping cars carried daily between Paris, Istanbul, and Athens, a daily through car for Istanbul was operated from Boulogne, where a connection was made with cross-Channel services from London. A daily Paris-Bucharest sleeping car operated in the *SOE* as far as Vinkovci, Yugoslavia. At Belgrade, through sleeping cars from Paris, Ostende, Prague, Berlin, and Vienna for Athens and Istanbul were picked up from the *Orient Express* and other connections. During the summer a shower bath, situated in one of the luggage vans, was available to *SOE* passengers. The equally plush *Rome Express* was the only other Continental train to offer this deluxe feature. Running time between Paris and Istanbul was reduced to an all-time low of 56 hours.

At Istanbul the *SOE* made a close connection with its intercontinental extension, the *Taurus Express*, which had begun operation in 1930, departing from Haydarpasa Station across the Bosporus from the *Simplon-Orient's* Sirkeci Station terminal. A special boat, in the charge of a Wagons-Lits/Cook interpreter, took through passengers and their baggage across the Bosporus between the two terminals. In the event the *Simplon-Orient* arrived late, provision was made for delaying departure of the *Taurus* for a maximum period of 1 1/2 hours. Running three times a week across Turkey, the *Taurus Express* carried through sleeping cars for Mosul, Iraq, and Tripoli, Lebanon, with the two sections diverging at Aleppo, Syria. Beyond Mosul and Tripoli connecting services took passengers on to such points as Baghdad, Tehran, Damascus, Beirut, Jerusalem, and Cairo.

The several *Orient Expresses* enjoyed an unequaled reputation for the mysterious and the romantic. It was said that everyone on the train had "a veiled mystery in his past and a sinister purpose in his future," and the *Orient Express* became a favorite with fiction writers, whose thrillers populated the Wagons-Lits cars with endless spies, adventurers, and inscrutable strangers. The *Orient* provided a setting for such novels as Graham Greene's *Orient Express* and Agatha Christie's

Murder on the Orient Express, and played a starring role in the Alfred Hitchcock film *The Lady Vanishes*. The fictional spy James Bond—007—rode the train in *From Russia with Love*.

In real life the *Orient Express* never quite equaled its literary reputation. No one was ever murdered on the train, although in 1948 an American naval attaché, Capt. Eugene Karpe, disappeared from the *Arlberg-Orient* under mysterious circumstances. His body was later found in a tunnel in the Austrian Alps. On an earlier occasion, the *SOE* connection from Athens was held up by brigands in southern Yugoslavia.

It isn't difficult, however, to imagine the international intrigue that must have taken place among the diplomatic couriers and foreign agents who rode in the paneled compartments of the *Orient Express* during such tense times as the "phony war" days in the winter of 1939, when the *SOE* continued to run from Paris to Athens and Istanbul, and incongruously still carried the through sleepers from Berlin south of Belgrade.

After the war, nothing was ever the same for the trains plying the route to the Orient. East-West tensions and the visa complications that ensued, as well as other difficulties of travel behind the Iron Curtain, discouraged all but the most determined travelers. The *Orient Express*, the *Arlberg-Orient*, and the *Simplon-Orient* all resumed operation at the end of the war, but the palmy days of the prewar era never returned. No longer did the train operate with solid Wagons-Lits consists. Ordinary coaches were added, and as the train approached their eastern European terminals, the once imperious expresses became no more than one or two through cars carried in what were often little better than locals. For example, under the winter 1961–1962 timetable in effect at the *Simplon-Orient's* discontinuance, the train began its eastward trip auspiciously enough by ripping off the 197 nonstop miles over the celebrated Paris-Dijon speedway at an average speed of 77.8 mph; but by the time the train reached Bulgaria, its average speed had declined to only 23 mph, and the final leg of the trip, across northeastern Greece and European Turkey, was made at an overall average of less than 14 mph.

The *SOE* in particular fared badly in the postwar period. After irregular operation from 1942 to 1944, regular service had been resumed early in 1946 between Paris and Venice, and was extended later in the year to Sofia, then in 1947 to Istanbul. The initial Paris-Istanbul running time of 105 hours was almost double that of 1939. Paris-Athens service, interrupted by the severe wartime damage to the Greek railway system and the postwar Communist rebellion, was not restored until 1950.

After 1948 frequent Bulgarian-Turkish border incidents disrupted the *SOE* service to Istanbul, and it was finally suspended altogether. A weekly through service was restored in 1953, and several additional Paris-Istanbul sleepers were routed via Thessaloniki. By 1957 the *SOE* was operating three times weekly over its original route.

In its last years, the *SOE* became largely a France-Italy service. Under its final schedule, the *Simplon-Orient* operated daily from Paris's Gare de Lyon with through sleeping cars, *couchettes*, and coaches for Rome, Naples and Venice. The connection from London was made daily by means of Wagons-Lits parlor cars

An enormous M-alpha class 2-10-2 stood in the Hellenic State Railways station at Thessaloniki,
ready to depart for the south with a 12-car train 2, the Athens connection for the *Tauern* and
Simplon-Orient expresses.

operated in the London-Paris *Golden Arrow.* These cars ran directly to the Gare de Lyon from the *Golden Arrow's* Gare du Nord terminal. A sleeper and coach operated twice weekly from Paris to Belgrade and three times weekly to Athens. Through service to Istanbul, consisting of a single sleeper and coach, ran twice a week.

The *Simplon-Orient's* intercontinental connection, the *Taurus Express,* fared better in the postwar period. Completion of a new standard-gauge route from Mosul to Baghdad during the war permitted the operation of through Istanbul-Baghdad cars for the first time. A new standard-gauge line between Tripoli and Haifa had been completed during the war, establishing an unbroken route from Turkey to Egypt; but the Arab-Israeli war and the subsequent Arab blockade prevented reestablishment of Istanbul-Cairo service.

In the early 1960s declining earnings from all Wagons-Lits through services to Eastern Europe brought the fortunes of the several *Orient Expresses* to a low point. Although the name remained, the original *Orient Express* ceased to operate into Hungary and Romania in 1961, when its run was cut back to Vienna, with a Paris-Prague section diverging at Stuttgart. A year later the *Arlberg-Orient Express* was cut back from Bucharest to Vienna and renamed the *Arlberg Express.* Through service from Western Europe to Budapest and Bucharest was no longer available.

In 1962, too, the proud *Simplon-Orient* name vanished from Continental timetables and was replaced by the *Direct-Orient Express.* The latter continued on a reduced scale—and a slightly slower schedule—the Paris-Istanbul and Paris-Athens through cars formerly operated in the *SOE.* A revival of the pre–World War I *Simplon Express* retained the *SOE's* daily Italian services on a nearly identical schedule.

Lessening of East-West tensions and growing trade between Western and Eastern Europe brought a revival of Paris-Bucharest *Orient Express* service in 1965. Eager for a direct link with Paris, the Romanians requested restoration of the service, agreeing to cover any losses the Wagons-Lits company might incur. Effective with 1965 summer timetable changes, the *Orient Express* reappeared as a Paris-Bucharest schedule, with daily through coach service and a four-times-weekly through Wagons-Lits sleeper.

Orient Express service between Paris and Istanbul did not fare so well. Mounting losses and operating problems brought an end to through *Direct-Orient Express* service in May 1977. Thereafter passengers for Istanbul had to travel in the *Simplon Express* to Belgrade, spend the night there, and continue on to Istanbul the next day in the *Marmara Express.*

I never got to ride the real *Orient Express* in anything like its true glory of the years before World War II. I can at least lay claim, however, to having ridden one of the very last *Simplon-Orient Express* trips into Istanbul just before it was replaced by the lesser *Direct-Orient Express* in 1962. By this time, of course, the *Simplon-Orient* was primarily a Paris-Italy service, and the only equipment that went through to Istanbul was a single coach and a Wagons-Lits sleeper. But even so, it was still the *Simplon-Orient;* it said so on the name plate on the side of the cars.

Having learned of the fabled train's impending exit, I planned a journey from Istanbul that would put me on board the *Simplon-Orient* for the overnight return trip. The journey began at Istanbul's Sirkeci station on the afternoon of May 12, 1962, where I boarded a diesel car local for the 6-hour, 169-mile journey across Thrace, or Trakya as the Turks call it, to the Turkish-Greek border at Uzunkopru (literally "Grape Bridge"), where I planned to board the *SOE* for the last leg of its eastbound journey from Paris.

It was past 9 P.M. when I arrived at Uzunkopru, but I still had more than two hours to wait for the eastbound *Simplon-Orient*. The station was a big, two-story frame structure with a fancy Turkish State Railways TCDD emblem outlined in light bulbs. Inside the station were a restaurant, offices for police and customs, and a station agent's bay where a telegraph key clacked intermittently.

A row of tea houses, stores, and a barber shop stood opposite the station. I sat outside in the warm spring evening in a little garden next to the station, listened to a man playing Turkish music on a flute in a nearby cafe, and enjoyed a cheese sandwich dinner I'd bought from a platform vendor. The lights of a Greek village twinkled in the darkness on the far side of the river that formed the border.

A Turkish 2-8-0 brought the *Simplon-Orient* through cars across the river from Greece around 10 P.M., more or less on time. The equipment had traveled only a few miles in Greece, having come across the frontier from Bulgaria at Svilengrad, some 50 miles away. In addition to the single Paris-Istanbul Wagons-Lits sleeping car, the consist included a first- and second- class SNCF (French National Railways) *couchette*—a car with seats that converted into narrow berths—coming through from Paris, SNCF and TCDD baggage cars, and a string of freight cars.

The nameplate on the side of a *Simplon-Orient Express* Wagons-Lits sleeping car in Istanbul's Sirkeci Station enumerated the principal points along the train's long journey across Europe from Paris to the edge of Asia.

The *Simplon-Orient* equipment would complete its long journey to Istanbul in TCDD train 9, an all-stops local that originated at Edirne, some 25 miles to the north on the Greek-Turkish border. The last revision of boundaries between the two countries had left the rail line between Edirne and Uzunkopru on the Greek side, so the local arrived, like its *SOE* connection, across the bridge from Greece, right on time at 10:50 P.M.

The station switcher assembled the train while the usual border formalities were completed. When the little 0-6-0 was finished, the local had been filled out to a consist that included a TCDD box car; a postal car; one third-class and two first/second-class coaches; the through sleeping car, *couchette* and SNCF baggage car from Paris; and 20 freight cars.

For the final segment of its long journey, which had begun with a high-speed dash down France's Paris-Dijon speedway, the *Simplon-Orient* had become little more than a mixed train.

Motive power for the run to Istanbul was a sturdy looking 2-8-0 Consolidation, whose low driving wheels promised more pulling power than speed. A little research would reveal that the elderly machine was built for the Ottoman Oriental Railway, the predecessor company for TCDD's European lines, by a German builder in the mid-1920s.

I settled into my compartment in the Paris-Istanbul Wagons-Lits. It was an aging 11-compartment Z class Wagons-Lits car manufactured by a French builder in 1927, and only slightly modernized with some light, simulated wood finish Formica-style interior paneling. Customs and other border-crossing formalities finally complete, the station agent raised a signal wand with a red target, the engi-

neer answered with a shrill whistle blast, and at 5 minutes before midnight the train moved off slowly into the night. I soon drifted off to sleep as the sturdy Consolidation took us across the rolling hills of Thrace at a brisk pace.

I awoke to a bright spring day somewhere east of Cerkezkoy in eastern Thrace. Patches of yellow wildflowers and bright red poppies added a colorful accent to the lush green fields that swept across the rolling hills. There was no restaurant car, and bread, preserves, and a cup of tea served by the Wagons-Lits attendant would have to suffice until we reached Istanbul.

Up ahead I could see that two more coaches had been added to the train during the night. These had come off a connecting branch line train from Kirklareli, in northwestern Thrace, at a junction with the main line at

Late on a May evening in 1962 the *Simplon-Orient Express* through cars from Paris had just come across the Greek border into the Turkish frontier station at Uzunkopru. Soon they would begin the tedious last leg of their journey to Istanbul in the consist of train 9, an all-stops local that originated in nearby Edirne.

Alpullu. The train was now double-headed. The big 0-8-0 switcher that had joined the 2-8-0 was another, and even older, holdover from Ottoman Oriental days, built before World War I by Germany's Henschel.

Approaching Hadimkoy the train slowed to a walk as the two locomotives struggled up a long grade. We paused briefly at a handsome old stone station set in a grove of trees, and then resumed the journey over a line that now turned southward toward the Marmara Sea coast. The track followed the water's edge around a long arm off the sea and then climbed away to the east toward Istanbul. Furious noise and billows of steam and smoke came from the head end as one of the locomotives lost its footing during the start from a station stop on the long grade.

Soon we pulled alongside a platform at Halkali, the outer terminal of an Istanbul suburban electrification completed by French suppliers in 1955. A train of suburban MU cars waited on an adjacent platform, and ranks of 2-8-0s and big German-built 2-10-0s stood outside a nearby engine house. Up ahead our two steam locomotives were cut off the train and turned on a nearby wye. A diesel switcher moved in to pull off the long string of freight cars at the head end of the train. I noted reporting marks as diverse as the DB of the German Federal Railways and Interfrigo, the international refrigerator car line.

Train 6 began to look a little more like a crack international express as one of TCDD's big B-B electric locomotives backed onto the train. One of three built by

Soon after dawn, a pair of Turkish steam engines labored up a long grade on the plains of Turkish Thrace with train 9 from Edirne, on the Greek and Bulgarian borders. Bringing up the rear of the all-stops local to Istanbul were the twice-weekly *Simplon-Orient Express* through cars from Paris. Soon the train would be following the Marmara Sea coastline through the Istanbul suburbs into Sirkeci Station on the edge of the Bosporus.

France's Alsthom for the 17-mile electrification completed in 1955, the sleek box cab electric was a near-duplicate of some of SNCF's most modern electric motive power.

The electric had us underway again at 7:45 A.M., and we were soon paralleling the Marmara coast toward the Bosporus and our Sirkeci station terminal. To the north I watched a PanAm Boeing 707 roll to a stop at the end of the runway at Istanbul's Yesilkoy airport. Graceful wooden houses dating to nineteenth century Constantinople stood in sharp contrast to the big masonry and concrete apartment buildings that were under construction everywhere in the fast-growing suburbs along the railroad. It was the first day of Kurban Bayram, a Moslem sacrificial holiday, and families were gathered in fields along the line for the ritual sacrifice of a lamb that began the holiday.

Near Yedikule the double-track line threaded through a breach in the ancient city wall of Constantinople and then paralleled the ruins of the old wall along the shore of the Marmara. We passed Yenikapi ("new gate") and Kumkapi ("sand gate"), and then curved around Seraglio Point below the walls of the Ottomans' splendid Topkapi Palace that overlooks the entrance to the Bosporus from the Marmara. The sleek buff and white ferries that link European and Asian Istanbul darted in and out among ocean-going tankers and freighters steaming up and down the Bosporus.

Its long journey from Paris at an end, the *Simplon-Orient Express* rolled past rows of electric suburban trains in a storage yard and braked to a halt at the platforms of Sirkeci Station. Sirkeci was a fitting terminal for a long international journey across Europe. To one side, high-level platforms in a modern addition served the suburban trains, but the *SOE* ended its run in the original nineteenth century terminal. A canopy of an orange, translucent material bathed the platforms in a bright, warm light. There was a small landscaped garden at the head of the two tracks for long distance trains. The main terminal building was an eclectic, ornate structure of red brick and white stone trim. A high mansard roof over the center section was flanked by minaret-like clock towers. Windows were surmounted by circular openings set high in the walls and inset with stained glass designs.

Baggage was lowered through open windows to waiting porters, and the train's passengers headed for the cab stand. Some, perhaps, would board a ferry for the short trip across the Bosporus to Haydarpasa station to continue a journey into Asia on the *Taurus Express*. An equally appropriate ending to an *Orient Express* journey would have been a stay in the Pera Palas Hotel, the elegant Istanbul hostelry overlooking the Golden Horn that was completed by the Wagons-Lits company in 1892 just to assure that the train's passengers would have suitable accommodations on their arrival in Constantinople. Instead of either, however, I set out in search of breakfast.

The Journey Today

The last train carrying the magic *Orient Express* name all the way across Europe to Istanbul was the *Direct-Orient Express*, which made its last run in 1977. Surprisingly, however, there is still an *Orient Express*, but today's train operates only from Paris to Vienna and Budapest. For travelers continuing to Istanbul there

Sleek French-built electric locomotives powered the trains from Europe over the last few miles into Istanbul. Glimpsed through an opening in the old Constantinople city wall, train 9 brought the twice-weekly *Simplon-Orient Express* through cars into their eastern terminal at Istanbul's Sirkeci Station. Looming above the train in the distance were the domes and towers of the Ottoman sultans' Topkapi Palace.

144

are through sleeping cars originating at Budapest, but it's a long, slow journey, and there are no restaurant cars. The luxury of the great *Simplon-Orient* of the pre–World War II period can still be experienced on a deluxe cruise train service, the *Venice Simplon-Orient Express*. Made up of restored period equipment, the train operates in a London-Paris-Venice service once or twice weekly from March through November.

Their journey at an end, passengers on the Wagons-Lits sleeping cars of the *Simplon-Orient Express* handed their luggage down to porters on the platform at Istanbul's Sirkeci Station.

"Yet there isn't a train
I wouldn't take"

Despite the turmoil of the Vietnam war, the trains still ran whenever they could. At the height
of the fighting in the northern area in 1966, this little meter-gauge train bravely headed north
from Da Nang toward Hue and Quang Tri every day at noon. Steel plate armored the locomotive
cab against ambushes, and a flat car was pushed ahead of the locomotive to detonate any land
mines.

III.
Asian
Journeys

Ali Shan's oldest Shay was ready to go to work in the pre-dawn darkness of January 4, 1974. No. 12 headed the forestry railway's train 131, scheduled to depart at 6 A.M. for the highest railway station in the Far East (see p. 219).

Into Asia on the *Taurus Express**

To devotees of railway travel, there have been few names among those of the world's great international express trains more likely to embody the romance and excitement of far rails and far places than that of the *Taurus Express.* Certainly few trains could match the romantic and historic associations of the places visited by this Turkish express on its long journey between Istanbul and Baghdad. On its three-day journey from the great capital of the Emperor Constantine and the Ottoman sultans to the city of the Arabian nights, the *Taurus Express* traveled across a historic land where Assyrians, Babylonians, Hittites, and Romans once lived, and which bore the traces of 70 centuries of civilization.

The *Taurus Express* began operation in 1930 as an Asian extension of the celebrated *Simplon-Orient Express*, offering connecting services for Beirut, Cairo, and Tehran as well as Baghdad. For much of its 1632-mile journey between Istanbul and Baghdad the train followed a route which had assumed international importance around the turn of the century, when it was a part of the famous German "Berlin to Baghdad" railway project. In 1899, when rails extended only from Istanbul to Konya, in central Turkey, Kaiser Wilhelm II obtained a concession from the Ottoman sultan for a 1550-mile railway extending from Konya via Baghdad to Kuwait. Although some 1200 miles of the route were in operation as early as 1918, it was not until after World War II that an Istanbul-Baghdad through rail service became possible.

When the *Taurus Express* began operation early in 1930, passengers completed an Istanbul-Baghdad journey by means of a motor car link operated by the Wagons-Lits company between Tel Kotchek, on the Syria-Iraq border, and Kirkuk, where a connection was made for Baghdad over the meter-gauge Iraqi railway system. By early 1939 the *Taurus* was able to reach Mosul, Iraq, where it connected with an extension of the meter-gauge line from Kirkuk. Early in the war a new standard-gauge route via Baiji was completed, and the *Taurus Express* finally was able to operate through all the way to Baghdad.

In the years before World War II, *Taurus Express* connections provided convenient services to many other Middle East and South Asian destinations as well. Passengers for Tehran traveled via Wagons-Lits motor cars that operated over a

*Reprinted with permission from issue No. 2/1962 of *European Railways* magazine.

487-mile route between a link with the Iraqi meter-gauge system at Khanikin, on the Iraq-Iran border, and the Iranian capital. Beyond Baghdad an Iraqi railway connection took passengers to Basra, at the head of the Persian Gulf, where steamer services for Karachi and Bombay were available.

A section of the prewar *Taurus* operated south from Aleppo, Syria, to provide a service to Beirut and Cairo. Passengers traveled beyond Tripoli, Lebanon, to Beirut and Haifa, Palestine, on a connecting motor car service and then returned to Wagons-Lits equipment to continue by rail to El Qantara, Egypt. There, they transferred to motor cars once again to cross the Suez Canal and complete the journey to Cairo.

From Istanbul's Haydarpasa station on the Anatolian shore of the Bosporus, the route of the *Taurus Express* extended eastward along the north shore of the Sea of Marmara, then turned south to climb upward through the Sakarya River valley to Eskisehir, on the Anatolian Plateau. Originally, the train's route extended from Eskisehir to Adana, on the Mediterranean coast, via Konya. Following completion of a direct route from Ankara to Adana in 1933, however, the *Taurus* was rerouted via the Turkish capital.

A day out of Haydarpasa, with the long run across the Anatolian Plateau behind it, the *Taurus Express* rejoined the original Baghdad route at Ulukisla to follow it through the Taurus Mountains to Adana, where the rails extended eastward again across the Mediterranean coastal plain. At Fevzipasa the train divided, part of it following the original route, which dipped south across the Syrian border to Aleppo and then back into Turkey, while the remainder stayed within Turkey, operating via Gaziantep and rejoining the original route at Karkamis over a new line completed in 1960. Eastward from Karkamis the route of the *Taurus* followed the Syrian border for more than 200 miles to Nusaybin, where it cut across the northeastern corner of Syria into Iraq, and then followed the historic Tigris River southward through Mosul to Baghdad.

A November 1961 journey from Turkey's Mediterranean coast to Izmit, on the Sea of Marmara, gave me an opportunity to ride the westbound *Taurus Express* over a substantial part of its route. The train operated four times weekly in each direction. Twice a week, departing Istanbul on Thursdays and Sundays, the *Taurus* went all the way to Baghdad, and twice weekly it operated to points within Turkey only, operating on Saturdays to Gaziantep and on Tuesdays to the Mediterranean port of Iskenderun, which was reached by a branch from the main line east of Adana. Through sleeping cars and first-, second- and third-class coaches were operated to all of these points, and, in addition, the Thursday Baghdad train carried a through sleeping car for Beirut, which operated beyond Aleppo via Homs and Tripoli. Through coaches for the train were provided by the Turkish State Railways, while restaurant and sleeping car equipment was operated by the Wagon-Lits company.

By comparison with the international express trains of Western Europe, the *Taurus Express* operated on a leisurely schedule. Requiring a full three days (73 hours, 30 minutes eastbound and 71 hours, 35 minutes westbound) for the journey, the *Taurus* averaged less than 25 mph for the 1632-mile trip.

My trip began at Adana, a little over midway in the train's long journey from Baghdad, and it would include two of the most scenic portions of the train's route,

On a bright winter morning in 1961, the *Taurus Express* steamed past Lake Saponca, east of Izmit, Turkey, on its long eastward journey from Istanbul's Haydarpasa Station to Baghdad. A handsome German-built (Henschel 1937) 2-8-2 express Mikado powered the train.

Climbing upward through the Sakarya River valley toward the Anatolian Plateau, an eastbound *Taurus Express* crossed a high stone arch viaduct on the 2.5 percent grade above Bilecik in October 1961. One of the usual German-built express 2-8-2's headed the ten-car train. Beyond the tunnel in the distance can be seen the smoke plume from the train's three-cylinder 2-10-0 Decapod helper.

as well as some surprises in the way of motive power. Precisely on schedule at 3 P.M., the *Taurus* rolled in from the east for a scheduled servicing stop and a change of motive power. A big French-built, former SNCF three-cylinder 2-10-0 Decapod powered a seven-car consist that included a baggage car, sleeping car, and two coaches which had come all the way from Baghdad; two coaches that had originated at Nusaybin, on the Syrian-Turkish border; and the restaurant car, which had originated at Gaziantep.

For some time the *Taurus* had been regularly operated between Adana and Ankara with diesel-electric power, and I fully expected to see one of TCDD's five 1980-hp, C-C General Electric units back on to the train. But instead of the diesel we got another of the three-cylinder 2-10-0's. Later I learned that TCDD had withdrawn the GE units from their regular assignments for a series of tests under a wide variety of operating conditions throughout the system that would evaluate the U.S. diesel-electrics against three new 2700-hp diesel-hydraulics that had just been delivered from German builder Krauss-Maffei.

On a November afternoon in 1961, the engine crew on train 603, the westbound *Taurus Express,* waited for departure time at Adana, on Turkey's Mediterranean coast. Locomotive No. 56726 was a big French-built, three-cylinder 2-10-0 Decapod that had once worked trains on the French National Railways.

Three-cylinder Decapod No. 56726, which headed the *Taurus* out of Adana, was not a particularly handsome or fleet-looking locomotive, but its big boiler and low driving wheels seemed eminently suited for the assault on the snow-capped Taurus Range to the north. The 2-10-0 wheel arrangement was easily the most numerous type of locomotive in Turkey; TCDD used them for both heavy freight and passenger service on all parts of the system.

Following a shrill blast from the locomotive, the *Express* accelerated smoothly away from the platform. For the first few miles the train traveled westward across the fertile coastal plain. At Zeytinli we took siding briefly to await the eastbound weekly Iskenderun section of the *Taurus*, which soon came through behind another 2-10-0.

At Yenice the main line curved abruptly north toward the mountains, while a branch continued westward to Mersin, where the recent completion of a large modern harbor had given a new importance to the line. During a brief station stop we met a Mersin-Islahiye local, eastbound behind a 2-6-0 Mogul, and passed a westbound freight powered by still another of TCDD's versatile 2-10-0's.

Northward from Yenice station, the *Taurus* headed straight for its namesake mountain range. Black smoke blasted upward from the roaring, off-beat exhaust of the three-cylinder locomotive as the train began climbing through low foothills. As the grade gradually grew steeper, the 2-10-0 settled into a slow, steady pace. In a field beside the track a Moslem peasant knelt in prayer, oblivious to the

Village children came to watch as the westbound *Taurus Express* began the climb into its namesake Taurus Mountains at Yenice, Turkey. A husky, French-built 2-10-0 Decapod made easy work of the seven-car express.

roaring passage of the express. At a little station labeled simply "Durak" (halt, or stopping place) an eastbound freight resumed its downgrade run to the coastal plain even as we rolled through the passing siding.

The route up into the Taurus was not an unusually difficult climb (the seven-car train required no helper) but it was a long one; the line climbed almost continually for some 70 miles north from Yenice. As the rails climbed higher the hills became increasingly rocky and rugged, and only scrubby bushes and occasional pine trees covered the steep slopes. Now and then the train slammed through a short tunnel, filling it with oily black smoke that rolled upward from the top of the arched portal after we passed.

Nearing the top of its climb the *Taurus* followed a long, rocky ridge, from which I could look down hundreds of feet on little villages of flat-roofed stone houses that reminded one of North African houses or the pueblos of New Mexico. Far to the south the Mediterranean could barely be seen in the gathering dusk. After skirting the east end of the ridge the train crossed a high viaduct, passed through a little village, and then, as the grade finally dropped off, gathered speed as it plunged into the first of an almost continuous series of long tunnels that carried the railway through the heart of the Taurus range.

Completed in 1918, this section of the old German-built Baghdad railway represented what was easily some of the most difficult engineering work involved in its construction. Originally, the builders had planned to drill a single long tunnel under the range. Instead, in a section of only 8 miles they built several massive concrete arch viaducts and drilled a dozen tunnels totaling more than 7 miles to complete the crossing. For some 10 to 15 minutes the train traveled almost continuously through the tunnels, occasionally emerging briefly between towering cliffs so high one had to look almost straight up to see the sky.

Finally the tunnels were past, and we stopped at the little village of Belemedik while the 2-10-0 took water. Small boys ran up and down beside the train selling cups of *buz gibi su* ("ice-like water"). I lowered a window and inhaled cold, fresh mountain air—refreshing after the smoky ride through the tunnels.

By this time night had fallen, and the remainder of the journey through the mountains, following the Cakit River through its rocky gorge, was hidden in darkness. At Pozanti a "Posta" train from Istanbul rumbled past with a long string of mail cars, jam-packed coaches, and freight cars. Portions of the train would eventually reach Nusaybin, on the Syrian border, and Kurtalan, at the end of a long line into southeastern Turkey. We continued the long climb from the Mediterranean coast, finally reaching a maximum elevation of 4845 feet above sea level at Ulukisla

Dinner on the Wagons-Lits restaurant car was, as always, excellent. Menus on the cars operated by CIWL's Turkish branch were customarily Turkish-oriented. Big slabs of *ekmek*, the substantial bread that is a staple of the Turkish diet, were served from a basket. Olive oil was liberally used in the salad and in cooking the chicken main course. Following the main course a spinach *borek* was served. This was a small triangular spinach-filled Turkish pie with a flaky crust made up of paper-thin layers of a dough called *yufka*. A dessert of fresh fruit and thick, sugared Turkish coffee completed the substantial meal.

It was almost 10:30 when the *Taurus* reached Bogazkopru, the junction with the system's principal route extending into eastern Turkey, which eventually branched into several lines. One reached the Black Sea port of Samsun. Another extended through Erzurum to the USSR frontier. Until recently this line had included a 52-mile stretch of 0.75 meter gauge between Horasan and Sarikamis, east of Erzurum, and then 74 miles of Russian 5-foot gauge through Kars to the border. In 1961, however, TCDD completed a new standard-gauge line replacing the narrow gauge, and converted the broad gauge to standard as far as Kars. The remainder of the line was scheduled for conversion in 1962. Still another branch from this route to the east extended to Mus. By the end of 1961 completion of a new 62-mile line under construction would extend it to Tatvan, on the western shore of Lake Van. Later on, a car ferry across the lake and a planned route through the Khotur River canyon would link TCDD with the Iranian rail system.

Alongside the *Taurus* one of TCDD's numerous Czech-built (1949) Deca-pods waited with a long Haydarpasa-Sivas train, which soon went steaming off to the east through the pitch-black night. On another track another 2-10-0, this one a U.S.-built (Vulcan) class, waited with a short connecting train for Kayseri, just a few miles away on the main line to the east.

My sleeping car accommodation was in an old and somewhat shabby but nonetheless comfortable, Wagons-Lits second- and third-class car, which contained five second-class (two-berth) compartments at one end, and four third-class (three-berth) compartments at the other.

Dawn found the *Taurus Express* running over an hour late as it wound through the bare, treeless hills of Anatolia approaching Ankara. Drab little houses were clustered on the steep hillsides of villages, where throngs of peasants waited on the platforms for the commuter trains that would take them to their day's work in the city. At Kayas a backward-running Alco 2-8-2 waited to follow us on the single track into Ankara with a string of the modern Austrian-built suburban coaches which TCDD used in this service. At Cebeci, where double track began, a big 2-10-0 with an eastbound suburban train accelerated away from the platforms as we cleared the line. Soon the old citadel of Ankara, perched high on a hilltop, became visible to the north through an early-morning haze. Then the *Taurus* slipped past the tall, modern office buildings of Yenisehir ("new city") and the big Ankara locomotive depot, and at 7:20 A.M., an hour and 20 minutes late, the train came to a halt in Ankara terminal.

Here, TCDD had another surprise in store for me. Ordinarily, the train was powered between Ankara and Istanbul by one of the railway's German-built (Henschel, 1937) express 2-8-2's. Instead of the Mikado, what at first appeared to be one of the Czech-built 2-10-0's was waiting to take the place of the 2-10-0 that had brought the train over the 420 miles from Adana. As the fresh locomotive backed on the train, however, it became apparent that it was something quite special. Turkish motive power was normally quite well kept, but this 2-10-0 was immaculate. It was freshly painted in TCDD's standard glossy black, with red trim on the pilot, running gear, and tender trucks, and white wheel tires, and its brasswork gleamed with a high polish.

A brass plate on the cylinder jacket identified the 2-10-0, No. T56202, as Turkish-built in 1961 at the railway's Sivas shops, with the serial number 0001! Unlike other Turkish locomotives, it bore a name, *Bozkurt* ("Gray Wolf"), which was displayed in chromium letters on the valve gear frame on each side. The name and a wolf's head emblem, together with a brief explanation of the locomotive's Turkish origin, were lettered on the smoke deflectors.

Later I obtained further details of TCDD's new steam power. Two of them had been completed late in 1961. The other, the *Karakurt* ("Black Wolf") was built by TCDD's Eskisehir shops. Virtually identical to some 176 previous 2-10-0's constructed to the railway's railway plans and specifications by builders in Germany, Great Britain, and Czechoslovakia, they weighed 170 tons in working order, including tenders, were fitted with 57-inch driving wheels, and were rated at 1800 hp. Both of the new locomotives were equipped to burn oil fuel. Except for main frame members, which were furnished by Krupp, they were entirely Turkish in fabrication. They represented not only Turkey's first home-built steam locomotives, but probably its last as well, for TCDD planned to purchase only diesel or electric power in the future.

For its scheduled engine change at Ankara, the westbound *Taurus Express* of November 9, 1961, got the maiden run of this glistening new Turkish-built 2-10-0 Decapod instead of its customary express 2-8-2 Mikado. No. T56202, *Bozkurt* ("Gray Wolf"), had just been turned out by the Turkish State Railways' Sivas shops.

With the *Taurus Express* running an hour and 15 minutes late leaving Ankara, the new 2-10-0, which I had been told was making its maiden passenger trip, had a good opportunity to show its mettle. Except for double track in the Ankara and Haydarpasa suburban zones, the entire route between Ankara and Istanbul was single track, and none of it is yet equipped with modern signaling or CTC, and in making up time the *Taurus* had to contend with a heavy eastbound traffic flow.

At Sincan, the end of suburban double track, we were delayed to wait for the overnight Haydarpasa-Ankara *Anatolia Express,* and by the time we had met the following, all-sleeping car *Ankara Express* at Esenkent, the next station, the *Taurus* was better than an hour and a half off schedule. Gradually, then, the 2-10-0 began to gain time, until the dispatcher decided to hold us at Yunusemre for the westbound Ankara-Haydarpasa *Bosporus* diesel train, which was rapidly overtaking us on its considerably faster schedule. A pretty hostess leaned out as the red and cream, three-car trainset (built by MAN of Germany), running in multiple with the identical Ankara-Izmir *Aegean,* paused beside us to register and receive orders. By the time the *Taurus* was on its way again, we were an hour and 43 minutes behind schedule.

Northwest of Eskisehir, site of one of TCDD's largest car and locomotive shops and junction point with lines to Konya and Izmir, the route passed through a scenic setting rivaling that of the passage through the Taurus, as the rails descended from the Anatolian Plateau to the Plain of Izmit and the shore of the Sea of Marmara.

At Karakoy the route began a precipitous descent down a mountain gorge into

157

The long journey from Baghdad nearing an end, the westbound *Taurus Express* sped alongside
a mountain stream near the village of Karakoy as the train began the descent from the Anatolian
Plateau toward the Plain of Izmit and the Sea of Marmara and its final dash into Istanbul's
Haydarpasa Station.

Bilecik over ten miles of 2.5 percent grade which included 13 tunnels, two high stone arch viaducts, a long steel bridge, and a horseshoe curve. Bluish smoke and the unmistakable odor of hot brake shoes rose from the trucks as our engineer gently eased us downgrade into Bilecik, where the eastbound *Taurus* waited for us to clear the line. The customary Henschel 2-8-2 headed the eight-car train and a sturdy-looking three-cylinder 2-10-0 was cut in at the rear to help the train up to Karakoy. Three shrill blasts from the lead engine were answered from the helper, and the eastbound *Taurus* roared out of town under a thick canopy of black smoke.

The "Gray Wolf" had gradually been regaining some of its lost time, and by cutting short the scheduled stop at Bilecik we departed only 55 minutes behind time. North of Bilecik the train wound through the towering cliffs of a narrow gorge, and then joined the Sakarya River to follow it down a lovely valley through the Geyve Gates. Red peppers hung out to dry added a dash of color to the trackside villages. Women squatted beside the track as they shelled dried beans. Near one village misfortune struck for a shepherd as the locomotive sliced through the center of a flock of sheep that bolted blindly across the rails in the path of the train.

At Arifye, where the route turned to the west again, we waited briefly for the arrival of a Sivas train eastbound behind a Czech 2-10-0. Two more identical Decapods waited in sidings with freight trains. Sunset tinted low-hanging clouds with soft purple and orange, and a bluish mist hung over the hills and water as the *Taurus* sped along the south shore of Lake Saponca, a long freshwater lake east of Izmit. Arrival at my Izmit destination was just 42 minutes late. After a very brief stop, the "Gray Wolf" accelerated smartly out of the station, giving every indication that a little more time would be made up during the remaining 55 miles into Haydarpasa.

The Journey Today

The *Taurus Express* still operates today, but Middle Eastern conflict has largely derailed the train's once prestigious international character. Now restored to its original, shorter route via Konya, the train operates three times weekly between Haydarpasa and Gaziantep, near the Turkish-Syrian border. A restaurant car and sleeping cars, now operated by TCDD rather than the Wagons-Lits company, operate between Haydarpasa and Gaziantep. What international service that remains is provided by through coaches operating between Haydarpasa and Aleppo (Halab), Syria, via a connecting train from Fevzipasa. Unfortunately, the train makes the spectacular crossing of its namesake Taurus Mountains at night in either direction.

All Aboard for *Ankara**

Until 1923 Ankara wasn't much more than a minor city lost in the arid reaches of the Anatolian plateau of Asian Turkey. Then Mustafa Kemal Ataturk, the great Turkish leader who created a vigorous new republic from the post–World War I shambles of the once-mighty Ottoman Empire, chose Ankara as the capital city of the New Turkey. In the several decades of the city's new eminence, the procession of government bureaus, banks, business firms, industries, and other enterprises that followed the seat of government to Ankara had transformed it into Turkey's second largest city.

But if Istanbul, the former Constantinople, which served for almost 16 centuries as the capital, in turn, of the Byzantine Empire and the Ottoman sultans, was no longer the political center of Turkey, it remained supreme as the nation's largest city, principal seaport, commercial and industrial center, and the favorite city of 24 million Turks. It followed that Turks traveled often between the two cities.

In 1961 there were several ways that this multitude could cover the 220-odd airline miles between Istanbul and Ankara. The fastest, of course, was to fly. The Turkish Airlines (THY) would take you between the two cities in just a shade over an hour by jet-prop airliner for the equivalent of $19.44. For travelers not quite so rushed, THY offered DC-3 service, which took a half hour longer and cost $2.77 less.

Thanks to liberal U.S. aid to Turkey's highway program, the second fastest way between Istanbul and Ankara was by bus. For those with limited travel budgets and steady nerves, Pullman, Jet, Rocket, or any of several other free-wheeling bus operators who competed fiercely for the traffic would barrel you over the 281 miles of asphalt between the two cities in 8 hours or less for just $3.88.

We, of course, were going to take the train.

By Turkish State Railways (TCDD) the journey was all of 357 miles long; and the running time varied anywhere from 8 hours 50 minutes on the fast daytime *Bosporus* diesel rail car service to better than 19 hours aboard a plug local. The spread in fares was equally great, ranging upward from the equivalent of $3.35 for a third-class coach seat on local trains to a top of $15.87 for first-class sleeping-car accommodations.

Easily the most elegant of the several daily trains scheduled between Istanbul and Ankara was the *Ankara Express,* one of two expresses operating in overnight service. Even though it could hardly equal the renown of such celebrated Turkish name trains as the Istanbul-Baghdad *Taurus Express* or the Paris-Istanbul *Simplon-Orient Express,* the train nonetheless could claim a certain distinction. For while

---

*© 1961 Kalmbach Publishing Co., reprinted with permission from the December 1961 issue of *Trains* magazine.

Railway journeys into Asian Turkey from Istanbul began
with a steamer crossing of the Bosporus to the
neoclassic splendor of Haydarpasa Station on the Asian
shore. Inside, great stained glass windows and ornately
decorated high, arched ceilings gave the terminal an
air of solemn grandeur.

the *Taurus* included ordinary coaches in its consist and the *Simplon-Orient*, within Turkey at least, was no more than a few through cars cut into an all-stops local to the Greek border, the *Ankara Express* boasted a solid sleeping-car consist. It was Turkey's only all-sleeper train and, for all I could find to the contrary, the only such train in all of Asia.

Patterned after the Wagons-Lits company's celebrated Calais-Mediterranean *Blue Train*, a Haydarpasa-Ankara all–sleeping car train was inaugurated on July 1, 1927. For almost two decades the train ran as the *Anatolia Express*; it was renamed the *Ankara Express* on May 1, 1946.

Scheduled for a leisurely after-breakfast arrival in Ankara, the *Express* departed from Istanbul's Haydarpasa station at 8:40 every evening. Since Haydarpasa is separated from Istanbul proper by the Bosporus, the great international waterway dividing European from Asian Turkey, a journey to Ankara began with a magnificent twilight ferry crossing to the Anatolian shore.

Galata landing, on the Golden Horn, was the starting point for the elegant white steamers that made the crossing, and it was easily among the busiest points in all Istanbul. Great crowds of pedestrians hurried back and forth across Galata Bridge, which spans the Horn at its junction with the Bosporus. Little red four-wheel trolleys crept cautiously across the

Ready to begin its overnight journey to Ankara, the all-Wagons-Lits *Ankara Express* waited for departure time on Track 3 at Istanbul's Haydarpasa Station in February 1961.

bridge through streams of trucks, buses, taxis, and horse carts, and then ground up the Pera hill through narrow cobbled streets. Passenger ferries with tall, rakish yellow stacks churned through the dense water traffic of the Bosporus with almost reckless speed, arriving and departing from the landing every few minutes, discharging and loading masses of commuters bound to and from the Istanbul suburbs that lie across the Bosporus and line both sides of the 12-mile channel all the way from the Sea of Marmara to the Black Sea. Nearby, at the Galata Quay, oceangoing liners loaded for more distant points in the Black, Aegean, and Mediterranean seas.

The 15-minute crossing to Haydarpasa was a splendid beginning to a railway journey. In North America, to my mind, it was equaled only by the now-defunct crossing of San Francisco Bay by Southern Pacific's ferries. To the north the Galata Tower topped the Pera hill, as it had for over six centuries. To the west, on the hills of the historic old Stamboul district, the domes and minarets of Saint Sofia and Sultan Ahmet Mosque—the "Blue Mosque"—were silhouetted against the evening sky. High above the Seraglio Point towered the walls of the Topkapi Palace, once the residence of the Ottoman sultans. Down close to the shore line red electric commuter trains followed high-voltage catenary into Sirkeci station, the Istanbul terminal for Turkey's European railway lines. Perched on a little island close under the high bluffs of Uskudar on the Asian shore stood the Tower of

Leander, near the point where legend has it (incorrectly, say most historians) that Leander drowned in an attempt to cross the Bosporus.

At Haydarpasa the steamer slipped in behind a long stone breakwater and tied up next to an ornate tile-faced little building, whose Oriental architecture was in rather marked contrast to the vaguely neoclassic "chateau" style of the adjacent railway terminal. Jutting out from the shore on a short mole, and bent in a U-shape around the stub-end terminal tracks, the Haydarpasa station was a towering four-story stone structure with a high-pitched roof, turreted corners, and great stained-glass windows over the entrances. It was completed in 1908, and rebuilt in 1917 after being heavily damaged in an ammunition explosion and fire.

By the time the connecting ferry steamer was in, train 6, the *Ankara Ekspresi*, was already spotted on Track 3 in the terminal. Steam still ruled in Turkey, and regular power for the train, as well as for most express passenger trains operating over the Haydarpasa-Ankara route, was one of a series of fast (top speed about 60 mph) 2-8-2 Mikados built by Henschel of Germany in 1937. Because of a need for light axle loadings and because of low schedule speeds, TCDD favored such multi-axled wheel arrangements as the 2-8-2 and the 2-10-0 Decapod for passenger service. The 2-10-0, as a matter of fact, was widely used on TCDD as a dual-service locomotive for freight and heavy passenger trains. In comparison with North American power of the same wheel arrangement, they were small locomotives. TCDD's express Mikados, for example, carried no more weight on their drivers (80 tons) than a typical U.S. light Pacific.

In appearance these Turkish 2-8-2's were striking machines. A big pair of smoke deflectors and a cab raked in above the window sills provided an appropriately dashing aspect for an express locomotive. In a few details, such as a horizontally barred pilot and a big headlight mounted high on the smokebox front, it was possible to find similarities to, say, Pennsylvania Railroad practice, but such other features as an additional pair of headlights mounted on the pilot beam, or piston rods protruding through the front of the cylinders, were purely European.

Their grooming was immaculate. The glossy black boiler jacket was bound in polished brass; running boards and running gear were lined in red; and the engine number, TCDD initials, and the Turkish star and crescent were mounted on the cab sides in brass.

Everything behind the buffers of the Mikado's modest tender was strictly a Wagons-Lits operation. The regular *Express* consist included a W-L baggage and mail car, a restaurant car, and four sleeping cars—increased to six sleepers during the winter season. The entire train was uniformly finished in the standard dark blue livery, with yellow trim, of the international sleeping car company.

The sleeping cars were all a standard Wagons-Lits 11-compartment car, built in Belgium. Their interior furnishings had a durable, ageless quality about them, not unlike that of one of Mr. Pullman's old standard open-section cars. The compartments were paneled in polished dark wood, and had heavy tufted brown upholstery and thick flowered carpeting. Second-class passengers shared occupancy of a compartment (each makes up into an upper and a lower); a first-class ticket bought single occupancy. Each sleeper rated a brown-uniformed Wagons-Lits attendant, who was required to speak one language (most knew English or French) in addition to Turkish.

As the minute hand on the big platform clock swung toward 8:40 P.M., a final announcement in rapid Turkish came over the station public address system. Someone blew a whistle, and the engineer answered with a shrill peep from the engine. A uniformed stationmaster held up a green lantern, steam jetted across the platforms from open cylinder cocks, passengers leaned from lowered windows to shout frantic last-minute farewells, and almost imperceptibly the sleepers were moving.

Among the chief delights of a journey on the *Ankara Express* was the mid-train restaurant car, which was operated by a Wagons-Lits staff. The interior of the car, built by Britain's Metropolitan Carriage, was rather ornately finished in mahogany paneling, with fanciful inlays in colored woods, and fitted with heavy bronze parcel racks and lamps. If the dignity of the interior decor was somewhat compromised by advertising placards displayed on the walls, the food was first rate.

Almost as soon as the train was underway a bell-ringing waiter passed through the sleepers to announce dinner. You *could* order from an extensive à la carte menu, but those who knew went for the table d'hôte dinner, which usually came to around 12.50 Turkish lira ($1.40) and took close to 2 hours to consume. The cuisine was more Turkish than European. A typical menu might include a thick Turkish soup, *shish kebab* (lamb, tomatoes and green peppers grilled on a skewer), French fries, a fresh vegetable, a mixed salad doused in olive oil, a Turkish *borek* (a small meat and cheese pastry fried in olive oil), fresh fruits, and a glass of heavily sugared tea or a demitasse of thick Turkish coffee. Any one of the several excellent Turkish wines stocked on the diner complemented the meal very nicely.

By the time dinner was over, No. 6 was well beyond the double-track territory that winds through the string of Istanbul suburbs along the Marmara coastline. Occasionally a suburban train, generally headed by a tank engine, slammed by on the way into Haydarpasa. The rolling stock employed in this commuter operation, incidentally, was rather interesting. Almost all of it was made up of aged four-wheel, open-platform wooden coaches. A close look at some of them revealed such intriguing details as journal box covers lettered with the initials or names of such TCDD predecessors as the Chemin de Fer Ottoman-Anatolie, or the Baghdad Bahn.

The Haydarpasa-Ankara route followed by the *Express* was one of Turkey's oldest railway lines. The first section, between Haydarpasa and suburban Pendik, was opened in 1872, and the entire route to Ankara was completed in 1892. The route was also one of the busiest on the entire Turkish system, and was receiving a number of improvements to accommodate a growing traffic. Except for double track in the Istanbul and Ankara suburban zones, the line was single track throughout. Then operated by train order, the entire route was getting U.S.-made centralized traffic control (CTC). Double-track territory was being extended in both suburban zones, and several important realignment projects were under construction. New, heavier rail was going in over the entire route in preparation for Turkey's first full dieselization. A recent U.S. loan would buy 32 U.S.-made export road-switchers—enough to convert over half of the traffic on the route.

Clear of the suburbs, the line went to single track, curved past the tumbled ruins of a castle once occupied by Hannibal, then dropped down to water's edge to follow the orchards, vineyards, olive groves, and charming villages of the Marmara coast into Izmit. Full enjoyment of this splendid scenery must wait for a westbound trip on the *Express*, which negotiated the Marmara coast line during daylight hours.

Izmit was reached at 10:45 P.M., the *Express* paused momentarily at the station for a few passengers, then the 2-8-2 gathered speed on tree-lined boulevard trackage that sliced through the heart of the city. Ignoring the thundering passage of the train, a few late customers sipped sugared tea in brightly lighted teahouses along the nearly deserted main street. Izmit, a thriving provincial capital and the center of a booming industrial area at the eastern end of the Marmara Sea, had a history even older than that of Istanbul. As the ancient Nicomedia, it was once the capital of the Roman Empire under the Emperor Diocletian.

East of Izmit the rails flowed through a low valley between high hills and mountains, skirted the south shore of a long freshwater lake, then abruptly plunged south through the Geyve Gates to the narrow Sakarya River Valley to begin a long climb to the Anatolian plateau. The slope was gentle at first. Then at Bilecik, where chunky 2-10-2 tank engine helpers waited for tonnage traffic, the 2-8-2 went to work in earnest.

By daylight the journey through the Sakarya Valley and up the winding grade above Bilecik was spectacular, but I'll always remember it best the way it looked at 2 A.M. one February night the first time I rode the *Express* to Ankara. The mountains were covered by a fresh white snowfall and illuminated by a full moon. I lowered the compartment window and contemplated the sight and sound of the 2-8-2 up ahead as it pounded steadily upward through almost continuous curvature, occasionally spanning a deep ravine on high stone arches, or slamming into a short tunnel. The sharp bark of the exhaust was softened by the blanket of fresh snow, and now and then the canopy of steam and smoke that drifted lazily back from the engine reflected a flaming orange as a sweating fireman hurled soft coal into the firebox.

Dawn found No. 6 rolling steadily eastward across the Anatolian plateau to Ankara. It was a wide-open, bare terrain that had as many aspects as there are seasons: I found it strikingly similar to the UP's Wyoming or Utah countryside. By winter it was a rolling, snow-covered prairie, stretching almost endlessly in every direction under a cloudless sky, and hardly broken by as much as a single tree. In the spring the fresh green of new crops pushing through the reddish soil alternated with fields of vivid wildflowers. By midsummer the hills were dry and dusty, and peasants worked under a hot sun in the grain fields, tediously harvesting and threshing their crops by hand. Cattle and sheep grazed in the meadows, and now and then you could see a gypsy tent camp alongside a little stream. At the country stations big grain elevators lined the sidings, and after the late summer harvest laborers shoveled sugar beets into four-wheel gondolas.

Breakfast in the restaurant car was typically Turkish. The usual "complete tea" breakfast included a big pot of tea, toasted slabs of Turkish bread, a sort of pound cake, butter and marmalade, and a big slice of *beyaz peynir*, a soft, salty white cheese made from goat's milk. For those accustomed to more substantial fare, fresh fruits and other extras were available.

Briefly the rails rejoined the Sakarya River, left behind the night before dur-

"Yet there isn't a train
I wouldn't take"

Early on a September morning in 1960, and little more than an hour away from its Istanbul terminal, the westbound *Ankara Express* steamed past the ruins of Hannibal's Castle on the shore of the Sea of Marmara near Gebze.

ing the long climb to the plateau, to follow the stream through a narrow rocky canyon. Near the little station of Yassihoyuk was the site of ancient Gordium, where Alexander the Great cut the famous Gordian knot; legend held that whoever separated it would rule all Asia.

At Sincan, while the *Express* waited in a siding, small children scrambled up and down beside the cars shouting for old newspapers, which were much in demand in news-starved rural areas. Westbound from Ankara, a three-car diesel-hydraulic trainset slipped by on the main line on its daily journey as the Ankara-Haydarpasa *Bosporus*. Running MU with it was an identical trainset, which operated five days a week as the Ankara-Izmit *Aegean*. The two trains would diverge to their separate routes at the big junction point of Eskisehir.

Pull wires twanged, the long-armed German-style semaphore swung up to the clear position, and the Mikado glided through switch points to resume the main line. On an adjacent siding a light Lima (1942) 2-8-2 waited to follow the *Express* into Ankara with a train of center-door suburban cars.

East of Guvercin the *Express* was on suburban double track. Powered by a 2-8-2 identical to ours, the *Taurus Express* rolled west out of Ankara on the last leg of its long journey from Baghdad to the Bosporus.

Flat, spread-out factory buildings began to appear beside the tracks. Monotonous developments of identical houses extended in precise rows across the dry plain. Except for the red tile roofs and the stuccoed walls characteristic of Turkey, suburban Ankara could have been suburban Anywhere.

Closer in to the city, tall modern apartment buildings became frequent. The rails dove under a big superhighway bridge. A long suburban train, preceded by a tender-first U.S. Mike, scurried by on the westbound main.

On time at 9:10 A.M., the sleepers jolted through special work, slipped by the large state railways headquarters building, and ground to a stop under the big train shed of the modern Ankara terminal. Luggage was passed through lowered windows to waiting porters, tips were pressed into the hand of the Wagons-Lits attendant, and we joined the crowd headed for the cab stand.

The Journey Today

Still an all–sleeping car train, the *Ankara Express* continues to offer a premier overnight service between Haydarpasa and Ankara. The Wagons-Lits company is gone from Turkey, and the train's sleeping and restaurant car services are now operated directly by TCDD. With the completion of electrification over the entire route in the early 1990s, the train is now much faster than it was in 1961. The *Ankara Express* now takes just 9 hours 5 minutes for a 352-mile journey that took 12 hours 30 minutes 40 years ago.

168

In addition to sleeping car passengers, the *Ankara Express* transported urgent mail that rode in a postal car just behind the locomotive. Baggage men unloaded the mail car soon after the train's arrival in Ankara on a November morning in 1960.

China by *Rail**

Perhaps nowhere outside of the Western Hemisphere is there so American a railroad system as there is in China.

In their physical details, the Chinese railroads have an air of familiarity that is owed in large part to an American heritage. The trains of China share with their North American counterparts such standards as rails laid to standard gauge (4 feet, 8½ inches), Association of American Railroads–pattern automatic couplers, and Westinghouse air brakes. But although the appearance of Chinese motive power and rolling stock is strikingly North American, the American visitor finds himself in a curious time warp, for the Chinese railroad scene is like that of America 40 years ago.

Ubiquitous Chinese steam locomotives look as if they could have rolled out of the erecting halls of Schenectady or Eddystone in the 1920s or 1930s (as, indeed, a few of them did). Except for their shovel noses, the big Dongfeng 3 ("East Wind 3") diesels that head so many of China's long-haul passenger trains have the appearance of early Fairbanks-Morse passenger units, a circumstance not just coincidental. The standard double-truck Chinese box car rolls on three-piece cast steel trucks that could be straight out of an AAR standards book, and the typical Chinese passenger car, like the Soviet design from which it was derived, is a remarkable lookalike to our own late 1930s rib-sided, West Milwaukee–built *Hiawatha* coaches.

BY RAIL TO THE GREAT WALL

Occupying a special place among early Chinese railways was the 125-mile Peking-Kalgan (Beijing-Zhangjiakou) railway, which was distinguished both as the first important line designed and built entirely by Chinese and by its construction through the difficult terrain of Nankou Pass northwest of Beijing on the way to Mongolia. Unlikely as it seems, the chief engineer for the Peking-Kalgan line, Zhan Tianyou, was a Yale University graduate. Sent to the United States as a young man to study, Zhan graduated from Yale in 1883 and then spent several years in an English technical school before returning to China to work under British engineer C. W. Kinder on the Imperial Railways of North China.

Zhan, chosen to build the new line, began surveys in the summer of 1905, and construction started a few months later. The first 34 miles of line to Nankou went relatively easily across the plain around the capital, but beyond Nankou the

---

*Portions of this article © 1986 Kalmbach Publishing Co., reprinted with permission from the October and November 1986 issues of *Trains* magazine.

Railway journeys from Beijing begin from this great central station. Crowds waited for train time on the square in front of the station in April 1983.

railroad builders faced much more formidable terrain as they followed the old Imperial North Road and a river through the 13-mile Nankou Pass. In less than 12 miles the line climbed 1641 feet on an average gradient of 2.5 percent, with maximum grades of over 3 percent. Great stone-faced embankments were required to protect the track from the waters of the fast-running river, and four tunnels totaling more than a mile in length had to be drilled. Even with 3.5 percent gradients, Zhan was able to attain the summit only with the aid of a great switchback near the top and a 3580-foot tunnel that burrows 200 feet below the Great Wall of China, which stretches along the mountain peaks at Badaling ("Eight Directions View").

I was able to see Zhan Tianyou's Nankou Pass handiwork first-hand aboard one of the special sightseeing trains that carry tourists from Beijing Station to Badaling for the Great Wall visit that is an obligatory part of any China tour. The line originally operated with formidable North British 0-6 + 6-0 Mallets and later acquired Alco 2-8 + 8-2's. Steam still operated across the Pass when I went there in 1981, but the tourist express was double-headed by a big six-axle, 5400-hp German (Henschel) diesel-hydraulic and a home-built 2700-hp Beijing-class B-B diesel-hydraulic passenger unit.

On a snowy November morning in 1981 a tourist express has just arrived at Badaling ("Eight Directions View"), where its passengers disembark for the obligatory visit to the Great Wall. Locomotive No. 3080 was a Chinese-built Beijing class diesel-hydraulic.

While we sipped tea from the big, lidded glasses that are a standard fixture of Chinese train travel, the two diesels labored up to the Great Wall through a mountain terrain lightly sprinkled with an early snowfall. At the Qinglongqiao ("Green Dragon") station, we paused briefly while one of the diesels ran around the train to head the consist backwards up the switchback to Badaling. From atop a stone pedestal in the station courtyard, a bronze figure of Zhan Tianyou, hand in pocket in a cutaway coat, surveyed the passing trains with seeming satisfaction. The diesels then urged the long train of dark green cars upward to Badaling and our hike along the battlements of the Great Wall.

LOCOMOTIVES FOR SALE

Despite the growing ranks of diesel locomotives rolling out of plants at Beijing, Dalian, Qingdao, and Shenyang, steam locomotives remained the principal motive power for the Chinese rail system, and in 1983 standardized Chinese designs continued to emerge from erecting halls at Datong and Tangshan.

The most popular of these standard units, and by far the largest class of steam power still operating in China, were the QJ, for Qianjin ("Forward") class 2-10-2; more than 4000 of them had been built since 1957. The QJ was based upon the Soviet LV-class 2-10-2 developed in the early 1950s, and—by American standards—was relatively small for a Santa Fe. With an engine weight of a little over

293,000 pounds and at a rating of 2980 hp at the wheel rim, the QJ was roughly equivalent in size and capacity to a typical U.S. Mikado. It was a straightforward, unsophisticated design, but came with such modern steam-power amenities as a welded boiler and frame, 59-inch Box-pok-like drivers, a Delta trailing truck, a mechanical stoker, pneumatic ash shakers, centralized mechanical lubrication systems, and air horns. Coal pushers were provided, according to the Chinese catalog for the QJ, only "at the request of customers." All-welded tenders were supplied in eight-wheel and twelve-wheel versions, with roller bearings.

Recent Chinese steam power production had been confined to the QJ and JS Jianshe ("Construction") class Mikado, which combined a Russian type boiler with a running-gear design derived from 1918 Alco 2-8-2's built for the South Manchuria Railway. Production of the QJ was concentrated at the Datong Locomotive Works in northern Shanxi Province, while the JS 2-8-2s were built at Tangshan.

Datong thus was that rarity in the world—a plant devoted to steam-locomotive production—and our visit there in 1983 was like a journey a generation back in time. Datong built a complete locomotive from basic materials, and we were led through a series of cavernous buildings where raw steel was being cast, welded, cut, and forged to form wheels, axles, frames, boilers, and fireboxes for QJ 2-10-2's. In a dim erecting hall, rows of the big Santa Fe's took shape as overhead cranes lowered boilers and cabs into place on completed frames. Outside, proud workmen opened the doors of a nearby engine shed, and a glossy new QJ rolled out into the sunlight. We marveled at the sight of a 1983 builder's plate on steam and then climbed into the cab for a test ride in a brand new 1983 QJ 2-10-2.

A proud fireman leaned out of the cab of QJ class 2-10-2 No. 6482 at the Datong plant in April 1983. The shiny, brand-new locomotive had just been rolled out for its first test run.

The February 7th plant at Beijing that we visited in 1981 was what the Chinese called a closed plant, manufacturing virtually every component of the diesel locomotives it built (the February 7th name commemorated a 1923 strike by Communist railway workers at Zhengzhou). We wandered through a sprawling series of machine shops, foundries, and erecting bays with our Chinese hosts, watching workers at a varied collection of European, Russian, and Chinese machines, new and old, produce the components that came together as a locomotive.

The Beijing class diesel built at the plant was a compact (54-foot) B-B unit powered by a single four-stroke V-12 engine that drove the unit through a hydraulic torque converter transmission and cardan shaft drive linked to all four axles through gear boxes. Designed exclusively for passenger service, the 2700-hp, 75-mph Beijing might be called China's F40PH. It comes in a rounded, double-end, box-cab carbody of vaguely European appearance. Chrome-plated Chinese char-

Inside the cavernous plant of the February 7th Diesel
Locomotive & Rolling Stock Repair Factory at Beijing,
a Beijing class diesel-hydraulic locomotive neared
completion in November 1981.

In the machine shop of the February 7th plant, a
machinist fashioned parts for a diesel locomotive.

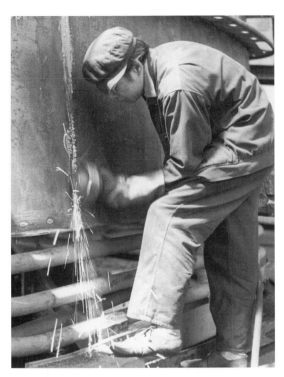

A worker at the Zhuzhou plant ground down welds on the front end of a Shaoshan 3 class electric locomotive.

China's electric locomotives came from this big Zhuzhou Electric Locomotive Plant in Hunan Province. Workers put finishing touches on Shaoshan 3 class electrics in April 1983.

acters for the class name ("North Capital") and a stylized rendering of Beijing's Tiananmen ("Gate of Heavenly Peace") decorated each end. Available colors seemed to be a sort of khaki or light blue, with red running gear. Very classy.

As we sipped a last glass of tea at the end of the visit, our hosts distributed copies of a glossy all-color folder offering the Beijing for export. ("We would like to serve for you!" concluded its sales pitch.)

"How much?" we asked.

"The government decides."

Electrification, too, was expanding rapidly on the Chinese rail system. Two batches of imported Alsthom electrics built in France powered China's earliest mainline electrification, which began operating over the Qinling Mountains into Sichuan in 1961, but since then, the Chinese had largely been turning out their own mainline electrics. Based on a prototype completed in 1958, the Shaoshan 1 class electric locomotive had been in series production since 1969 (the name, "Shao Mountain," commemorated the Hunan Province birthplace of Chairman Mao).

We visited the big Tianxin locomotive plant in Zhuzhou, Hunan, to watch brand new SS1 locomotives taking shape on the erecting floor and older units cycling through the plant for periodic overhauls. The Shaoshan 1 is a big, blunt-faced box-cab unit that looks like the heavy-duty mountain hauler it is. Powered by six 700-kw traction motors, the 152-ton, C-C SS1 develops a 5700-hp, 743,000-pound traction force hourly rating. Silicon rectifiers supply the DC traction current, and big banks of roof-mounted dynamic brake grids provide the braking capacity needed for mountain tonnage.

By the beginning of 1984, the Tianxin plant had delivered close to 400 of the Shaoshan 1 electrics, and production had reached a level of about 100 locomotives annually. By 1984, production was shifting to the even larger Shaoshan 3, a 6539-hp, C-C unit that had been in prototype test operation since 1979. And even as the Shaoshan 3 was moving into series production, engineers at the Zhuzhou plant were beginning development of an even more powerful Shaoshan 4 prototype, an eight-axle unit capable of developing around 8800 hp.

JOURNEY TO THE YALU

The main railway station at Shenyang, in Liaoning Province, stood at the edge of a broad station square that was teeming with pedestrian and bicycle traffic. On this warm July morning in 1985 it was the starting point for a journey from the one-time capital of Manchuria, now known simply as North-East China, south to the very edge of reclusive North Korea. Our destination was Dandong ("Red East"), a booming provincial city on the north bank of the Yalu River opposite the North Korean city of Sinuiju.

The handsome Shenyang station was a reminder of the early twentieth century, when the city, then known as Mukden, was the hub of the Japanese-controlled South Manchuria railway system. Built of red brick and stone in a classical architectural style, with a massive domed rotunda at the center, the building was typical of Japanese colonial architecture of the time. The Shenyang-Dandong

Kuai Che ("Fast Express") waiting on Track 1 was made up of a boxy Chinese-built Dongfanghong 3 ("East Is Red 3") diesel locomotive and a long string of the Russian-patterned olive green coaches that are a ubiquitous feature of the Chinese rail system.

The rail line that we would follow had an interesting history. Built as a Japanese military railway during the 1904–1905 Russo-Japanese war, the line later became part of a through route between Japan and Europe, linking steamship services between Japan and the southern tip of the Korean peninsula with the Trans-Siberian railway. The line had been cut at the demarcation line between North and South Korea since the Korean War, but international through trains still operated over a part of the route several times a week between Beijing and the North Korean capital at Pyongyang.

Our five-and-a-half-hour, 170-mile journey south across Liaoning Province to the Yalu began in a lush landscape of rice paddies and fertile fields. Neat little houses of red brick or stucco, with tiled roofs, dotted the countryside. Soon the train began climbing gradually into forested mountains, thundering through tunnels and then soaring on high bridges over deep valleys, where full, brown rivers meandered toward the sea.

An hour and a half into our journey we made a long stop at Benxi, a furiously busy industrial city of iron, steel and cement works. A smiling dining car staff leaned out a window to have their picture taken, and a young woman held up her baby, all dressed up in red, yellow and blue, for a photograph. But Benxi's factories belch out enough smoke and gases to make it one of the most polluted cities on earth, and we were happy soon to be on our way again.

It was time for lunch, and we headed for the train's dining car, a handsome vehicle paneled in wood with lace curtains at the windows. We took a seat and the white-jacketed staff served an excellent lunch of rice, soup, shrimp with scrambled eggs, and fish with cucumbers, accompanied by an over-

A journey to the Yalu River began from Shenyang, where this handsome, erstwhile South Manchurian Railway station was a reminder of Manchuria's era of Japanese control early in the century.

sized bottle of China's popular Tsingtao beer. Racks on each table displayed bottles of Great Wall wine and Chinese Riesling for sale. Eschewing these offerings, a man at an adjoining table drank heavily from a bottle of fiery maotai white liquor in his handbag. Another lunch patron enjoyed a large bowl of noodle soup in the Oriental manner, slurping it noisily and then all but disappearing into the bowl as he tipped it up to savor the last few drops.

We thought the brass band that waited on the Dandong station platform was a bit much, but soon learned it was there to greet, not us, but a "sister city" delega-

Benxi, in Liaoning Province, was a busy station stop for Shenyang-Dandong
Kuai Che ("Fast Express") train 321 in July 1985.

Waitresses from the dining car staff leaned out to view the activity during
Kuai Che train 321's stop at Benxi.

This bombed out railway bridge across the Yalu River between China and North Korea remains as a reminder of the bitter war in Korea more than four decades ago. Trains now cross the newer bridge to the right.

tion arriving from Eastern Europe. The much smaller group that was there to meet us swept up our luggage and carried us off through the city's broad, tree-shaded streets to comfortable accommodations in the Dandong Guest-house.

The next morning our hosts announced that we would go for a cruise on the Yalu River. The starting point for the trip was a dock in the Yalu River Park, where we joined a crowd of Chinese tourists aboard a handsome white launch and were seated under a striped awning

Against a backdrop of the Phoenix Mountains of the Korean Peninsula, fast express 298 slowed for a station stop at Fenghuangchen on its way from Dandong to Shenyang. An "East Is Red 3" diesel locomotive headed the train.

on the upper deck. The Bach *Mass in B Minor* was playing loudly over a public address system as we pulled away from the pier.

The big white boat cruised slowly down the river, passing under two bridges that were reminders of the bitter Korean War of the 1950s. One was only the rusting, bombed-out remains of the railroad bridge that had once linked the railroad systems of China and Korea. American warplanes had destroyed it after People's Army "volunteers" came streaming across the Yalu to join the North Korean forces against the United Nations armies in 1950. Just upstream from this remnant of that conflict, a shiny steam engine shunted slowly across the new bridge that had taken its place, interchanging freight cars between the two countries.

THE CHENGDU-KUNMING RAILWAY

One of the proudest accomplishments of post-revolutionary China's years of railroad construction is an extraordinary line completed in 1970 across the Sichuan-Yunnan Plateau and the rugged mountains of the Liangshan range between Chengdu and Kunming, the capital cities of Sichuan and Yunnan provinces. Beginning at an elevation of 1837 feet at Chengdu, the 675-mile line climbs to 6890 feet at its highest point, and 40 percent of its length consists of tunnels or bridges. Foreign railroad engineers, say the Chinese, called the route a "forbidden zone" for railroad construction, and it was conquered only by the most extraordinary effort over 12 years of work.

Our Chinese hosts in Beijing introduced us to this remarkable railway with a film of its construction. If the propaganda was on the heavy-handed side ("the Chinese people, armed with Marxism, Leninism, and Mao Zedong thought, can overcome all difficulties"), the real message of the film was in its portrayal of the successful completion of an exceptionally difficult construction task.

A geography of lofty mountains, deep ravines, and swift rivers offered difficulties enough, but the builders also faced such geologic complexities as karst caves, underground rivers, gas pockets, silt and salt deposits, and faults. Drifting sand, mud and rock slides, and magmatic explosions were among the obstacles, and one-third of the line was located in a zone where frequent earthquakes registering 7 or greater on the Richter scale occur. In the 20,930-foot Shamulada Tunnel, the line's longest, builders discovered an underground river that dumped 12,000 tons of water a day into the bore. Weather conditions were often extreme; in another tunnel, along the Jinsha River, tunnelers encountered hard rock at temperatures of over 100 degrees. At many points, winds of Beaufort Scale force 10 (55 to 63 mph) or greater were common.

In the end, the Chengdu-Kunming railway builders had bored more than 200 miles of tunnels, and built 653 bridges of stone, steel, and concrete.

Armed with this background, I approached a 1981 journey over this remarkable railroad with understandable anticipation. The 24-hour journey aboard Chengdu-Kunming express No. 289 began with deceptive ease, as the long train rolled south across fertile plains under what seemed to be a perpetually overcast Sichuan sky ("dogs bark when the sun comes out," according to an old Sichuan

A pair of China's big "East Wind 3" diesel-electric locomotives headed southbound express train 289 into the mountains of southern Sichuan Province on the Chengdu-Kunming railway.

saying). But it was soon evident why two of the big East Wind 3 diesels headed our 15-car train. Fertile plains gave way to hills, and then the diesels began climbing in earnest as we followed the deep valley of the Dadu River upward into the mountains.

For hour after hour the train twisted and turned through a succession of tunnels, deep gorges, and high bridges, past little houses of crude brick or mud,

181

"Yet there isn't a train
I wouldn't take"

It was late afternoon and shadows were lengthening as train 289 followed the Chengdu-Kunming railway into the mountains of southern Sichuan in November 1981.

A cheerful dining car waitress served passengers on express train 289 during its journey of 675 miles and 24 hours over the Chengdu-Kunming railway.

The institution of the Railway Post Office car still flourishes in China. This was the postal clerk on the Chengdu-Kunming R.P.O. car on express 289.

roofed with rough shakes or thatch, and terraced rice paddies that clung to the steep mountain slopes wherever a toehold was available. At small mountain towns, for which the railroad provides the only link to the outside world, crowds of passengers boarded or alighted from the dark green coaches, and mail bags were exchanged at the door of a Chinese Railway Post Office car just ahead of our sleeper in the train. At one station, farmers had appropriated the station platform to spread crops of red pepper and grain for drying. At the high plateau town of Puxiong—the highest station on the line—colorfully dressed Yi people, one of the many Chinese national minorities, gathered along the platform to watch the activity of No. 289's servicing stop.

Fighting for elevation, the line crossed and recrossed itself. At one point a series of spectacular spiral tunnels carried the track to three successively higher points. At Xin Liang, the line descended into a valley on a series of steeply sloped horseshoe curves, changing direction twice in semicircular tunnels.

As the day ended, the train ran through high valleys, the mountains to the west brightly silhouetted by the setting sun. Later, a full moon came up from the east, the lights of little towns twinkled in the valleys, and I finally drifted off to sleep, only dimly conscious of the changing background sound as the train ran through tunnel after tunnel, and climbed or descended what seemed to be countless grades.

At dawn we were far into Yunnan, passing through an ever-changing countryside of pine and eucalyptus forests, rice paddies, and cultivated fields, against a backdrop of hills and mountains on all sides. The dining car crew served up a breakfast of eggs, French toast, sweet cakes, and coffee. Soon the train slipped past the broad expense of Dian Chi, the great lake to the southwest of Kunming, and then braked to a stop in the city's busy station, where loudspeakers broadcast a welcome of atonal Chinese music. Our journey over China's remarkable new railroad had come to an end.

THE NARROW GAUGE TO VIETNAM

At Kunming, we got a look at an interesting meter-gauge vestige of French colonial days in Southeast Asia. China's narrow gauge to Vietnam goes back almost to the turn of the century, when the French built the Yunnan & Indochina Railway to gain access to the rich trade of Central China. The railway never amounted to much as an international trade route, and the trains didn't run to Vietnam anymore, but the little railway still carried a busy traffic across the plateau of southern Yunnan Province.

The idea of a railway from the South China Sea into the heart of Yunnan goes back at least as far as 1885, when the French gained possession of Tonkin, the northern part of what became known as French Indochina, primarily for the foothold it gave them on the way to Yunnan. Construction of the railway began before the end of the century. The first 240-mile section, extending from the port of Haiphong up the valley of the Red River through Hanoi to the Chinese border at Lao Cai, was a relatively easy task. The remaining 200 miles to Kunming (then Yunnan-fu) was a much more difficult proposition. First, the French had to extract a concession for the line from the reluctant Chinese. That finally in hand, they then faced the formidable task of constructing their railway through

Ready to set out from Kunming over the meter-gauge railway to Vietnam, diminutive "East Is Red 21" class diesel-hydraulic locomotive No. 013 headed a special train for Yiliang in November 1981. The well-polished locomotive carried special red flag emblems designating a model crew.

the rugged mountains and deep gorges that lay between the Red River and the Yunnan plateau. Over much of a section of more than 50 miles, ruling grades of 2.5 percent and curves of more than 17 degrees were required. Rock slides, washouts, an inhospitable climate, and labor problems plagued the work, and not until 1910 did the builders finally reach their goal at Kunming.

Operation of the railway continued under French control until 1943, the Chinese told us. But aside from the meter gauge that was the standard for French Indochina, little remained to mark the railway's French origins. Motive power and rolling stock were now all Chinese-built, and only in the distinctive forms of the French colonial architecture of an occasional lineside building did the railway reveal its past.

At the North Kunming station for the narrow gauge, the Chinese had ordered up a mixed extra south for our party. At the head end was one of the Dongfanghong 21 ("East Is Red 21") class B-B diesel-hydraulics that replaced all steam power on the meter-gauge line in 1979. The Qingdao locomotive works built 42 of the 1150-hp units for the line. Our locomotive—No. 013—carried special red flag emblems for a model crew. A visit to the cab revealed a Chinese version of the

185

"Yet there isn't a train
I wouldn't take"

Near Sanhacun, in Yunnan Province, passengers on the meter-gauge line to Vietnam looked down from a high escarpment for this splendid view of Gao Shan Ho ("High Mountain Lake").

The uniform of the well-attired engineman on the narrow-gauge train to Yiliang was complete even to white gloves. A hotplate for the teapot and a vase of plastic flowers on the dash added a homey touch to the locomotive.

comfort cab, with a vase of plastic flowers mounted on the dash next to the speedometer and a built-in electric hot plate for the inevitable teapot.

At the rear of the train were three lace-curtained sleeping cars that were diminutive versions of their standard-gauge counterparts, complete even to the *Hiawatha*-like ribbed sides. The cars had been built in 1975 for Kunming-Hanoi through service, the Chinese told us, but hadn't run beyond the Vietnamese frontier since 1979. That was when the Vietnamese destroyed the bridge at the border in the brief war between the two countries, and international traffic had been cut off ever since.

Four freight cars, added to the train to take advantage of the special run, were cut in between the sleepers and the diesel.

Shortly after 9 A.M., the little East Is Red unit urged the train into motion to begin a 2½-hour, 41-mile journey that would take us to Yiliang, the site of the meter-gauge line's principal engine terminal. It was a pleasant trip through a prosperous looking semi-tropical countryside of carefully tended fields, rice paddies, bamboo groves, and orchards. Precise rows of eucalyptus trees frequently lined the track.

Despite meter gauge, single track, and a closed border, China's railway to Vietnam carried an impressive traffic. The track was heavy and well-ballasted, and there was a steady flow of northbound freight and passenger trains in sidings along the way. Annual traffic over the 260-mile line, the Chinese told us, amounted to 650 million ton-miles, more than 20 times the traffic volume at the time the French relinquished operation of the line.

Near Sanhacun station, the rails climbed upward over the range of bare hills, and then emerged on the edge of a high escarpment overlooking a splendid mountain lake named Gao Shan Ho ("High Mountain Lake"). Then the track plunged downgrade on a twisting, turning run of 2.5 percent grades and 35-degree minimum curves. We met double-headed diesels struggling upgrade with a northbound freight and noted occasional runaway tracks in case things got out of hand on the 2.5 percent descending.

The long descent was followed by a few miles of easy running through a verdant countryside, and then our mixed train south plunged into a deep gorge where the line vaulted from one side to another on high stone arches. I counted 17 tunnels in quick succession and looked down on little mountain villages deep in the gorge. Finally, the train emerged into a broad valley and rolled to a stop at the Yiliang station. In a spontaneous display of friendship, crowds of smiling Chinese applauded their foreign visitors as we descended from the dark green sleepers to the platform.

THE SHANGHAI SPECIAL EXPRESS

The long journey eastward began, curiously enough, to the rousing strains of Strauss waltzes blaring from loudspeakers on the Kunming station platform. Promptly at 4:40 P.M., twin Dongfeng 3 diesels urged the long train of dark green cars into motion; train No. 80—the Kunming-Shanghai *Te Kuai* ("Special Express")—was soon rolling along through the semitropical countryside of Yunnan Province in the warm sunshine of a late autumn afternoon.

All through the night and all the following day the big diesels droned eastward across Yunnan and Guizhou provinces, their high-pitched air horns wailing now and then for rural road crossings. It was a long journey across an alien land. In the neighboring "hard class" sleepers, Chinese in baggy khaki or blue jackets, and

During a long servicing stop at Mawei, in Guizhou Province, train 80, the Kunming-Shanghai Special Express, stood amidst the curious, humped mountains that characterize much of southern China.

trousers of uniform cut, reclined impassively in narrow, three-tiered bunks, sipping tea from big lidded cups. Recorded music played relentlessly from the train's loudspeaker system. For hour after hour, the express twisted and turned through a strange, mountainous countryside of great limestone formations, worn down by time, and then the terrain gradually changed to one with the curious, humped mountains of Chinese landscape paintings. Villages consisting variously of half-timbered structures with slate roofs, or mud huts roofed in tile or thatch, were huddled in the occasional mountain valleys.

Dinner in the diner, seldom a gourmet experience on Chinese trains, was exceptional—the best of our entire journey. The dining car crew emerged from the kitchen to bring a seemingly endless succession of courses—soup, pork dishes, chicken dishes, fish dishes, vegetable dishes, and rice, accompanied by big bottles of Chinese beer. The chef, a plump young man of jovial mien, was brought out for a round of applause.

For all the unfamiliarity of our fellow passengers and the strangeness of the geography on the train's two-and-a-half-day journey east toward Shanghai, there was a sense of familiarity to the trip. In our sense of isolation from the world beyond, like passengers on an ocean liner steaming for endless hours across a great sea, we were on very much a North American kind of railroad voyage, spanning great distances in what seemed to be a vast and endless land. It seemed an interesting coincidence, perhaps, that the land area of China (3.7 million square miles) was almost identical to that of the United States.

We left the train at Guilin, in Guangxi Province, to experience the celebrated boat trip through the incomparable scenery of the Li River. The big FD class 2-10-2's we observed hammering through the station with long freight trains had an interesting background. As American-looking a locomotive as I had ever seen, they were actually Russian in origin. First built in 1931, they appeared to have been closely patterned after two batches of modern steam power acquired the year before from Baldwin and Alco in the U.S. In the USSR the class was named for Felix Dzerzhinski, an early Bolshevik revolutionary and founder of the Soviet secret police, but they became known as the "Friendship" class when more than a thousand of them were sold to China in the late 1950s. By late 1981 these aging locomotives were running out their last miles on the Chinese system, but large numbers of them were still active on this east-west main line between Kunming and Shanghai across the south of China.

The next day at the Guilin Bei ("Guilin East") station we discovered a genuine American-built locomotive hard at work on switching duties. This was an elderly 2-8-2 Mikado that carried a November 1937 builder's plate from the Alco works at Schenectady, New York. Despite its age, the engine was well kept and polished, and it carried a red flag badge, signifying a model crew, on each side of the cab.

INTERNATIONAL TRAIN DELUXE

I returned to the West aboard what must easily have been China's classiest train.

The 107-mile rail route between Guangzhou (Canton) and Hong Kong had become one of the principal travel routes to China, and the Chinese had put their best foot forward on the international trains that operated over the line. After a 30-year interruption that began with the 1949 revolution, through train operation between the British crown colony and Guangzhou was restored in 1979. Service

Under the watchful eye of an immigration official, international passengers boarded Guangzhou-Kowloon train 95 at Guangzhou station in 1990. The capitalist wonders of Hong Kong were only a few hours away.

began with a single daily round trip, and by the date of my late 1981 journey had been increased to two daily through trains in each direction.

We boarded the earliest of the daily through trains, No. 91, at the broad platforms of Guangzhou's handsome new station (opened in 1974). Waiting outside the customs shed was a train unlike any other in China. The motive power, one of the sturdy East Wind 3 diesels, was familiar enough, but the remainder of the

Headed by a big "East Wind 4" diesel, 14-car train 91 set out along Guagzhou's Huanshi Road
on the international journey to Kowloon in 1990.

train was in sharp contrast to the heavy, rib-sided dark green cars that provide the
usual Chinese passenger accommodations. Aside from a head-end power car (for
the air-conditioning), baggage car, and diner, the 13-car consist was made up of
brand-new air-conditioned coaches that would have done credit to any North
American streamliner of the 1950s. Exteriors of the welded, high tensile steel cars
were finished in a handsome blue and ivory color scheme. Each car had reserved,

reclining seats for 68 passengers. Broad, double-glazed picture windows were fitted with both light blue drapes and lace curtains. Lace antimacassars were provided on each seat. Television sets mounted at the end of each car provided videotaped "in flight" announcements and entertainment. A uniformed female attendant greeted passengers at the door of each coach.

Promptly at 8:30 A.M., No. 91 slipped away from the high-level platforms to begin the 3-hour journey to Hong Kong. It was a pleasant run through a lush, semitropical countryside. I enjoyed a breakfast of French toast, ham omelet, and coffee in a handsome diner arranged in the standard 48-seat configuration of North American practice. We paused at Shenzhen, the Chinese border city, and then moved across the bridge into Lo Wu, in the crown colony's New Territories.

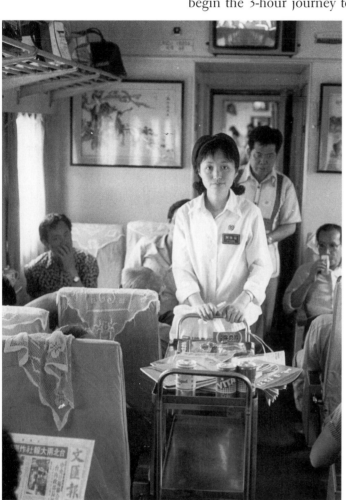

We were now on the rails of the British-run Kowloon-Canton Railway, which was in the midst of reconstruction into a high-capacity electrified suburban railroad. The long Chinese train threaded its way through track crews and wire gangs, and past construction sites for new suburban stations. In every direction, rising housing blocks for Hong Kong's burgeoning population explained the purpose for the railroad's transformation. The East Wind 3 rumbled through the long Beacon Hill Tunnel, and then the train descended toward Kowloon and the glittering Hong Kong harbor.

No. 91 came to a halt in the cavernous platform level of KCR's Hung Hom station in Kowloon (or Jiulong to the Chinese). The ordeal of immigration and customs over, we sank back into the luxury of a hotel limousine and began looking forward to the comforts of a few days in a Hong Kong hotel, and then the long flight home on PanAm 6.

Air-conditioning, reclining seats with lace antimacassars, and "in flight" television entertainment were among the features of China's deluxe international train to Hong Kong. This was train 91 in April 1983.

The Journey Today

All of my trips of the 1980s are still possible today on the still-expanding Chinese Railways, which expects to add more than 3000 route-miles to the 41,000-mile system over the next five years. Passenger trains are now operating at speeds up to 100 mph on some principal lines, and test trains for planned new high-speed lines have hit speeds as high as 150 mph. Operation with diesel and electric motive power continues to expand, but steam motive power can still be found in many parts of China and is likely to last well into the century.

China's international trains reached their Kowloon terminal at Hong Kong over the rails of the Kowloon-Canton Railway. Powered by an "East Wind 3" diesel, a northbound international run to Guangzhou headed into the Kowloon-Canton's newly completed Beacon Hill tunnel in 1981.

#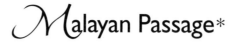

It was only March, but already Bangkok was beastly hot and humid; I consoled myself with the recollection that it was far worse in summer. After a false start I learned the drill, took a numbered slip, and sat down to wait my turn in the "advance booking office" at the main railway terminal. I was at the beginning of a trip that had been a long time in coming, and the prize at the end of a tedious wait was a sleeping-car ticket on the *International Express*, southbound on the first leg of a long journey down the Malayan Peninsula to Singapore in 1979.

I had long been intrigued with the idea of a trip by train through Malaya. In a lifetime of reading I had formed some enduring mental impressions of the place. In W. Somerset Maugham's short stories of Malaya, gin-soaked colonials carried on steamy affairs in steamy jungles. Articles in my circa-1935 copy of the *Railway Wonders of the World* described the opening of this corner of the British Empire by enterprising railway builders who overcame swamps, jungles and wild beasts (one photograph depicted the aftermath of a train-elephant collision). More recently, Paul Theroux in *The Great Railway Bazaar* had found congenial company and adventure on a journey down the peninsula that began on the self-same *International Express*.

The Malayan Peninsula is the southernmost extremity of the Asian continent, thrusting 850 miles southward into the South China Sea from the main land mass of Thailand. By rail, it's almost 1200 miles from Bangkok to Singapore, divided fairly equally between the State Railway of Thailand (RSR) and the Malayan Railways (KTM), both meter gauge. The first leg of the trip, on RSR's tri-weekly *International Express*, would cover the 721 miles to the Malaysian port of Butterworth in just under 24 hours. Beyond Butterworth, choices were available for travel to Kuala Lumpur and Singapore, but no matter what combination of trains was used, the through journey from Bangkok to Singapore would take better than 48 hours.

After briefly considering the uncertain comforts of that two-day passage through the jungles of Malaya, Dorothy had opted for two extra days of sightseeing in Bangkok and a Thai Airways ticket to Kuala Lumpur, and we parted amidst labored jokes about the exotic Asian beauties I was likely to meet in adjoining compartments on the *Express*.

Bangkok had three railway terminals, but only one amounted to much. Thon Buri, on the west bank of the broad Chao Phraya River that meanders through the Thai capital on its way to the Gulf of Siam, originated a modest collection of local and mixed trains, and a single daily rapid train for the south. Wongwien Yai Station, near the circle of the same name in the southwestern sector of the city, was

*© 1982 Kalmbach Publishing Co., reprinted with permission from the May and June 1982 issues of *Trains* magazine.

the Bangkok terminal for suburban rail car services operated over the rickety Mae Klong line. But the grand Bangkok Station near the center of the city on Rama IV Road was the terminus for the *International Express* and just about every other train of consequence.

Bangkok Station, impressive and of European character, was completed in 1916 for the Northern lines of the Royal Siamese State Railways. A colonnaded entrance, flanked by elaborate masonry towers at each corner, fronted on Rama IV Road. Its great train shed was supported by steel arches. Both ends of the shed were glazed, and the use of alternating panels of clear and colored glass in the north end, above the tracks, gave a dramatic effect. A two-story structure along the east side of the shed housed railway offices. This wing of the station once also contained the Rajadhani Hotel. The main entrances to its lobby, bar, and restaurant opened right off the platforms, and a second-floor lounge and the corridor leading to the hotel rooms were open to the splendid arched train shed. But alas, what was once a train-watcher's ideal hostelry was now closed, its rooms given over to offices.

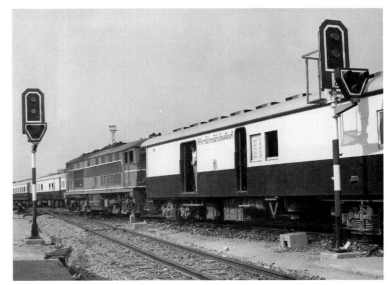

On a March afternoon in 1979, State Railways of Thailand train 11, the *International Express,* was ready to depart from Bangkok Station for the long journey down the Malayan Peninsula to Butterworth, Malaysia. A big French-built diesel powered the 11-car train.

Bangkok Station once had standard-gauge tracks. The British engineers who planned Siam's Northern Railway built it between 1892 and 1922 to 4-foot, 8 1/2-inch gauge. But elsewhere in Southeast Asia, meter gauge (3 foot, 3 3/8 inch) prevailed, and the Siamese links to both the Burmese and Malayan railways were built to the narrower gauge. The Siamese government converted the entire system to meter gauge by 1930.

The daily passenger count at Bangkok Station was about 20,000 passengers, and traffic had long since outgrown the original structure. Platforms for the six tracks under the train shed extended beyond its cover, and another four tracks had been added to the west.

Train 11, the *International Express,* stood on Track 10, the last of these tracks, and its 19-car consist extended several car lengths beyond the umbrella sheds. A long overnight sleeping-car express for Chiang Mai, far to the north, was on the adjacent track. Most of the other platforms were occupied by the ubiquitous Japanese-built, U.S.-powered (Cummins) diesel rail cars that RSR favored for its local services.

Motive power for my *Express* of March 31 was one of the railway's newest and biggest diesels, a 2250-hp, French-built (Alsthom) C-C unit powered by an engine—a 16-cylinder, V-type, SEMT-Pielstick PA4-185—with a name that sounded as if it belonged on a sports car. The French build some handsome rolling stock, but it had been my observation that their export diesels tended toward the utilitarian in appearance. Certainly this Thai Alsthom fell into that category. No. 4146 was a rather awkward-looking box-cab machine finished in two shades of brown;

her flanks were a patchwork of windows and grilles. But she could pull more than anything else the railway had, which was why she headed the heavy international consist.

It was hard to characterize Thai motive-power policy. How does one explain a railway that installed some of the world's first road diesels in 1930, yet acquired new wood-burning steam power as recently as 1950 (and was still running it through the 1970s)? And in its post–World War II dieselization, the railway had acquired a multinational fleet of makes and models that was downright bewildering. The roster could doubtless be explained by the strings attached to foreign-aid programs and international financing deals which help keep the developing world going, but it must have created a nightmare for the RSR motive power parts man.

In addition to the French C-C's, the Thai system included diesel-electrics from two U.S. builders (Davenport and GE) and two international combines (Henschel with Swiss engines and Hitachi with German engines). In addition, one British (Hunslett) and two German (Henschel and Krauss-Maffei) builders had supplied diesel-hydraulic road locomotives and switchers. The latest Thai order, I was told, continued the international tradition: Thirty near-duplicates of the big Alsthoms, financed by a French-German loan, were being built by a German (Krupp-Henschel) consortium with Alsthom's Pielstick engine and an Alsthom transmission.

The 19 cars behind No. 11's big French diesel were a mixed lot. Two head-end cars tucked in behind the locomotive (peeping sounds from several cartons of chicks in one of them suggested that some kinds of express were universal) were followed by a single through second-class coach for Butterworth, a dozen second-class and three first-class sleepers (destined, variously, for Thung Song and Haad Yai, in Southern Thailand, as well as Butterworth), and two diners. The train was made up entirely of blue-and-white Thai equipment except for a single Malayan Railways first-class sleeper at the rear.

I checked my ticket and headed for car ADNF, the Malayan sleeper. Despite a builder's plate that revealed Malayan origins (Sentul Shops, Kuala Lumpur, 1961), the car was determinably British in lineage, with rounded sides and tapered ends, and a heavy steel, truss-rodded underframe. The car was finished in a rich maroon with yellow striping and lettering, and a silver roof. The regal Malayan Railways logo, a tiger holding a three-legged device bearing the Moslem star and crescent, was painted on each side. I wasn't quite sure of the meaning of this device. A Malayan acquaintance in Kuala Lumpur suggested, somewhat doubtfully, that the three legs represented the three principal races of Malaysia—Malay, Chinese, and Indian ("A tiger, rampant, savaging a dousing rod," was the way Paul Theroux described it).

The Malayan porter made himself scarce while I dragged my baggage down the narrow corridor to first-class compartment 7. It was paneled in varnished dark wood. A transverse seat-berth was upholstered in a medium-green fabric that was showing its age. Brown and yellow curtains at the small window incorporated an elaborate design that managed to combine the Malayan Railways' rampant tiger, Moorish domes and minarets of the Kuala Lumpur station, and a steam locomo-

198

tive. Among the amenities were a wash basin and a large piece of crockery in a cabinet labeled "komod." At one end of the car I found a lavatory and a shower bath. The *Super Chief* and the *Crescent* had nothing on this train!

Glory be! There *was* an exotic Asian beauty in the next compartment! Almost as quickly, I noted that there was also a very flinty-looking man sharing the compartment with her, and I quickly set aside any fantasies of James Bondian romantic interludes in the cars of the speeding *International Express.*

Promptly at 4:10 P.M., a shrill whistle announced departure time, the turbocharged Pielstick wound up, and the train lurched into motion. I organized my baggage and set out to explore the train. The adjacent Thai first-class sleeper was a much newer car of Japanese origin, but its bright surfaces of polished metal and plastic laminate lacked the charm of the aging Malayan sleeper. An older Thai sleeper, however, was something else. Louvered wooden doors and windows substituted for air conditioning. In the bathing compartment in the center of the car stood a big stoneware crock with a glazed dragon on its side, from which one dipped cool water for a bath.

The train glided northward on welded rail, following color light signals through the Bangkok suburbs, and paused briefly at Bang Sue, the great freight yard serving Bangkok. When I had first seen it in the middle 1960s, Bang Sue was a flat yard switched by ex-U.S. Army 2-8-2's; but now diesels shoved cars over a hump with automatically controlled pneumatic retarders (the only yard of its kind in Southeast Asia, my State Railway hosts had told me proudly a few days earlier).

The *International Express* turned westward toward the late afternoon sun and crossed the Chao Phraya River on the great Rama IV Bridge that linked the once-separated northern and southern Thai railway lines. The river has been an artery of commerce for centuries, and its broad surface was alive with tows of bulbous teak barges moving ponderously down to the wharves of Bangkok. Sleek water taxis propelled by curious, long-stemmed outboard motors darted through the slow-moving freight traffic like nervous dragonflies.

The trackside scene was typically Southeast Asian: coconut palms, banana and mango trees, and all manner of lush tropical vegetation intermingled with truck gardens, flower beds, and rice paddies. Water buffaloes, sheep, and goats grazed. Ducks swam among the lotus growing in ponds of rich brown water.

Small boys flew kites. Naked brown children swam in the "klongs"—the Thai canals that serve as roadway, bathing place, and sewer. And wooden houses, a few picturesquely thatched in palm fronds but most roofed in the rusted, corrugated iron that has become a Southeast Asia standard, stood on tall stilts. Big ceramic water jugs stood outside each house.

Nothing sets the countries of Asia apart more readily than the architecture of their Buddhist temples. Those of Thailand, where they're called *wats*, are a pervasive part of the landscape, characterized by steep roofs covered in brilliant red, yellow, and green tiles, and pointed pagodas gilded in gold.

No less than its motive power, the lineside installations of the Thai Railway conveyed an impression of diverse national origins. At Taling Chan Junction, where our line joined that from Thonburi station, semaphores were European in style, but each of the wood-framed country stations we passed was painted in a

199

standard color scheme of box-car red and cream that would have looked at home in rural North America. Khaki-uniformed station agents gave operations a Japanese air of military precision.

Nong Pladuk Junction was much as I remembered it from an April 1966 visit. Monkeypod trees surrounded an interlocking plant and a sleepy wooden station that presided over a four-way junction. The main line of RSR's Southern Line formed the east and south legs. The other two were now only short branches, but rich in history or future possibilities.

The Nam Tok branch followed the Kwai River northwest 80 miles toward the Burmese border. During World War II, the Japanese pushed this line—the notorious "Death Railway"—through Three Pagodas Pass into Burma with Allied POW labor at a fearful price in human lives. That railway, celebrated by the novel and film *The Bridge on the River Kwai*, was gone beyond Nam Tok, but RSR, capitalizing on the film's popularity, offered a weekend excursion on the branch, including a visit to the Kwai River bridge at Kanchanaburi, the POW cemeteries, and the Nam Tok waterfall.

The Suphan Buri branch to the north didn't really go anywhere, and never had . . . but someday it might. Suphan Buri was one of two proposed starting points for a rail link between Thailand and Burma, and detailed surveys have been completed to Mae Sod on the Burmese border. The projected line was part of a grand Trans-Asian Railway scheme that would join Europe and Southeast Asia with an unbroken chain of railways. The idea of rails between the Straits of Dover and Singapore, the dream of British colonials, had been around for more than 50 years. In the 1970s it had been taken up by the United Nations Economic and Social Commission for Asia and the Pacific (ESCAP), and a few days before, I had discussed the project with U Shwe Shane, a soft-spoken Burmese who was a coordinator and consultant for the project with ESCAP in Bangkok.

He told me the project would require 1200 miles of new line, as well as integration of railways built to standard, broad, and meter gauges with a diversity of braking, coupling, loading gauge, and axle-loading characteristics. The political problems were greater. Plans for completing the Iran-Pakistan link, forecast for 1985, had collapsed with the Shah. And early closure of the sizable gaps that separated the Burmese Railways from India and Bangladesh to the west, and from Thailand to the east, was unlikely, given the xenophobic policy of the Burmese government, which did not favor opening through land routes of any kind.

It seemed unlikely that trains would soon be running through Suphan Buri on their way to Europe, yet the thought was intriguing.

The sun was a bright red disc dropping toward the horizon as I walked forward to the *International Express* dining car. Like most Asian diners, it was a utilitarian eating place, lacking any pretensions of elegance save for a flower vase on each table. Stained tablecloths evidenced a steady business since departure from Bangkok. There was no air conditioning, but warm, moist air rushing through open windows, and a battery of whirling ceiling fans, made it comfortable enough.

Instead of the traditional hot towel of East Asia, the waiter brought a scented, moist-paper towelette in a plastic wrapping imprinted with pictures of steam trains. The menu listed a wide variety of fried and boiled rice dishes, eggs in several forms, and such exotica as a sweet and sour fried vegetable sandwich, while the beverage list offered soft drinks, beer, Mekhong whiskey, and Hennessy brandy.

My fried rice and chicken came with a sliced cucumber, a fried egg, and a powerful Thai hot sauce of uncertain origin. The best part of dinner was a big bottle of excellent Singha Beer, a heavy lager produced by a Bangkok brewery. Dessert was a banana. My after-dinner coffee was served in a water glass. Curious. The tab: a modest 37 baht—about $1.82.

The train rolled southward in the gathering twilight through palm forests, bamboo groves, and sugar cane fields. We passed a painted statue of a seated Buddha, and then a brightly lighted *wat* where some sort of Buddhist festival was in progress. With the sun safely below the horizon, the Malayan sleeper's air conditioning finally began to win its struggle against Thai heat and humidity, and I slept in comfort as we followed the Gulf of Siam down the Malayan Peninsula.

The sun came up April 1 from behind dark clouds over the Gulf, silhouetting palm trees and stilted houses in a misty dawn. Shaving in the fast moving metergauge sleeper was an adventure, but I survived it without major wounds. The *Express* was a good two hours late as we paused briefly in the early dawn at Surat Thani, about 400 miles from Bangkok. The pace of life here was slower than in the capital. A line of trishas—a sort of bicycle ricksha—waited for passengers outside the station; ordinary taxis were nowhere to be seen. Occasionally I saw men wearing the native *sarong* instead of the western dress common in most of Thailand.

We moved on through a now hilly landscape, passing the precise ranks of rubber trees in the great rubber estates of the Peninsula; poor-looking villages; and the splendor of an occasional ornate *wat* standing in contrast to the shabby houses around it.

Breakfast consisted of a plate of toast, a banana, and another water glass of coffee. Not much, but only 13 baht, about 64 cents.

In Bangkok, my Thai railway hosts had assured me that RSR steam had not been active since 1977, with 39 of the newest locomotives held in reserve against another oil supply crisis. But the power-short motive-power officer at Thung Song Junction didn't know that, and a shiny Japanese-built 2-8-2 on station switching duty nosed up to the rear of our train to drop two second-class sleepers. Dead steam power stood in long ranks east of the station. A Caterpillar-powered Davenport B-B switched diminutive box cars nearby.

The *International Express* moved on through a rolling countryside covered with dense jungle growth, frequently interrupted by neatly aligned trees of rubber plantations. Palms grew on the low ground beside the track. Later in the morning, the terrain leveled out again. The rice paddies were still dry, with only the stubble of last year's crop, but beds of bright green seedlings were almost ready for planting. Water buffalo and cattle grazed together in trackside fields.

Haad Yai Junction was the last major stop in Thailand. Here the RSR's Southern Line divided. One leg angled off to the southeast to link up with the Malayan Railways' east coast main line at Sungei Golok; the other, taken by our now-diminished *Express,* joined the Malayan system's west coast route.

Food, drink, and souvenirs were all on sale to *International Express* travelers from platform vendors at the Hatyai Junction station in southern Thailand.

The border station at Padang Besar was the sort of place Paul Theroux would call flyblown. We halted opposite a large, grubby concrete station, and I disembarked for the usual tiresome border-crossing formalities.

A stern "Immigration Warning" tacked on the wall sounded a less than cordial welcome:

Malaysia Welcomes Bona Fide Tourists but not Hippies.

*You are therefore advised at all times to dress, behave,
and live decently in hotels as becoming a bona fide tourist.*

*If you are found dressed in shabby, dirty, or indecent clothes,
or living in make-shift Shelters, you will be deemed to be a Hippie.*

Any "hippies," the notice concluded, would be given 24 hours to leave the country, or would be prosecuted, and furthermore, would not be permitted to enter Malaysia again.

The immigration inspectors seemed to be taking it seriously. A group of youthful European travelers ahead of me were obliged to show that they had onward travel tickets and adequate funds, and were questioned intensively concerning their travel plans.

Oh, oh, I thought, I'll bet they're going to hassle me, too. Even though I was well started in my 50's, you see, I was *very* youthful looking for my age.

But an immigration inspector briefly flicked open my passport, glanced without interest at my respectable middle-aged countenance, stamped the passport, and waved me on. So much for illusions of youthfulness.

A maroon, Japanese-built box-cab diesel replaced the Thai locomotive, and the *International Express* rolled southward into a Malaysian countryside that was much the same as that I had just left in Thailand, but subtle differences in the railway architecture recalled the British colonial origins of the Malayan Railways. Culverts and bridges were carefully laid up in brick; wayside semaphores were in the British style; and the fussy, Victorian fretwork of a signal box at Bukit Mertajan was as English as anything at lineside on British Rail.

An acquaintance in Bangkok had warned me that the station at Butterworth was little more than a waterfront shed, so I had an early supper of fried rice, pork, and beer in the dining car before our arrival.

Shortly after 7 P.M., not quite an hour and a half behind schedule, the *International Express* braked to a stop in the Butterworth terminal. The Malay porter made himself scarce again, and I lowered my baggage to the ballast several car lengths beyond the end of the too-short platform. An elevated walkway connected the modest station with the nearby ferry terminal. Two miles away across the Strait of Malacca, the lights of Penang beckoned, but exploration of that island resort would have to wait for another time. I queued up at the ticket window to buy the additional sleeping-car ticket I needed to continue my southward journey on the overnight sleeper train for Kuala Lumpur.

Malaysia had some splendid train names. My night train to Kuala Lumpur, for example, was the *North Star Night Express*, while its daytime counterpart was called the *Golden Arrow Day Express*. The Kuala Lumpur–Singapore night sleeper train carried the grand title of *Southern Cross Night Express*. My favorite train name, though, was that of the *Golden Blowpipe Night Express*, which ran through the aborigine jungle on Malayan Railways' east coast main line.

Train 5, the *North Star Night Express*, was a 16-car mixture of coaches, second- and first-class sleepers, a diner, and a baggage car. The style of Malayan rolling stock was very British, even to the use of destination roof boards. Color schemes were best described as varied. The same deep maroon, with yellow striping and lettering, of the *International Express's* single Malayan sleeper seemed to be the current standard, but other cars were finished in light green and yellow. The diner, in a cream and chocolate scheme with an orange stripe, was reminiscent of the old pre–British Rail livery of the Great Western, but its interior accommodations were utilitarian, with stand-up shelves along each wall rather than tables and chairs.

Our motive power was a 1971 British (English Electric-AEI-Metro Cammell) C-C box-cab diesel, 22127. The Malayan Railway—Keretapi Tanah Melayu (KTM) in Malay—maintained the worthy practice of naming locomotives, and these class 22 units carried Malayan place names. Train 5's engine was named for *Tanjong Bunga* ("Flower Cape"), a cape on the north coast of Penang Island. KTM's other two road diesel classes were named for Malayan flowers and rivers.

Indians, Chinese, and Malays ran the railroad, and I was intrigued by the elemental English that was their common language. Their common railway terms—*teren, seteseyn, tiket, nombor, peletform,* and the like—were easily understood.

I settled my luggage in a wood-paneled compartment in an elderly sleeper labeled "Dingin," denoting air conditioning. The dingin wasn't working, but an electrician summoned over the station's public address system finally coaxed it into operation by departure time. We were well out of Butterworth before it was cool enough to sleep.

I awoke to a misty, early-morning light filtering through heavy tropical growth as we rolled through a landscape of rubber plantations and jungle. Soon the night express was passing through the quickening urban surroundings of Kuala Lumpur—K.L. to knowledgeable Southeast Asia travelers—and shortly before 7 A.M. the train halted in what was clearly the grandest of the three great railway terminals of the Malayan peninsula.

The splendid station was an exotic buff and white stuccoed confection of vaguely North African style . . . all Moorish arches and towers and minarets, surrounded by meticulous lawns and gardens. The station's four tracks were enclosed within a British style walled and covered train shed. In the station, paddle fans revolved slowly in a high-ceilinged restaurant with Moorish arched windows, and an elderly open lift (elevator) led to the second-floor Station Hotel.

While handy for train-watching, the Station Hotel was decidedly down at the heels, so I headed to the nearest phone booth to book a room at one of the uptown tourist hotels. I could rough it with the best when I had to, but at age 50-plus, one finds that creature comforts take on a growing importance. A resourceful *teksi* driver managed to fit me, my baggage, and four Malayans into his subcompact cab, and I headed to the Merlin Hotel.

Later in the day I met KTM official Oon Paek Lim in the equally ornate Moorish palace that houses the railway's headquarters just across Jalan Sultan

The Malayan Railways' exotically named locomotive *Bunga Butang* (a Malaysian flower) stood in the ornate Moorish palace of a station at Kuala Lumpur with train 7, the *Magic Arrow Day Express,* for Singapore. Although vaguely American in appearance, the class 20 diesel-electric was actually built by Britain's English Electric in 1957.

Hishammuddin from the station. I asked him what he knew of the origins of the station, which was completed about 1910. "I think," said Oon, "that since Malaya was a Moslem country, this was an English architect's idea of what a Malayan railway terminal should look like."

During the several days I spent visiting KTM's Kuala Lumpur installation with Mr. Oon, I learned that Malayan steam power was not quite gone, even though the railway had been fully dieselized since the mid-1970s. Still on hand was one serviceable class 56 Pacific built for KTM by North British in the 1940s. For a modest minimum of 200 Malayan dollars (say, $95 U.S.), the 4-6-2 was available for "Down Memory Lane" excursions out of K.L. to the nearby Batu Caves or Port Kelang, trips popular with Australian steam fans.

I was tempted, yes, but the budget wouldn't quite make it.

Several mornings later, on April 5, 1979, I resumed my journey to Singapore on the 7 A.M. "ordinary train," No. 15. Mr. Oon was accompanying me as far as Gemas, where we would visit some of KTM's facilities at the junction with the east coast line. Dorothy, who had flown from Bangkok to K.L. to join me, had decided in favor of a few more hours of sleep and the later departure of the *Magic Arrow Day Express*, which I would join at Gemas.

No. 15 carried only second- and third-class coaches (KTM called them "Eksikutif" and "Ekonomi," respectively). The Eksikutif coaches were filled, and we found seats in an Ekonomi combine at the rear of the train.

I stood in the open rear door and watched the meter-gauge rails recede down the lush green trough of jungle vegetation and rubber plantations that lined the tracks. An occasional white sign beside the track told the engineer when to *wisel*. Track gangs of sweating Malays stepped back from their work as the train sped by. Here and there the sound pattern shifted from the clickety-clack of bolted rail to the smooth hiss of welded.

Mr. Oon brought tall glasses of hot tea, heavily sugared and mixed with milk, from a buffet in the baggage compartment. Most of our traveling companions in the third-class compartment were railway men, deadheading from one assignment to another. I sipped my tea, listened to their discussion of railroad operating problems, gripes about management, and retirement plans, and wondered again at the universality of their profession.

We stepped down to the platform at Gemas, and a local KTM official escorted us off to visit locomotive shops and a tie treatment plant.

The touring over, I climbed up on a pedestrian footbridge that spanned the yard to await the passage of the up *Ekspres Rakyat* en route from Singapore to Butterworth. The various day and night expresses may have had Malaysia's most exotic train names, but since 1976 the "People's Express" (as the name translated) had been KTM's premier passenger service. *Ekspres Rakyat* operated daily between Singapore and Butterworth, 489 miles, in a little over 13 hours. The seemingly modest 37 mph average wasn't bad for meter gauge and a schedule requiring nine intermediate stops, and it was a good 3 hours better than the combined running times of the two-day expresses operated over the same route. The rolling stock was a fleet of handsome new Japanese-built coaches that exemplified KTM's new one-class approach to passenger travel. All were second-class Eksikutif class,

206

In 1979 the Malayan Railways' premiere passenger train was the fast *Ekspres Rakyat* ("People's Express"), which made a daily round trip between Singapore and Butterworth. On April 5, 1979, train 18, the up *Ekspres Rakyat* from Singapore, came flying through Gemas. A big British-built class 22 box-cab diesel headed the 14-car train.

the only distinction being a choice between air-conditioned (Eksikutif Dingin) and non–air conditioned stock.

A feeling of expectancy hung in the humid air as *Ekspres Rakyat*'s passing time approached. Soon class 22 diesel 22122—*Changkat Tenggara* ("Mount Tenggara")—came roaring out of the south with the 14-car express. Gemas is not a scheduled stop, and the big C-C slowed only slightly while an engineman leaned out for the tablet held high by a signalman, and the coaches lurched through the special trackwork to follow the West Line north toward Kuala Lumpur.

Train 7 down—the *Magic Arrow Day Express*—was late and getting later. Mr. Oon and I repaired behind the swinging doors of the station restaurant and bar, a pleasant, high-ceilinged room cooled in Malayan style by whirling ceiling fans. We sat in rattan chairs and sipped Anchor beer brought to us by the aged Chinese barman from a big white refrigerator in the corner. A motorcycle parked in the corner, a dog sleeping on the cool concrete floor, and children running through at play gave the place an informal air. Signs on the wall advertised soft drinks, Anchor Beer, Hennessy Brandy, and Guinness Stout, and advised, inevitably, "Have a Nice Day," and—sternly—"Terms Cash."

We were joined by the Gemas station agent, an Indian, who explained that Indians were first brought to Malaya by the British to help run the railway. Thus, even though scarcely 5 percent of the Malaysian population is of Indian origin, close to half of KTM's officials are Indian. We talked of the tendency of sons of railway men to go to work on the railway and to marry the daughters of railway men. This led to a comparison of varying ethnic wedding customs. The Indian good-naturedly bemoaned the need to accumulate a sizable dowry for his daughter. Mr. Oon, an ethnic Chinese, remarked upon the Chinese custom that requires the groom to finance the wedding dinner, at which the number of tables is important. Frequently, he remarked, a father-in-law will secretly pay for the feast to save face if the groom is poor.

Finally, a good hour and a half behind schedule, No. 7 came in behind one of KTM's class 20 1500-hp C-C diesels. Although they were KTM's oldest diesels (English Electric 1957), they were easily its most attractive units, with a double-cab, vaguely American-style car-body that was a little reminiscent of Baldwin's double-cab Central of New Jersey DR64-20's. The railway named them after the flowers of Malaysia. Train 7 was pulled by the 22104, *Bunga Seroja*, or "Lotus Flower."

Despite No. 7's grand name, its 13-car consist was a mostly mismatched collection of second- and third-class coaches of varying styles and origins. One elderly, open-platform coach I noted still had door windows with elaborate Federated Malay State Railways tiger emblems etched in the glass. No. 7 was a mail train, and a postal car at the rear had letter drops in each side.

I joined Dorothy in the train's single Deluxe Dingin, just ahead of the postal coach. The car had big, reclining chairs in a 2-1 configuration, with tables between pairs of facing seats. The compartment was paneled in wood, the seats upholstered in faded light green fabric, and the windows draped in the same brown and yellow fabric, with elaborate tiger rampant, tower and minaret, and steam

208

locomotive pattern I'd observed earlier in my *International Express* sleeper. The car was roomy and comfortable, if a bit aged and worn.

No. 7, observing the truism that late trains get later, fell further and further behind schedule as we worked our way south to Singapore through a rolling countryside of more or less continuous rubber and palm oil plantations. The attendant brought us a lunch of fried rice, tomato sandwiches, and beer from the buffet car. A Pan Am flight crew, off for a Singapore outing during their K.L. layover, played cards, drank, and made bright remarks about train travel.

The two trainmen who came through checking tickets characterized the diversity of Malaysia. One, bearded and turbaned, was an Indian. The other, a Malayan, wore the black cap of a Muslim.

Johore Bahru, the capital of Johore State and our last stop before crossing to the island nation of Singapore, was a big, prosperous-looking place, with even a few modest office towers on its downtown skyline. We halted briefly while Malaysian Immigration made a cursory check. The station was handsome, a masonry structure with a domed tower roofed in red tile, and ornate iron grillwork over the doorways and supporting the station canopies. Two splendid tigers and the Muslim star and crescent were incorporated into the ironwork of the main entrance gate.

An open-air signal box on the platform controlled the station's approach and home signals. Each of the interlocking levers was marked with a carefully polished brass plate.

"Lotus Flower" edged out across the Johore Strait on the great causeway leading to Singapore Island, the meter-gauge track flanked by a six-lane highway on one side and by the great fresh-water pipelines that supply Singapore on the other.

Until the nearly 3500-foot Johore Causeway was opened, car ferries and launches carried freight cars and passengers across the Strait to a link with the Singapore Government Railway at Woodlands. Construction of the causeway began in 1920, and more than 1.6 million cubic yards of granite had been dumped into the waters of the Strait by the time the Governor of the Straits Settlements, the Sultan of Johore, and the various rulers of the Federated Malay States joined to celebrate its completion in June 1924.

From the windows of No. 7, Singapura—the Lion City—was a jumble of expressways, tropical vegetation, factories, tin roofs, laundry hanging on bamboo poles from the balconies of concrete apartment blocks, and a gaggle of geese marching through a backyard.

Singapore Station, the third of the three great stations of my Malayan journey, was totally unlike either the European style of Bangkok Station or the Moorish gaudiness of that at Kuala Lumpur. Opened in 1932, the massive masonry structure was finished in a buff-colored imitation stone stucco. A triple arched *porte cochere* stood over the entrance drive, surmounted by green tile eaves and four stone figures representing agriculture, commerce, transport, and industry. The tiger rampant crest appeared again on two stone shields above the outermost figures, flanking a pair at the center bearing the MR initials of the railway.

The main concourse of the station was a great arched vault painted in a light blue and white. Tiled murals of Malayan scenes were set high in the wall on each side, with the FMSR initials of the old Federated Malay States Railways and the omnipresent tiger crest at each end of the vault. The station restaurant and bar, a book stall, and ticket offices flanked the concourse.

Singapore, too, had its station hotel. The reception desk was on the second floor level, and all 34 rooms opened off balconies which enclosed the concourse on all four sides. The facilities appeared well kept and comfortable, and the price was right—the Singapore dollar equivalent of only $17 for a double.

But Dorothy and I had reservations in a splendid relic of British Colonial Malaya, just off the Singapore waterfront. Drawn on by visions of Singapore slings in the long bar and dinner in the Palm Court, we gathered our bags and headed for the cab stand to follow the ghost of Somerset Maugham to the Raffles Hotel.

The Journey Today

The *International Express* still operates daily between Bangkok and Butterworth, with onward connecting services available there for Kuala Lumpur and Singapore. A more recent addition to the route is the *Eastern & Oriental Express,* which operates through between Bangkok and Singapore with deluxe sleeping, lounge and dining car equipment. The train operates weekly via Butterworth and Kuala Lumpur on a fast schedule requiring 48 hours or less between the two terminal cities.

In 1964 Japan brought forth a new kind of railroad. Called the "Super Express of Dreams," the "Bullet Line," or, officially, the New Tokaido Line (NTL) of the Japanese National Railways (JNR), it was a 320-mile high-speed superrailroad between Tokyo and Osaka that had taken five years and the equivalent of a billion dollars to build. When it opened on October 1, 1964, just a few days before the start of the 1964 Olympic Games at Tokyo, the NTL's 210 km./hr. (130 mph) trains set new world speed records for railway passenger service, and its installations and equipment represented a level of railway technology unsurpassed anywhere in the world.

Taking its name from the ancient "Eastern Sea Road" highway connecting Tokyo and Osaka, the Tokaido route links Japan's five largest cities in a densely

---

*© 1966 Kalmbach Publishing Co., reprinted with permission from the April 1966 issue of *Trains* magazine.

A panned photograph captured an image of high-speed travel as an eastbound Osaka-Tokyo
Hikari "Super Express" roared through Atami on the Japanese National Railways' New Tokaido
Line at 130 mph in September 1965.

populated region that contains 40 percent of the total Japanese population and no less than 70 percent of its industry.

Faced with near saturation traffic on its existing 3-foot, 6-inch gauge Tokaido Line, JNR had begun studies for an entirely new railroad over the route in 1957. Once a decision was made to proceed, nine special teams were formed to plan the New Tokaido Line construction, covering overall standards for the new line, high-speed track structures, high-speed rolling stock, dynamics of high-speed rolling stock, high-speed braking systems, overhead wire systems, electrification, high-speed signaling, and automatic train operation. Over a six-year period these teams undertook study and research in some 173 areas of railroad technology.

The plan that emerged called for a new railroad at a 4-foot, 8 1/2-inch standard gauge that would operate with a conventional flanged-steel-wheel-on-rail technology, but little else about the new line would bear much resemblance to conventional practice. The line would be double track throughout and entirely grade crossing–free, operating between Tokyo's Central Station and a new terminal at Shin (New)-Osaka, with ten intermediate stations. Track would be welded steel rail attached by double elastic fastenings to prestressed concrete ties, and laid to extremely high standards of curve and grade for unrestricted high-speed operation.

Construction of the NTL through the densely populated urban areas and rugged terrain of the route required some 37 million cubic yards of cut and fill. A total of 66 tunnels, totaling over 42 miles in length, were drilled, the longest of them the 4.9-mile New Tanna Tunnel. There were some 3000 bridges, aggregating 35 miles in length, of reinforced concrete, prestressed concrete, or steel construction, and nearly 71 miles of line was placed on reinforced concrete elevated structure over urban or low agricultural areas.

The new railroad was powered by an advanced commercial frequency AC power system supplying 25 kilovolt power to trains through an overhead catenary system and high-speed pantographs. The NTL's signaling system included automatic train control (ATC) and centralized traffic control (CTC), with the entire line under the control of a single control center at Tokyo. There were no wayside signals, and the ATC provided in the cab of each train a continuous indication of maximum permissible speed. Interconnection of cab signals and braking controls provided automatic speed reduction to the permissible maximum.

Instead of using locomotive-drawn equipment, JNR elected to develop a series of high-speed multiple unit cars for the new line. This would reduce the loading on bridges and elevated structures, permit higher performance characteristics, and afford a faster turnaround at terminals. These were 82-foot, welded high-tensile steel cars, each powered by four 185 kilowatt traction motors mounted on four-wheel trucks. Wind tunnel tests were used to develop the most efficient aerodynamic shape for both the cross section of the cars and the front end shape. As a result of these tests, the cars were designed with slightly bulging sides and deep skirts below the floor level. Head-end cars were given the dramatic bullet-nosed shape that gave the railway its "Bullet Line" nickname.

A total of 360 cars were delivered in time for the line's October 1964 start-up, and another 120 were delivered the following year. Initially, these were arranged in 12-car trainsets, although the equipment and stations were designed for an eventual increase to 16-car trainsets. Two first-class cars in each train each seated 64 or 68 passengers in reclining seats arranged in a 2-2 pattern, while eight second-class cars each carried 110 passengers in non-reclining seats in a 3-2 pattern. Two coach-buffet cars were divided between second-class seats and a buffet section.

Opened with elaborate ceremony, the New Tokaido Line was an immediate success. Initial schedules provided for 30 trains daily in each direction, divided about equally between *Hikari* (meaning "Light") super express schedules and *Kodama* ("Echo") limited express schedules. *Hikari* trains, making intermediate stops only at Nagoya and Kyoto, were scheduled over the 320-mile Tokyo-Osaka run in four hours flat. *Kodama* schedules, stopping at all ten intermediate stations, were allowed five hours.

Spectacular as they were, NTL's inaugural schedules were only a modest beginning. New schedules placed in effect a year later increased the number of daily trains in each direction to 43, and this was increased again only a month later, on November 1, 1965, to 55 daily round trips. At the same time Tokyo-Osaka *Hikari* running times were cut to only 3 hours 10 minutes, while *Kodama* times were reduced to an even 4 hours. The new line proved highly reliable, and the fast, comfortable trains were soon drawing record numbers of passengers. In the NTL's first year *Hikari* trains ran at an average of about 92 percent of capacity, while the *Kodama* trains filled an average of about 80 to 86 percent of their seats. Already, too, JNR was laying plans for a 312-mile westward extension of the Bullet Line over its San-yo line route to western Honshu and Kyushu.

Intent on gaining a firsthand impression of 2-mile-a-minute railroading, I joined the crowds heading for the New Tokaido Line platforms at JNR's Tokyo Central Station one morning in early September 1965. A first-class basic ticket, super-express supplement, and seat reservation entitled me to a first-class seat on *Hikari* super express No. 9. Scheduled for a 10 A.M. departure, No. 9 was carded between Tokyo and Osaka in 4 hours flat, with intermediate stops at Nagoya and Kyoto.

The MU train waiting at Track 17 was arranged in the 12-car consist standard for all NTL trains. First-class accommodations were located mid-train in cars 7 and 8 (cars are numbered from the Osaka end). The remainder of the train was given over to second-class coaches; buffet sections took up approximately half the length of cars 5 and 9. Except for luggage racks in each car and small luggage compartments in first-class coaches, no baggage space was provided on the Bullet Train; checked baggage moved in narrow-gauge trains on the old Tokaido line. A bullet-nosed head-end car at each end of the train (plus reversible seating) permits a quick turnaround at terminals.

In their design of NTL rolling stock, Japan's rail car engineers, who had come up with some noteworthy MU equipment styling in recent years, had outdone themselves. The gleaming trains, finished in a handsome blue-and-ivory color scheme, presented an almost unbroken appearance. Resembling a cross between the wingless fuselage of a jet airliner and Union Pacific's M-1000 of 1934, the head-end cars were easily the train's most striking feature. A high cab surmounted the car's protruding bullet nose, which was fitted with a rakish pilot. Recessed twin headlights flanked the fiberglass disk capping the nose. The translucent disk,

The dramatic lines of JNR's Bullet Train equipment captured the fancy of the Japanese public.
Two small children gazed in awe at the airliner-like nose of a New Tokaido Line train at Tokyo
Central Station.

which was removable to expose an emergency drawbar, glowed eerily at night with reflected light from the headlights.

Perhaps as much for their dramatic appearance as for their breathtaking performance, the Bullet Trains seemed to have captured the fancy of the Japanese public in a manner unlike anything we had seen in our own country since the advent of the first streamliners—and perhaps not even then.

In the contest that selected the *Hikari* and *Kodama* names for NTL schedules, JNR drew an avalanche of more than 700,000 entries. At almost every departure time small children were brought forth to admire the handsome trains, and there was a steady stream of prospective passengers smilingly posing for snapshots beside the bullet-nosed head end. Japanese toy stores abounded with Bullet Train picture books and toy facsimiles that ranged from plastic pull trains for the toddlers to battery-operated tinplate versions for the older age group. In perhaps the ultimate accolade, the ad agency for one brand of Japanese cigarettes had forsaken the customary airline pilot or ship captain in endorsement posters in favor of a smartly uniformed NTL trainman puffing contentedly on the sponsor's product while a Bullet Train raced by in the background.

My Bullet Train accommodations proved to be exceptionally comfortable. The first-class coach was finished in beige and wood-grained plastic paneling, with a light gray ceiling in which were mounted continuous strips of bright fluorescent lighting. Windows were curtained in a dark blue material, and the aisle was laid with heavy blue carpeting. The roomy deep-cushioned reclining seats were upholstered in a gold material, fitted with spotless white linen antimacassars and arm rests, and equipped with adjustable foot rests and small tables that folded out of the arm rests.

Second-class Bullet Train accommodations, which I sampled on subsequent trips, were somewhat less luxurious. Seats were non-reclining and, by virtue of closer spacing and their 3-2 arrangement, considerably snugger than first class (overall, seating density in second-class spaces was nearly half again that in first class). There was no carpeting and the upholstery was a plainer blue-and-gray material. Otherwise, the cars were outfitted about the same as the first-class equipment. Everything on the Bullet Train, of course, was air conditioned.

As departure time neared, *Hikari* No. 9's dozen cars had filled almost to capacity. A warning bell clanged on the platform, air-operated doors hissed shut, and platform visitors waved and bowed low to departing friends. Precisely at 10 the motorman began feeding direct current to 48 hungry traction motors, and almost imperceptibly we moved away from the platforms.

Threading its way through downtown Tokyo on the New Tokaido Line's high elevated structure, the bullet-nosed *Hikari* paralleled JNR's narrow-gauge tracks on which multicolored MU trains from the Tokyo suburban lines shuttled to and fro with their commuter cargoes. The public-address system came to life with a musical flourish, and a lovely feminine voice (prerecorded, I later decided, when the same girl seemed to show up on every train I rode) welcomed us aboard and announced with utter assurance that we would (no hedging "are scheduled to") stop at Nagoya at 12:29 P.M., Kyoto at 1:34 P.M., and arrive at Shin-Osaka at 2 P.M. So confident is JNR in its timekeeping ability, I learned from the pocket folder distributed to NTL passengers, that the railway would refund the full price of my super-express supplemental fare should the Bullet Train be delayed an hour or more in reaching its destination.

A conductor and his assistant, white-gloved and smartly attired in blue-gray uniforms, bowed and politely asked to examine my tickets. Briefly *Hikari* No. 9 paralleled the new Tokyo Airport monorail, dropped to ground level as we passed NTL's Tokyo rail car depot and the big Shinagawa engine terminal and coach yard, then climbed back to elevated structure—built over a JNR narrow-gauge freight line—to provide a rooftop view of Tokyo's disordered sprawl.

Up to this point, New Tokaido Line speed had been moderate, but as we left the city behind, JNR began to deliver what I'd come for.

What's it like to travel at 130 mph by train?

The answer: on the Bullet Train at least, not much different from riding on any other train at half the speed. Outside, the scenery of the hilly countryside west of Tokyo began to blur past the double-paned window, but otherwise there was far less sensation of speed than I had expected. Thanks to NTL's super-smooth road-bed and welded rail, rubber cushioning, air springs, and extremely effective sound insulation, the Bullet Train seemed to float serenely along with remarkably little noise or jostling and only the slightest hum from the spinning traction motors. Entry into tunnels, even at maximum speed, was marked only by a barely notice-able increase in air pressure.

Taking advantage of arrangements made with JNR, I moved forward to a van-tage point beside *Hikari*'s motorman. Even here I found it difficult to accept the speedometer's 210 km./hr. figure; the high cab and protruding nose tended to minimize the dizzying sensation of ties unreeling in front of me at 130 mph. Only when an opposing train loomed up in the distance and plunged toward us at a breathtaking relative speed of 260 mph did I gain the full impact of Bullet Line speed.

Hikari's youthful motorman, selected only after thorough psychological and physical testing and carefully trained, was all business as he gripped the train's controls and watched for the slightest irregularity. Occasionally a warning bell clanged and the ATC panel in front of him flashed a speed restriction as *Hikari* entered a block in which break-in speed limitations were still in force. Automati-cally, the ATC-controlled dynamic braking decelerated the train until the new limit was reached. Starting and acceleration, however, were under the motor-man's control.

The scenery naturally moved by rather rapidly, but New Tokaido Line passen-gers still got a splendid panorama of central Honshu. Much of the time, when it wasn't in one of the 66 tunnels that comprise over a tenth of NTL mileage, the Bullet Line was above ground level on fill or elevated structure, according a clear view of the well-ordered fields and rice paddies of the Japanese countryside.

Between Odawara and Atami, *Hikari* dove in and out of one tunnel after an-other as the line followed the mountainous Pacific coast. Atami, a resort city popu-lar with Tokyoites, was glimpsed briefly before *Hikari* plunged into the long New Tanna Tunnel. Ordinarily at about this point Bullet Train riders got a splendid view of Japan's renowned Mount Fuji, but all I could see were heavy mists that shrouded the great volcano on this particular September morning.

Neatly trimmed hedgerow-like tea plants sped by the windows as we approached Shizuoka. According to the attractive "Train Window Panoramas" folder JNR distributed to its NTL passengers, the Shizuoka area produces most of Japan's tea, not to mention strawberries. At Hamamatsu, some 160 miles and not quite 2 hours out of Tokyo, we were due to overtake *Kodama* limited express No. 107 which had preceded us out of Tokyo by a half hour. Safely in the clear, the *Kodama* waited in the stopping track as we shot through the station's center through track with undiminished speed.

By now it was time for lunch, and I headed back to the forward buffet car. I took a seat at the narrow counter facing the windows and ordered a spaghetti lunch, coffee, and a bottle of Japanese black beer. The meal—catered on *Hikari* No. 9 by Tokyo's Imperial Hotel—was good, and the price moderate (380 yen, or a little over $1—no tipping allowed). A big speedometer on the end wall indicated we were doing 200 km./hr. (125 mph), and a device above the door at the opposite end of the buffet which indicated the train's position on a strip map of its route by means of a moving red thermometer-like line kept buffet patrons posted on *Hikari*'s progress.

For the economy-minded traveler JNR provided a pushcart service—staffed by young women attractively outfitted in gray and white uniforms—from which one could buy anything from boxed meals, tea, and cold drinks, to cigarettes and magazines, or even, if you were so inclined, a flask of Japanese whiskey.

While I lunched, *Hikari* had crossed Lake Hamana, where my Japanese companion had pointed out the eel-raising beds for which the lake is famous; had raced through the silk center of Toyohashi; and was now streaking past Nagoya's steel mills and heavy industry on the elevated structure that carried Bullet Line trains to their downtown station.

On the dot of 12:29 P.M. *Hikari* No. 9's disk brakes smoothly brought the big MU cars to a halt beside the platforms paralleling those of the adjacent old Tokaido line. Electric power dominated the narrow-gauge scene, but here and there a plume of soft-coal smoke betrayed the presence of JNR steam power.

Moments later *Hikari* was off and running again. Now the route headed inland away from the Pacific coast and between two mountain ranges, through Gifu-Hashima and Maibara. In little more than an hour *Hikari* had covered the 90-odd miles between Nagoya and its Kyoto stop. Another high

More than 42 miles of the 320-mile New Tokaido Line were in tunnels. Westbound Tokyo-Osaka *Hikari* ("Super Express") train 9 emerged from one of them at the coastal resort city of Atami, 65 miles west of Tokyo.

217

elevated structure afforded views of the ancient capital's celebrated temples. Below, green-and-cream trolleys clanged through crowded streets.

The last lap down the Yodo River valley into Shin-Osaka was run off in 26 minutes. Precisely on schedule at 2 P.M. *Hikari* nosed up to the bumpers of the elevated Shin-Osaka terminal, doors hissed open, and the Bullet Train's nearly 1000 passengers streamed down the platforms to lower-level taxi stands, Osaka city subway platforms, or connections at ground level with JNR's San-yo line trains for western Japan.

With his attention firmly fixed on the road ahead, the engineer of westbound *Hikari* "Super Express" train 9 gripped the controls as his train raced westward from Tokyo. Two engineers were assigned to each *Hikari* train, alternating at the controls.

The Journey Today

Japan's New Tokaido Line ushered in a new era of high-speed passenger trains for much of the world. In Japan itself high-speed Shinkansen routes, as they're now called, extend all the way from Kyushu to northern Honshu. Extensions planned or under construction will extend high-speed service to the southern tip of Kyushu, the northernmost island of Hokkaido, and across the north shore of Honshu. The newest fleet of high-speed trains, which entered service in time for the 1998 Nagano Winter Olympics, raised Shinkansen maximum speeds to 275 km./hr. (170 mph), while test trains with speed objectives up to 400 km./hr. (250 mph) are now operating. Today, the fastest *Nozomi* ultra high-speed trains operate over the New Tokaido Line between Tokyo and Shin-Osaka in as little as 2 hours, 30 minutes, an average speed of 128 mph for the 320-mile journey, even with intermediate stops at Nagoya and Kyoto.

Similar high-speed trains now operate in western European countries all the way from Spain and Italy to Sweden and Finland. In the U.S. the Washington–New York–Boston Northeast Corridor has been upgraded to modern high-speed standards. Russia, China, and Korea are among still other countries developing high-speed passenger rail systems.

218

Taiwan's Railway to the Clouds*

Alongside the big diesel-hauled express that had brought us to Chiai from Taipei on New Year's Eve of 1972, the *Chung Hsin Hao* (literally "China Prosperity Express") four-car diesel train that waited to take us on to Ali Shan seemed unprepossessing. Low and narrow, the little red-and-white cars stood there on thin narrow-gauge rails spaced only 2 feet, 6 inches apart, their engines idling softly.

But—as I soon found out—looks can deceive, for during the next four hours the intrepid little train would take us on a dizzying ascent of Taiwan's Ali Shan Forestry Railway to deliver us to the highest railway station in the Far East, nearly a mile and a half above sea level.

Despite its diminutive size, *Chung Hsin Hao* turned out to be a very nifty little train. Seats in the reserved cars were fitted with white antimacassars, and there was a rack at each seat to hold glasses for the hot tea that flowed more or less constantly throughout the journey. The train crew was smartly attired. A stewardess in each car was outfitted in an airline-like blue uniform, while the train's conductor wore a dignified dark gray uniform and a trainman's cap banded in yellow. The engineer had a vase of plastic flowers mounted on the windshield post.

The 45-mile climb through three climate zones to Ali Shan must be ranked as one of the world's great railway journeys. It began, gently enough, in the rich tropical countryside of Taiwan's western coastal plain. Masses of purplish bougainvillea, roses, and great groves of bamboo grew beside the tracks. We looked out at farmers wearing the traditional conical straw hats of China toiling in a patchwork of rice paddies, truck gardens, orange groves, sugar cane fields, and the like as the train climbed gradually toward the mountains to the east. My two sons chewed with relish on stalks of sweet, juicy sugar cane bought from a trackside vendor during a brief station stop.

The gentle coastal plain was soon left behind and we began to climb in earnest through the rugged mountain terrain that had made the construction of this little railway such a formidable task for its Japanese builders. Begun in 1907 during Taiwan's long period of Japanese occupation, the Ali Shan railway was built to tap the great stands of pine, cedar and cypress high on the slopes of the Chungyang Shanmo, the island's central mountain range. To reach their Ali Shan destination the railway's builders were obliged to drill 49 tunnels, the longest of them almost a half mile long, and erected some 114 bridges. Grades as steep as 6 percent (a rise of 6 feet in every hundred feet) were frequently required.

No ordinary locomotives would do for this sort of railroading, and the Japa-

---

*Portions of this article © 1978 Kalmbach Publishing Co., reprinted with permission from the February 1978 issue of *Trains* magazine.

High in the subtropical zone of Taiwan's central mountain range, *Chung Hsin Hao* ("China Prosperity Express") diesel car express 302 headed down to the seacoast at Chiyai from Asia's highest railway station at Ali Shan. The topography suggests why the Ali Shan Forestry Railway had to build 114 bridges and drill 49 tunnels to construct a 45-mile railway.

nese loggers turned to the Lima Locomotive Works of Lima, Ohio, for a fleet of the legendary Shay locomotives that had revolutionized logging railroading in much of the world. Patented in 1881, the Shay was the invention of a mechanically ingenious Michigan lumberman named Ephraim Shay. Confronted with the high costs of using horses to drag his timber out of the woods to the sawmill, Shay had built a little railway to do the work instead. But neither horse power nor an ordinary steam locomotive worked satisfactorily on the steep slopes and light rails of his logging road, so the resourceful Shay set out to design and build a special kind of steam locomotive that could do the job. The result was a curious-looking contraption that rode on ordinary trucks, instead of the big driving wheels of a conventional locomotive. Vertically mounted cylinders on one side drove a big crankshaft which was linked to the wheels of the trucks through a complicated-looking arrangement of shafting, universal joints, and bevel gears. The small wheels and swiveling trucks were easy on the light track that was typical of logging roads, and permitted the Shays to negotiate much sharper curves than a conventional locomotive, while the geared drive arrangement made the little engines remarkably powerful machines that could haul amazing loads on the steep grades of logging railroads.

Shay licensed his invention to a little machine works in Lima, Ohio, which ultimately grew into one of the leading American locomotive builders, largely on the strength of the remarkably successful Shays. Over a period of 65 years Lima sold nearly 3000 of them. Most went to logging roads in North and South America, but a goodly number of Shays turned up on logging railroads in such diverse locations as Japan, Siam, Australia, and the Philippines.

For the first section of the Ali Shan line completed between Chiai and Chu Chi, where the grades were a modest 3 percent or less, the Japanese contractors who built the line were said to have relied on some 0-6-0 and 0-8-0 tank engines built in the U.S. by Vulcan and Porter, as well as some similar machines of British and Japanese origin. But as the rails climbed higher into the mountains, something else became necessary.

The Ali Shan Forestry Railway saw its first Shay in 1908, when one borrowed from Japan showed up for tests. So successful were the results that the railway promptly placed an order with the Lima Locomotive Works for a batch of seven two-cylinder, 18-ton Shays. These were delivered during 1910–13, and a second order soon afterward added a dozen three-cylinder, 28-ton Shays to the roster during 1912–17. Just as they had at so many other locations on at least four continents, Ephraim Shay's patented locomotives proved to be just what was needed to bring the timber down from Mount Ali's heights, and they remained the forest railway's primary motive power for well over a half century.

Diesels began to invade the Shay's heretofore exclusive province on the slopes of Mount Ali during the 1960s, when the line bought some Nippon Sharyo diesel cars to accommodate the growing tourist trade drawn by Ali Shan's spectacular scenery. In 1969, 25-ton Mitsubishi diesel-hydraulic locomotives began to arrive on the property as well. These were appealing little double-truck machines driven through a cardan shaft drive, gearboxes, and side rods, but of course they seemed rather colorless alongside a Shay.

By the time I first made the pilgrimage to Ali Shan at the end of 1972, the diesel locomotives and rail cars like our *Chung Hsin Hao* had displaced Shays from regular main line service between Chiai and Ali Shan, but the geared steamers were still much in evidence. Almost all of the original fleet was still on the property. Some were stored in obviously unserviceable condition, but a goodly number of Shays were still in steam, operating out of engine houses at Peimen, just out of Chiai; Fenn Chii Hwu, part way up; and Ali Shan.

The heavy climbing on our journey to Ali Shan began abruptly some 14 miles from Chiai at an extraordinary piece of railroad engineering called the Mount Tuli (or Dwu Lih Shan) spiral. Here the Japanese engineers were obliged to construct a bewildering paroxysm of curves, tunnels, and steep grades to conquer the mountain's severe topography. In the space of less than 4 miles our little train plunged in and out of no fewer than 11 tunnels and whirled around two complete loops and a figure eight, all the while climbing steadily upward on a 5 percent grade.

Soon the trackside vegetation began to change as we reached more temperate elevations. At 800 meters—a half mile above sea level—a trackside sign advised that we'd passed into the subtropical zone. Bamboo groves were still plentiful, but now we began to see pine trees—and logging sidings—as well, and lush ferns and a kind of low purplish plant grew in the shade of the trackside forest. Passengers reached out from the slow-moving cars to pick the bright red poinsettias that grew wild in profusion along the tracks.

It had long seemed to me that a railroad—particularly a narrow-gauge line—can integrate itself with the landscape in a way that a highway cannot. This seemed especially true of the Ali Shan railway, whose builders had adapted it so intimately to the tumultuous terrain of the Taiwanese mountains.

Twisting, turning, and always climbing, the little train plunged through a tunnel one minute and skirted a sheer drop the next. Often now, as we neared an elevation of a mile above sea level, we looked down on clouds, and views of wooded, mist-shrouded mountains conveyed the mood of a misty Chinese landscape painting.

There was a long stop at Fenn Chii Hwu, roughly halfway to the top and seemingly the biggest place along the line. Outside a wooden engine house a pair of big three-cylinder Shays simmered quietly, while two or three more stood cold inside. Trackside vendors offered hot corn on the cob, tangerines, and a doughy sort of cake with a hot meat and onion filling. My hungry boys stocked up again.

Another *Chung Hsin Hao* diesel-car express, on its way down to Chiai, pulled into the station, and we resumed our climb to Ali Shan, looking down on the clouds and across great abysses at sheer, rocky mountain faces. At 1800 meters—well over a mile high—another trackside sign advised that we had now officially reached the temperate zone. There was a brief wait in a siding at the little mountain town of Shoeisheliau for a local train going down the mountain, and then we were on our way again, climbing through dense, dark forests.

Soon our little train began a final, prodigious leap to its Ali Shan terminal, see-sawing through a series of four switchbacks laid on a 6 percent grade. At one, the train paused briefly to let us examine Ali Shan's famous "Sacred Tree," a huge, gnarled Formosan cypress said to be 3000 years old. Then the climb resumed through one more switchback and a final corkscrew of a curve until at last the rails

222

Passengers looked down on clouds and mountaintops from the trains of the Ali Shan Forestry Railway. This was the view from *Jung Yu Hao* diesel rail car express 305 during the climb from Chiyai to Ali Shan in December 1972.

leveled out and our *Chung Hsin Hao* coasted to a stop in the Far East's highest railway station, 2274 meters—7460 feet—above sea level.

Just down the track from the station, two of the little two-cylinder Shays waited with steam up outside the engine house, ready for work in the yard or on the two logging branches that went on into the mountain forests beyond Ali Shan. Four other Shays, both large and small, were stored in the engine house and a nearby shed.

Over the next few days I watched the comings and goings of assorted diesel-

As they neared the end of the climb to Ali Shan, the little trains seesawed back and forth through a series of four switchbacks laid on 6 percent grades. Here, at one of them, passengers on *Chung Hsin Hao* express train 306 get a good look at the 3000-year-old "Sacred Tree."

Ordinary trains on the Ali Shan line consisted of diminutive wooden coaches pulled, or pushed
on the way up the mountain, by diesel-hydraulic locomotives. This local from Chiyai was nearing
the end of the climb to the Ali Shan terminal in 1973.

hydraulic locomotives and the red-and-white *Chung Hsin Hao* rail cars, but the main attraction for a railway enthusiast, or for anyone enamored of quaint machinery, was always the famous Shays of Ali Shan. One or two of them were usually simmering quietly at the little wooden engine house, or chuffing furiously as they rearranged freight cars for the journey down the mountain. Now and then one dragged a few logging cars off into the mountain forests, with perhaps a logger or two riding in a little red caboose-like car at the rear of the train. And although

The patented mountain-climbing locomotives devised by Michigan lumberman Ephraim Shay were wondrous mechanical marvels. A forestry railway engineman checked over the intricate machinery of two-cylinder, 18-ton Shay No. 18 at Ali Shan in January 1973. Ohio's Lima Locomotive Works had delivered the durable machine in 1913.

Ali Shan was the end of the line for the railway's passenger trains, the truly energetic enthusiast could arrange to ride a logging train on up the mountain to Tungpu, which was the starting point for the strenuous climb up 13,113-foot-high Yu Shan ("Jade Mountain"), Taiwan's highest mountain as well as the highest in all Asia east of the Himalayas.

Ali Shan would have been an engaging place even without the trains. There was an invigorating quality to the fresh, clear mountain air and the tranquility of the misty mountain forests. Once a rustic mountain logging village, Ali Shan had become more mountain resort than anything else. There were a number of modest inns, and the Forestry Bureau operated a comfortable hotel—Ali Shan House—that served up some splendid Shanghai cuisine. Paths through the nearby forest led to some pleasant ponds, modest Buddhist temples, a forestry museum, or down the mountain to the Sacred Tree. In March and April Ali Shan's famed cherry blossoms were a special attraction.

But the premier attraction for most Ali Shan visitors was the viewing of the splendid mountain sunrise. Every morning, visitors rose early for the trek to the "Sunrise House" pavilion at the top of nearby Chu Shan ("Celebration Mountain") to watch the sun rise over Yu Shan. More often than not, the event was obscured by mist and clouds, but the sight of the magnificent mountain sunrise above a sea of clouds—when one was at last fortunate enough to see it—made all the early rising worthwhile.

The Journey Today

Ali Shan remains a popular destination for both Taiwanese and visitors to the island, and the little *Chung Hsin Hao* diesel trains still make the three and a half hour journey up the mountain from Chiai. While diesel-hydraulic locomotives have long since displaced the engaging Shays of Ali Shan, one of the little steamers has been restored to operation for tourist traffic out of Ali Shan, and others are stored or on display along the line or preserved at other locations.

The oldest Shay still active on Ali Shan in 1977 was No. 12, seen here outside the Ali Shan
engine house. Lima had built the venerable locomotive some 67 years earlier.

Index

The author aboard the Turkish steamer *Tekirdag* on the Marmara Sea, part of a journey via train and ship from Izmir to Istambul in June 1989. *(Photo by Dorothy H. Middleton.)*

$\mathcal{W}$ILLIAM D. MIDDLETON is a 1950 civil engineering graduate from Rensselaer Polytechnic Institute and is a registered Professional Engineer in Virginia and Wisconsin. His professional career has included 29 years as an officer in the U.S. Navy's Civil Engineer Corps and 13 years as chief facilities officer for the University of Virginia. He has also been active as a transportation and engineering historian and journalist, with 15 books and nearly 500 articles to his credit. His published books include a number of titles concerned with the history of electric railways and rail transit in North America, and histories of New York's Grand Central Terminal and Pennsylvania Station. He has written about electric railways, cable cars and Penn Station for *American Heritage* and *American Heritage of Invention and Technology*. His most recent book is *Landmarks on the Iron Road*